Endorsements

I am forever blessed for having read Call Me Vivian. I felt the presence of God and his Holy Spirit speaking to me. I pray that God continues to use Katie Scheller to minister to his lost and wounded lambs.

—James Earl Quant Jr., inmate, Wyoming Correctional Facility

I try to make it a habit to write to an author when he or she has written something that has reached me and attached to my soul. I am so thankful that Jesus, in his awesome orchestrating abilities, allowed Katie's path and my path to converge by placing her book into my hands. All this time, I have been convinced that addiction was my problem. God has finally shown me that addiction is only a symptom of a much bigger issue: codependency. May the blessings of the Lord pursue and overtake you and may you be victorious in all that you set your hands to do.

—Amy Davidson, inmate, Weakly County Jail, Tennessee

I am touched and inspired by Katie Scheller's journey. The miracles and revelations that transpired in her life could only have come from the great God we serve. May the Lord continue to provide for The Vivian Foundation.

—Cynthia Houvenel, inmate, Federal Correctional Institution, California

I read Call Me Vivian and could not believe the similarities between Katie's life and mine. Thank you for the inspiration to never ever give up.

—Nicki Bibbs, inmate, Hampton Roads Regional Jail, Virginia

Katie's story feels so much like my own. I have resolved to use whatever time I have been given here on earth to draw closer to God.

—Angela Greer, inmate, Townsville Women's Correctional Centre, Australia

I'm fighting a war every day. I still have a lot of work to do, but thanks to Katie Scheller and Call Me Vivian, I understand I'm no longer doing it alone! God's got my back.

—Katy Judd, inmate, North Carolina Correctional Institution for Women, North Carolina

Call Me Vivian is such an uplifting, inspiring testimony for which I am grateful. My spiritual growth has been an uphill, vigorous one. This book has touched me and many others here at the institution. We need more inspiring women of Katie Scheller's caliber.

—Viviana Rivas-Gunn, inmate, Washington Corrections Center for Women, Washington

I have distributed Call Me Vivian to our chapel and state libraries, and every unit has several copies as well. This book is not only touching inmates but also staff. I saw our chaplain walking on campus and carrying Call Me Vivian. He has since expressed what a wonderful book it is. Your continued generosity of sending so many books to our facility has blessed countless women and their families.

—Pamela Smith, inmate and Angel Network Librarian at the Washington Corrections Center for Women, Washington

Call Me Vivian gave me hope and a great outlook on life. God gives the toughest battles to the strongest soldiers.

—Crystal Morris, inmate, Martin County Jail, Florida

Call Me Vivian gave me hope when I felt like there was none. It was an easy, relatable story and helped me realize I don't have to keep struggling.

—Janelle Jesuca, inmate, Martin County Jail, Florida

Call Me Vivian was like a divine intervention from God. I totally felt the Holy Spirit speaking to me and could not believe what I was reading; it was like I was reading pieces of my own story. I know that all things are possible with God.

—Giuliana Bosco, inmate, Vista Detention Facility, California

I was feeling hopeless when Call Me Vivian gave me a second wind.

—Sonya Pittman, inmate, Aliceville Alabama Prison Camp

I loved Call Me Vivian. It made me cry, laugh, and grow closer to the Lord. I can't explain it, but this book drew me closer to God. I am so excited that he is in control of my future.

—Daniel Kiss, inmate, Mid North Coast Correctional Centre, Australia

I finished reading Call Me Vivian, and Katie Scheller's journey was compelling. Her inspiring message surely transformed some of the women's hearts to trust God for their future.

—Faye Boyd, Forgiven Ministry, Inc. and One Day with God camp volunteer

Katie Scheller presented Call Me Vivian and her story at the Milwaukee Correctional Institution for Women. She is a powerful source of inspiration and an undeniably spirit-filled woman. The gospel is weaved into Katie's message, and her story shows that overcoming sin is possible by filling the void in your heart with the one and only true source of love: God.

—Diane Rolfs, ministry lead of Eastbrook Church Prison

Call Me Vivian

A True Love Story

KATIE SCHELLER

BroadStreet
PUBLISHING

BroadStreet Publishing Group, LLC
Racine, Wisconsin, USA
BroadStreetPublishing.com

Call Me Vivian
A True Love Story

Cover design by Chris Garborg at GarborgDesign.com
Typesetting by Katherine Lloyd at TheDESKonline.com
Author photo by Mike Steinbach at BachPhotography.com
Special thanks to Chad Bernhard for bringing The Vivian Foundation logo to life

Printed in China
20 21 22 23 24   7 6 5 4 3

Dedication

For my sister Susie
"It is pleasant to see dreams come true." (Proverbs 13:19)
I could not have done this without you!

This book is dedicated to all those
who struggle with codependency.
The security you crave can only be found in the Lord.

Introduction

A s I stood on the tarmac, the cold January temperatures and brisk wind made my entire body shiver. I looked down at the red welts that had already formed on both of my wrists. The handcuffs were painfully tight, as were the chains that were wrapped securely around my waist. The heavy restraints prevented me from raising my hands more than a couple of inches.

"Scheller, stand here!" barked the US marshal as he held his clipboard, taking inventory of the nearly one hundred federal inmates who just made the seventy-five-mile one-way trip to the Tampa International Airport. Given I was surrounded by a dozen federal agents wearing bulletproof vests and carrying high-powered sharpshooting rifles, I started moving in the direction he was pointing. The metal cuffs around my ankles and short chain between my feet made walking extremely difficult, but I eventually made it to my assigned spot.

I was one of two female inmates from the Federal Correctional Complex in Coleman being airlifted to the Federal Transit Center in Oklahoma City. While I stood in my designated area, dressed in my khaki-colored elastic-waist pants, a brown short sleeved T-shirt, and blue slip-on tennis shoes, the same US marshal was diligently studying his paperwork as the damp air chilled me to the bone.

Just when I did not think it could get any worse, it did. I silently began to pray that somehow the light mist would wash away the black Sharpie marker that had just been placed on my hand. The dreaded X meant I was heading to the Grady County Jail in Chickasha, Oklahoma. Chickasha is thirty-five minutes southwest of

Oklahoma City, but it might as well have been a million miles away. "Shady Grady" was the last place on earth I wanted to spend my one-year anniversary in prison.

"God, I don't deserve this," I prayed quietly. "The punishment just doesn't fit the crime." Unfortunately, the chains and shackles, armed guards, and prison-traveling clothes told a different story.

What was a nice girl like me doing in a place like this? How did something that felt so good and seemed so right twenty years earlier turn into my worst nightmare? Why did a mother and grandmother on the fast track in corporate America end up in federal prison?

Sad but true, there was only one answer to all three questions: it was a matter of my heart. And like so many women who fall in love, convinced they are going to live happily ever after, I let my heart determine the course of my life.

As I closed my eyes, just trying to escape the horror of being on Con Air, my mind drifted back to 1992, the year it all began.

1

It was a long shot and I was on cloud nine. I could not stop smiling. I had just been offered the job. To say I was thrilled was an understatement. As one of more than fifty internal applicants for the Staff Resource Planner position in the Transportation Department at SC Johnson, I knew I could do the job and I was confident the door would open for me.

As I shared the good news with my coworkers, the look of surprise and bewilderment on their faces was quite telling. Apparently, I was the only one optimistic enough to believe I would actually get the job. I chuckled as I walked past the long list of our favorite sayings that were scribbled on loose-leaf paper hanging near my workstation in research and development. My favorite was, "Work goes where it gets done," and a close second was, "A woman would rather have beauty than brains, because a man can see better than he can think."

My new boss was Milt Morris and I tried to find out what I could about him prior to my interview. He was in his early fifties, had been with the company for more than thirty years, and loved to play golf. I figured I probably should not mention the rumors I heard about his girlfriend who worked in customer service.

Milt seemed like a nice-enough guy, and he was willing to give me a chance for a fresh start. I had recently completed my undergraduate work in business administration and marketing, compliments of our company-sponsored degree program.

Milt and I hit it off when we met—he made me feel at ease. We laughed throughout the hour-long interview and I remember telling him something that I felt was important as he contemplated who would be the best candidate for the position. "If you like me," I said, "then hire me. And if you don't, that's fine, because I'm not going to change. What you see is what you get."

It was almost as if I had offered up a challenge to Milt, and I could see the wheels turning in his head. As strange as this sounds, I could also feel some sort of chemistry beginning to form between the two of us. There was something intriguing about Milt besides his tantalizing cologne, confident demeanor, and impeccable dress. As I would later find out, Milt found some things intriguing about me too. Apparently, it was my sailor dress and great-looking rear end that got me hired. It was true. Milt Morris could see better than he could think.

At the time I had no clue about what I was getting myself into, and neither did Milt. A successful, powerful businessman with an insatiable sexual appetite had just hired an adventurous, risk-taking young businesswoman who was looking for love. It was the perfect storm.

~

On October 14, 1993, I took a business trip to a regional distribution center in Dallas. But for me, it started long before that fateful day in the Lone Star State. Why do women have a knack for remembering dates like this? I imagine most life-altering moments are hidden somewhere in our psyche. This date, however, was etched into my brain, my heart, and my Franklin planner.

Over the last year, the occasional workplace flirtations between Milt and me had moved from slightly embarrassing comments to desired daily banter. The chemistry we shared had evolved from an awkward experiment to a hormonal interaction on the verge of explosion.

My suitcase was packed for my first business trip alone with Milt. Some casual clothes, two dresses, a few pairs of sexy panties, white thigh highs, and a pile of justifications for my impending actions. As we enjoyed a delicious dinner at the Marriott Quorum, my confidence began to wane. What was I thinking? Milt was sixteen years my senior and almost old enough to be my dad. Oddly enough, thoughts of my dad crossed my mind, but none of my husband.

After we had already said good night, I knocked on Milt's door with a transparent excuse of needing help with my phone card. His need to feel needed saved this deceitful damsel in distress, and my ulterior motive was the key to bypassing any barriers that stood between us.

One look at the thigh highs and the night's decadent events proceeded without interruption. The sex was absolutely incredible. Darkness, silence, and satisfaction filled the room. I was lying on the boss's bed wondering what to do next, my gaze transfixed on the ceiling as my thoughts drifted: *A new fringe benefit? Steamy sex with your supervisor?* I smiled as I imagined that the value of that perk would be dependent on who was doing the calculating. But like most transactions, I also had a standard disclaimer: *When you fall in love with me and ask me to marry you, the answer is always no.*

～

Corporate America. A place where illicit love affairs are part of many company cultures but never talked about. Getting to know your colleagues in the biblical sense can be encouraged and even sometimes expected in many work environments. And why should that come as a surprise? We spend more time at work than we do at home.

When I was just twenty years old, the company hired me to work in the factory—a second-shift line job that got me out of the house and earning a decent wage. I worked my way up in the organization and somehow managed to earn my bachelor's degree while working full time and raising a family. I continually challenged myself—always looking for more, that "something" that would make me feel complete and whole.

I invented and launched successful products that generated millions of dollars in revenue. I reorganized operations to save equal amounts of money. I pushed my subordinates to achieve or leave. I was the poster child for the knocked-up dropout teenager who made it big in corporate America.

As cliché as it sounds, I worked hard and sometimes I wanted to play hard too. And playing with a menagerie of men was yet another accomplishment. The one thing I made sure of was that regardless of my partner, the minute any relationship crossed the noncommittal line and even remotely resembled love, I took off running.

The truth is that I was afraid of love, so I chased after anyone I thought would provide that powerful emotion that eluded me. But the words I so desperately needed to hear—*I love you*—scared me to death.

So what does one do when she finds herself in bed with the boss who is now sound asleep and snoring? I failed to plan for that scenario, so I improvised. I got dressed, quietly left, and questioned what I had just done. I stood in a hot shower, allowing one type of steam to cleanse my body from a different type of steam.

Then I lay awake for a long time, all alone in my own bed. I thought about my husband and my kids, somehow validating my immoral actions. Sleep finally overtook me and I woke up the next morning wondering what would happen that day.

It was a repeat of the previous night. The sordid affair had begun. The lust-filled weekend was the escape I needed from my stressful work responsibilities and my unhappy marriage. If only I had heeded the lyrical advice of Texan and country singer Johnny Lee, because in hindsight I was definitely looking for love in all the wrong places.

～

Sunday night arrived and I returned home from Dallas. I was back home with my family, and the reality that was my life: my three kids and my husband, Tom. No dog. No white picket fence. But a fairly typical family and home if viewed from the street.

Tom and I had married back in 1976, meeting about a year and a half before we exchanged vows. He was a first-year teacher and an assistant track coach at my Catholic high school and a doctor's son. He somehow convinced me to see him socially before I even graduated. The lure of a secret relationship had been a consistent stumbling block in my life.

My relationship with Tom blossomed quickly, as is typical when a teenager's heart is involved. I spent one semester at a state university before I felt a five-hour drive was too far from the object of my infatuation. So I did what anyone would do—I dropped out of college and went to work. Before long, I was eighteen years old, engaged, and pregnant. My focus was on planning a wedding and my expanding waistline. Unfortunately, however, I failed to notice the warning signs of a love-starved marriage.

~

When I returned to work on Monday, the game had changed. I had a secret. And so did Milt. But the next few months were heavenly. Lunches, gifts, compliments, and, yes, many more hotel rooms. I became alive with anticipation and excitement. I was fervent about my work and absolutely thrilled with my new social life. One thing was certain: our sexual compatibility was off the charts. The passion and romance I felt every time we were intimate convinced me I had found my soul mate.

I thought I was in the driver's seat for getting my needs met, but there was only one problem. Milt really did have a girlfriend who worked in customer service. His girlfriend was a showy number, larger than life with lots of bling and high-end taste. She had big demands and a bigger mouth. When she walked into a room, she expected everyone to notice, and most people did.

With my competitive spirit, my next challenge was to see if I could get her out of the picture. The race was on, and no doubt I was going to win. The chase was almost as much fun as the catch. I would have Milt all to myself.

Subconsciously, I strategized. I had a game plan. The aggression that I used to leave on the basketball court with the neighborhood boys now manifested itself in my adult life. Girls' athletics were on the cusp of mainstream when I was finishing high school. Title IX was in its infancy, and sports-minded females were still presumed to be lesbians. Good competition was beginning, but the opportunities were limited. In the early 1970s, women were encouraged to burn their bras, but not really taught what to do after that. Donning a Nike sports bra and ripping off your shirt like Brandy Chastain's victory celebration were far-fetched ideas for women in my era. But the thrill of victory and the sense of accomplishment pushed me throughout my life. Milt was another goal for me to reach and win.

I worked hard to win Milt over, and then it happened. Only six months after our first sexual escapade, and much sooner than I expected, if I expected it at all, I told Milt I loved him. I had said it! It felt so good. What a special moment it was. I was falling in love for the first time in my life and experiencing emotions I did not even know existed deep within my heart.

∼

Initially, I worked for Milt during a three-year assignment where I was responsible for scheduling the outbound finished goods. It was a very stressful job that required late nights and long weekends, but I loved it. The job played to my strengths. I was able to fully utilize my planning and organizational skills and also leverage my outgoing personality. It was a match made in heaven.

Milt had established a partnership program with the domestic transportation carriers, and I thoroughly enjoyed the social aspect of the job. The fulfillment I was not getting at home, I received at work. We enjoyed dinners and golf, sporting events and gifts, and friendships that would last a lifetime. It was a special place to work, and I was convinced I had the best job in the company. The only problem was that I had fallen in love with my boss, which wasn't necessarily a good thing.

Milt still had his girlfriend. During the years I shared my lover, I justified it because I needed Milt. I needed his touch, his kind words, his encouragement, and his company. I would be willing to patiently wait knowing that I was not necessarily his top priority but confident I would win him over in the end. The girlfriend had to know we were romantically involved, although I thought we did a pretty good job hiding it in the beginning. But then again, how could she not figure it out?

Milt's mode of operation was generous but not overly creative. If she got an expensive watch, so did I. If she went on a shopping spree, then I did too. If she got new earrings, guess who got them too? If she got laid, then so did I. On Sunday mornings, when we should have all been in church, we took turns grocery shopping with him. Double the fun, double the expense, double the trouble? Quite frankly, I am not sure where Milt got all of his energy. How he managed to keep both of us happy, play golf at least three times a week, travel for work, and run the department was simply amazing.

~

A wonderful opportunity to move to the marketing department presented itself in 1996, yet I felt so conflicted. It meant I had to leave a job I loved and take a chance on fulfilling a lifelong dream by working as a marketing associate in Air Care New Products. I would also have to leave Milt. I cried as I pondered the decision, but I chose to realize my dream.

Milt and I continued our relationship, however. And he also sustained his affair with the girlfriend. For the next three years, I used every bit of my vacation to travel with him on his business trips. We went to some wonderful places throughout the country. One trip in particular, I will never forget.

Milt was at a conference in California at LaCosta Resort. He went to play golf, and when he returned we spent the rest of the day at the pool. As I removed my sunglasses and looked to my right, I could not believe who was sitting just a few chairs away: Julia

Roberts. Like *the* Julia Roberts—you know, from *Pretty Woman*, which just happens to be one of my favorite movies. Ironically but appropriately, I really did not see Julia Roberts. Rather, I saw her character, Vivian, the kept woman. And somehow Milt, in spite of his age, appearance, and stature, started to look like Richard Gere.

That was how Milt treated me, and I wanted him to rescue me the way Edward Lewis rescued Vivian. In fact, I *needed* Milt to rescue me. I wanted to be the princess, not the prostitute. I wanted the fairy-tale ending, not to play second or third or even fourth fiddle. At that time, I somehow convinced myself—and I was absolutely positive—Milt and I were going to live happily ever after.

~

Following my marketing assignment, I completed a brief stint in the research and development department. The door called opportunity opened once again. Milt's voice sounded over the phone: "Hey, I need an export manager. Are you interested?"

By this time, I had received a nice promotion in research and development, so it would be a lateral career move. I threw my name in the hat, knowing I had the inside track. In June of 1999, I accepted his offer, and, once again, we had a direct reporting relationship.

Corporate travel took us around the world as I managed the international side of the business. Whether in Denmark, Mexico, Puerto Rico, Japan, or Racine, Wisconsin, his yin complemented my yang. If his left hand might have missed something, my right hand compensated. Together, we achieved outstanding results in the boardroom as well as the bedroom. The fairy tale continued. I was being groomed for what I knew of Milt's job, and although it was not a slam dunk, I liked my chances.

Milt and I were finally a couple. The girlfriend gave him an ultimatum, demanding a full-time commitment, and he said no. Clueless and in love, I could not see the big picture that was going on around me. I was looking at the world through rose-colored glasses, not ruby-colored ones. Did I mention that Milt was married too? Sad but true, I was still the other woman even though the girl-friend was now out of the picture.

Milt's wife was handicapped, having suffered a stroke in 1990 prior to me meeting him. He carried a tremendous burden and a sense of guilt regarding her condition, yet he always made sure she had proper care and assistance given his work, travel, and social schedules.

I know what you are thinking: *How could either one of you have done this to this poor woman?* Believe me, you can justify just about anything when you are insecure, which we both were. It was almost like she was not a real person. I managed to make her part of my pretend world, part of the fairy-tale story I was living out.

Milt and I were deeply in love, and it showed. We were both longing to be touched, we both wanted to be wanted, and we were two people who used each other to boost our feelings of self-worth. It was easy to excuse our infidelities.

As Milt expanded his carrier base, I met new friends. Together, we often traveled with his business associates and their wives or girlfriends. Milt and his buddies arranged trips to Amsterdam, Hawaii, and Las Vegas. We played golf at some of the best courses in the world and stayed at the finest hotels. The gifts, winnings from gambling, romantic dinners, and lovemaking—it was incred-ible. I even taught Milt how to dance.

This vast, marvelous world Milt exposed me to compared only to that which I had seen on television or read about in a love story. It was a level of luxury I had never experienced before. Escargot and Dom Perignon were a far cry from the potato pancakes and powdered milk I grew up with.

I came from humble roots—my father was a teacher while my mother stayed home when we were young. We were raised with wholesome values and family-centered activities. With six children to feed, clothe, and educate, hand-me-downs were the norm for the kids, and extra part-time jobs were the norm for my dad. Yet my parents never turned away anyone—not the two neighborhood girls who lost their mother to cancer, not my cousins who needed a peaceful place to hang out, and not any other wayward souls who stumbled upon our family. To this day, their back door is open to those in need, the cookie jar and candy drawer are usually filled, and there is always room for one more porch sitter. The unconditional love they provided and modeled must have sustained me through all my years of despair and searching. In my lowest moment, I was one of the wayward souls who found refuge back in their home.

I typically knew right from wrong, but when I was with Milt I lost all control. I was like Pavlov's dog, but instead of receiving food when the bell rang I was answering the phone, setting up our next tryst, and getting paid. At times, I did not even know who I was—I actually felt worthless. I struggled with the lies and deceit I regularly fed my family. Other days I hated myself and despised the things I had done. But my ongoing behavior showed otherwise. I could justify and excuse my indiscretions because of the financial security and love the relationship provided. Sex was still a substitute for the feelings I was afraid to express.

My marriage had failed. I let it linger much longer than I should have. Finally, I could not continue to live a lie anymore—not with my husband or with myself. I decided to take a drastic measure.

~

Every time I seriously contemplated leaving my husband, I would find myself making a rather large purchase to somehow justify staying together. My behavior was irrational, but it allowed me to convince myself that I could not afford to get divorced because of the exorbitant price tags of some of these items. One time I bought a new car, another time it was a player piano, and out of sheer desperation I bought a lake lot with plans to build a beautiful home on the shores of Lake Michigan.

But no matter how hard I tried to make myself feel better with all of this stuff, none of it filled the void in my soul. My husband and I talked about building the lake home, but I could no longer live the lie. I did not love Tom, and I did not want to be with him—I wanted to be with Milt. How I was behaving in my marriage was far from acceptable and so unfair to Tom. It was time for a change.

We sold the lake lot, which gave me the freedom to finally make the decision I knew I should have made years earlier. In November of 2001, I put a reservation on a condominium in a subdivision called Hidden Creek and went home to tell my husband of my decision to move forward without him. It was a difficult conversation, but my mind was made up—I wanted out. I was in love with another man, my boss of all people, and no one was going to convince me otherwise.

Over the course of the next ten months, while my condo was under construction, our marriage was strained ever further, due to the fact that I was still living at home. My husband was in denial about my decision to leave and, as a result, there was virtually no discussion about my choice to build a new house and move on with my life. There was a fair amount of stress that I carried, but most of it was due to job pressures and the demands that came with building a new home. I worked hard to be as nice as I could during this time, and I did not immediately file for divorce but decided to separate and see how things would work out. I thought it would be easier on everyone, especially our children, as they got used to the idea of Tom and me living apart.

I was excited that my new life was about to begin. In September of 2002 I moved into Hidden Creek, separated from my husband, and began the next season of my life.

~

I was convinced given Milt's involvement in the construction of my condominium, approval of the interior furnishings, and willingness to provide the financial support I needed, that someday we would be together. So there I was, alone in a big, beautiful house, trying to convince myself I was happy. In essence, my new living arrangements did not change a thing in my heart. My life continued to be placed on hold, waiting for the next phone call from Milt.

It was an interesting time in my life. There were times when Milt would love to flaunt our affair and then there were other times he did not want anyone to know. Even though I was separated, Milt's car would always have to be pulled into the garage or I would have to pick him up somewhere because we were still feeling the pressure that came from sleeping with the boss. The independence we enjoyed when I first moved into my new place was beginning to fade since many of my new neighbors were also employed at the company.

But one thing was certain: the only person Milt seemed to be deathly afraid of when it came to spending time with me was his wife. I could never figure that one out, but nonetheless if his wife said jump, then he would ask how high. If she said be home at five o'clock, then he was home at five. And Milt became incredibly nervous if he thought he would be even one minute late.

Milt was leading a double life, which was also taking a toll on him. He knew it and I knew it, and yet we accepted the situation and did nothing to change his circumstances. Clueless and in love, I convinced myself that I had the best of both worlds. I no longer had to deal with an unhappy marriage, and I did not have to put up with Milt on a full-time basis either. Life was pretty good, or at least I thought it was. In retrospect, however, it was one of the loneliest times of my life.

~

The affair started very innocently. I began to look outside of myself for a person who would provide me with the emotional and life stability I lacked. Unfortunately, I did not know how to have emotional intimacy in nonsexual ways. Given my confusion, when I used love and sex as a way to cope rather than a way to grow, my partner choice became skewed. I was fearful of being alone or rejected, and out of emotional desperation I chose to embrace an inappropriate relationship that made me feel special.

I did not realize that the loneliness I experienced throughout my adult life was the result of my own lack of responsiveness. I would give in to the demands of others and focus on their needs because I did not want to hurt their feelings, and, more importantly, I did not want to be alone.

Lonely people submerse themselves in as many projects as possible and keep themselves busy to hide from their pain. Although there were only twenty-four hours in a day, I worked full time, raised three children, ran the household, volunteered at sporting events, coached my daughter's basketball team, exercised virtually every day, and went to night school for eight years. I continually challenged myself, always looking for more, that "something" that would make me feel complete. Unfortunately, I was not going to find it until I dealt with the emptiness in my heart.

~

In 2003 Milt decided to build a new home. He was impressed with my condo, and my designer provided input into the architectural features of his new residence. Milt's desire was to build an upscale one-level handicap-accessible home because of his wife's disability and her difficulty maneuvering stairs. The two-story house where he lived was in desperate need of updating, and although I was only invited to his home on a few occasions, I was surprised that a man in his position did not live more extravagantly.

Fast-forward to the twenty-first century. The home he built for his wife was not only extravagant but also over the top. Milt did not spare a dime on the design, construction, furnishings, or the accessories. The sprawling brick ranch, which sat on a quiet cul-de-sac among equally impressive homes, belonged in *Architectural Digest*.

During the year his home was under construction, the two of us spent virtually every day watching the progress. The house was handicap accessible, and he was so happy that his wife would have a home that would accommodate her needs. Milt and his wife met with the design firm on many occasions, and he was always anxious to share their selections with me. He was so proud of his new house, and I was happy for the two of them—this was the type of home they deserved.

The stress of building, however, along with the pressure of making final selections on a tight timetable, was driving a wedge between them. They were beginning to have some significant issues just prior to the home's completion.

Milt told me he was contemplating leaving his wife. Her behavior was erratic, and it seemed that no matter how hard he tried to please her, she was not happy. Milt became so frustrated that he was ready to raise the white flag and throw in the towel at the same time. When I heard him say that we should build a home together, I could hardly believe my ears. Did I just hear him right? I immediately began to look for a subdivision that would meet both of our needs, and we even went so far as to have some preliminary floor plans completed.

Was this really happening? After years of waiting for him to be completely mine, was there finally going to be a change so we would be together? Given his wife had her dream home, maybe it was possible for Milt to move forward minus the guilt. He continued to give me money for our future purchases and life together.

I was in pretty good shape. Milt had bought virtually all of the furnishings for my new home and I paid for everything in cash. He gave me money for my divorce settlement and I put the cash in the bank. Every time he gambled and won, which was quite often, he shared his winnings with me. When Milt came back from a trip that I did not attend, there was a gift of jewelry. He even gave me money for a down payment on a car. The average person could have figured it out right away, but I didn't. I was too busy being Vivian.

~

My divorce was finalized in January of 2004, just prior to Milt and his wife moving into their new home. It was a dwelling they both loved but a residence they would only enjoy for a short period of time given there were some significant changes about to take place.

I knew better than to give Milt an ultimatum, but I was finally free. The two of us talked about marriage, but there were only empty words that I somehow heard as promises. There were no commitments—in fact, there never would be.

When you are having an affair, you get all of the good stuff and none of the bad. But eventually you start to question whether or not you would really want to wake up with this person every morning. Then you question if he is being honest with you and whether or not you can trust him. You think you will become his top priority, but that never happens. So you continue to sit at home waiting for your phone to ring. When he finally does find the time for you, it's on his schedule, not yours. This was no way to live, but for close to twenty years this was my life.

Something big was indeed on the horizon and the roles would soon be reversed. It would be Milt that needed me to rescue him. But I had yet to realize that Milt would never be climbing up the fire escape with a bouquet of roses like Edward Lewis. Rather, I would be trying to escape a decade-long nightmare that I was plunged into as a result of our relationship and his unrelenting control over me.

2

I t was October 18, 2004. I was scheduled to take a business trip to a regional distribution center in Dallas, Texas. Does this sound familiar? This is where it all started, and this was where it was going to end. My suitcase was once again packed for a trip with my boss, but any plans we had of sleeping together that night were going to have to be scrapped.

That morning, prior to leaving for the airport, the two of us had a meeting with the vice president of worldwide sourcing and procurement to share the presentation I was going to be giving at a global conference the following week. As I was sharing my international plan, Milt was suddenly pulled out of the meeting. I figured it was because that was the day the upper management team received their bonus payments. I finished my presentation, and it was obvious we were done as the vice president and I were engaged in small talk.

Within minutes, I was led into a conference room and greeted by the senior vice president of human resources and a private investigator from the company's law firm. I was given a letter and told I was being placed on administrative leave with pay because I was suspected of violating company policy. They also told me that my office was being searched, Milt Morris had been fired, and there was a lawsuit filed against him.

If I had been smart, I would have kept my mouth shut and left; however, I did not feel that was an option given both individuals began to question me. Not too long after that, a postal inspector joined the meeting and, when he threatened to send me to jail like

Martha Stewart, I had had enough. I thought, *What in the world is going on? Why would the post office want to search my office? And what is happening with Milt?*

I signed a statement the private investigator had written on my behalf, and they let me go after two hours of questioning. I was escorted to my car and told to turn over my company credit card, parking tag, and office keys, and leave the premises. It would be the last time I drove out of our manufacturing facility. In reality, however, not only was it the perfect storm, but it was also the beginning of my worst nightmare.

~

After being pummeled with a blizzard of questions about my personal life, as well as what I knew about supplier gifts and Milt's mode of operation, I was experiencing my own personal whiteout. I was scared, confused, and in absolutely the worst place I could possibly be. Afraid I would be fired, I lied about accepting gifts from suppliers, yet for some reason I admitted to the affair that I had been having with Milt. My title quickly changed from the US import/export services and compliance manager to the woman caught in adultery. I was in trouble, my job was in jeopardy, and I did not know what to do.

Milt was scheduled to retire in fewer than three months, and his boss had told me just a few days earlier that the management succession and development team had selected me to replace Milt as director of transportation. Why would the company fire a guy who had worked for them for forty-three years, managed the transportation department for well over a decade, and was routinely told he was doing an excellent job? And why did Milt's boss tell me that I was getting a promotion when in actuality I was being placed on administrative leave? It did not make sense.

I was determined to find out what was going on; someone had to know. So I made a few phone calls to see if anyone had any clue as to what was transpiring, and the only information I could glean was that there was yellow crime-scene tape outside our offices. A short time later I received a phone call from Milt, letting me know he got fired. I pleaded with him to tell me something I did not already know. I was at a loss for words and so was Milt.

I chose to head over to a friend's house and did not hear back from Milt until the following day. When he finally did call, he told me he had retained a lawyer. I was more than familiar with his attorney's name: Gerry Boyle. This was big time. Boyle was nationally recognized, and I had seen this guy on television many times before. Milt told me Gerry wanted to see me. Why would some celebrity lawyer want to see me? "Milt, what in the world is going on?" I asked. "Why do I need to meet with Gerry Boyle?"

"Well, given the gifts I have given you and because of our relationship," Milt said, "Gerry thought it would be best for you to have legal representation." Great. Just great. Boyle proceeded to set up a meeting for me with an attorney named Mike Penkwitz.

That same day, the senior vice president of human resources called to cancel a meeting she had set up the previous day. I had been expecting to meet with her and an attorney who was hired by SC Johnson as part of their investigation. I questioned whether or not my attorney could attend, and she replied that company policy prohibited me from having legal counsel present. I felt as if I was being backed into a corner with no place to go. And, unfortunately, it was going to get a lot worse before it got better.

Up to this point I had been threatened to be sent to jail like Martha Stewart, I was pretty sure I was going to be fired for violating company policy for accepting supplier gifts, and even if I wanted to cooperate I could not have legal representation present. Not only was I backed into a corner, but I was also between a rock and a hard place. Given my no-win situation and based on the advice of Mr. Boyle, I had a letter delivered to the company stating that I would not comment until I knew the status of my employment.

The next day I met with Mike Penkwitz at the Wisconsin Club and was told that until we knew what was going on, I was done talking. We were going to have to be patient and wait to see what developed. In the meantime, however, it was suggested that I get a tax attorney because of the gifts Milt had showered upon me. Within a few days I had spent $25,000 to retain two lawyers. The million-dollar question remained unanswered, however: what did they know that they were not telling me?

~

During the next four weeks, the game of cat and mouse continued. It was like a championship chess match as each side contemplated their next move. My diet mainly consisted of McDonald's breakfast burritos, Diet Coke, and sleeping pills. I had lost seven pounds because of the stress of all that was going on, and for the first time in my life I was feeling really depressed.

The legal baton had been passed to my tax attorney, a gentleman by the name of Michael Cohn. This would be the first time I met him. Michael's office was located in downtown Milwaukee, across from the federal courthouse, and his workplace setting was very formal. In many ways it reminded me of a doctor's office, which is probably where I really needed to be in that moment. I sat in the waiting room before being greeted by Michael and led down a long hallway into a conference room that overlooked Lake Michigan.

Michael began the meeting by explaining why I needed his services. He then asked me how much money Milt had given me over the course of our relationship. A subpoena would be necessary to accurately answer that question, so until I could review my financial documents I only guessed. As I would later find out, my estimate was not even close. Apparently that happens in these types of cases.

Michael then wanted to know where Milt got his money. I told him that it all came from gambling. He insisted that Milt could not have possibly made that much money gambling, yet I argued he did. I explained that Milt would play cards every Wednesday night, and on the way home he would call me to tell me how much money he had won or lost. He also gambled on golf courses and would frequent casinos. When he won, he gave me money.

Regardless of how hard my attorneys tried to help me see the truth, I could not see any faults in Milt. And, unfortunately for me, modern-day research supported the view that the blindness of love is not just a figurative manner. Love officially renders you stupid. "There is none so blind as those who will not see."[1] Matthew Henry's quote was almost as relevant as one from William Shakespeare—"Love is blind."

According to a study by the University College London published in *NeuroImage* in June of 2004, scientists have shown that there is a degree of truth in the old adage that love is blind. They have found that feelings of love lead to a suppression of activity in the areas of the brain controlling critical thought. It seems that once we get close to a person, the brain decides that the need to assess their character and personality is reduced. Professor Robin Dunbar, an evolutionary psychologist at the University of Oxford, argues that the rational parts of the human brain shut down when experiencing love.[2] I spent so much time with Milt and I was so blinded by love that I might as well have had a lobotomy. As hard as I tried to look at the situation objectively, I could not see the truth.

~

In the midst of the uncertainty of what was happening with SC Johnson, I was blessed with a gift from heaven—my third grandchild. Colin was born, and my son Mike and his wife, Kelly, had their hands full as they now had three boys all under the age of four.

Colin would eventually become my inspiration—the little boy who taught me what life is all about and how we cannot take one

1 Matthew Henry. *Brainy Quote: www.brainyquote.com/quotes/m/matthew_henry. html*, (October 21, 2015).
2 "'Love is not only blind, it also makes you stupid' UK research claims." June 16, 2012. *News.com.au: http://www.news.com.au/lifestyle/real-life/love-is-not-only-blind -it-also-makes-you-stupid-uk-research-claims/story-e6frflri-1226397515433* (October 21, 2015).

day for granted. His circumstances provided the motivation and fueled my desire for a faith-based life. Unfortunately, Colin would have to endure some arduous times for his grandma to learn this valuable lesson.

With love and great anticipation, I headed to Green Bay to meet my newest grandson. No day is better than the day you get to hold your child or grandchild for the very first time. We were so blessed, and I had to keep this in the forefront of my mind, thanking God for this miracle. The other distracting things going on in my life did not matter in that moment. The stress of my job situation was nowhere to be found on this special day.

I returned to Racine only to be summoned back to Green Bay three days later. Colin was back in the hospital with complications. Our six-pound, fifteen-ounce bundle of joy was in the neonatal intensive care unit at Bellin Hospital. Colin had an IV and was undergoing a septic workup when I arrived. He was so sick, continually vomiting, and the concern on all of our faces was evident. I tried to put a positive spin on the situation, but that was easier said than done. You never think about how delicate life is until you find yourself in a situation wondering if your grandson will survive.

Through God's grace, additional medical intervention, and some much-needed nutrition, Colin was sent home a week later. The doctors never determined exactly why he was not gaining weight, but at the time it did not seem to matter. He was healthy and he was home. We were grateful for his stability.

Just five days after rejoicing and celebrating Colin's recovery, I was fired from my job. But it would take me years to understand that this was a blessing in disguise.

～

I would be less than honest if I did not tell you that the next few months were terribly stressful. Although I was collecting unemployment, I needed to find a job because my expenses were far greater than the income the state of Wisconsin was providing. I went into survival mode and determined the best thing to do was to sell my condominium and everything in it.

In spite of my upheaval, I found many reasons to be thankful during this period of time. I had the opportunity to visit my kids and grandkids and share special time with my family. One of the only things I initially regretted about losing my job was the guilt I felt for always putting the company first. I missed quite a bit while my children were growing up due to my increasing job responsibilities as well as the time commitment that was necessary to generate the results the company required. It was time I could never get back, and I was so angry at myself because of it. Here I was, working for a family company, and I sacrificed time with my very own family to climb the corporate ladder.

It was something that I could not change, but I vowed that it would never happen again. There was a reason my tax attorney, Michael Cohn, told me to go read the book of Ecclesiastes:

> I came to hate all my hard work here on earth, for I must leave to others everything I have earned. And who can tell whether my successors will be wise or foolish? Yet they will control everything I have gained by my skill and hard work under the sun. How meaningless! So I gave up in despair, questioning the value of all my hard work in this world. (Ecclesiastes 2:18–20)

As I readied my home for sale and pounded the pavement looking for work, news of the lawsuit filed in Racine County Circuit Court was beginning to hit the newspapers. The suit accused Milt of engaging in racketeering and accepting bribes. Well, at least I had something I could ask my attorney: "What is racketeering?" In case you are wondering, racketeering is obtaining or extorting money illegally or carrying on illegal business activities.

The civil lawsuit accused Milt of paying inflated shipping rates and paying for services not rendered. The company claimed money had been exchanging hands during card games and that carriers paid for travel and jewelry, though they did not name the carriers involved. It was not until January of 2005 that the transportation companies were finally named in the lawsuit. They were businesses owned by two of Milt's best friends.

~

I sold my home in Wisconsin and began looking for a home in Florida. Florida bankruptcy laws would protect my primary residence, which, given my situation, seemed like a good idea. I was lucky to make a nice profit on my condominium, and the new owners bought most of my furniture and accessories. The sale allowed me to look for a house in the $300,000 price range. In the meantime, Milt and his wife purchased a home in Tampa, and it should not come as a surprise that is where I decided to relocate.

After leaving the airport, I drove to the north side of Tampa into a neighborhood called Tampa Palms. As I wondered how I would go about looking for a home, I saw a sign for a real estate company and headed in their direction. Meeting an agent at the door, I told her I was new to the area and interested in buying a condo or townhome, preferably on a golf course with nice amenities and a large garden tub.

We quickly realized I could not get on a golf course in my price range, but she was confident she had something that might work. We drove to a new development called Palma Vista, and I immediately knew this was exactly what I wanted. The townhomes backed up to a nature preserve; there were two swimming pools, a clubhouse, and a fitness center; and you could tell the builder was top notch. After looking at the four models, I quickly settled on the one that had the master bedroom downstairs, turned to the agent, and told her I wanted to buy this particular unit.

She looked at me in total amazement, as this may have been

the easiest commission check she would ever earn. I had been in Tampa for fewer than two hours, looked at one place, and decided to buy it. We proceeded to put an offer in that day.

The real estate market was booming in February of 2005, and the same week I bought my unit the developer sold six other townhomes. Two days after finalizing my paperwork, the price of each floor plan increased by $50,000. God was nice enough to steer me in the direction of this development and help me be decisive. Let's just say that God had me right where he wanted me.

~

During this same time period, I continued to look for work. One Sunday as I was reading the employment section of the *Milwaukee Journal*, a particular ad caught my eye. A company called Lamplight Farms was looking for a customer service manager. The job description was a perfect match for my skill set and experience.

There was only one problem: I had just signed a contract on a new townhome in Tampa, which would be completed in early April. I thought, *What the heck. Nothing ventured, nothing gained.* I had to apply for two jobs each week in order to maintain my unemployment benefits—this was one of the two jobs I selected.

I submitted a very impressive resumé and cover letter, and continued to move forward with my life. My real estate agent in Racine was fine-tuning the offer on my condominium, and the closing date was set for March 1. As I packed my remaining personal items, I was excited about my big move. I could not wait to get out of Wisconsin. But as I was about to find out, it did not matter what I wanted to do; God had other plans.

After shutting the door at SC Johnson, he opened the door at Lamplight Farms. I accepted their offer and began working on March 7, 2005, as their new customer service manager.

~

Lamplight Farms was an interesting place. Owned by WC

Bradley, it was a fairly small company yet privately held. Yes, I found myself at another family company. But this time I knew with certainty that God had a hand in my employment. WC Bradley's company philosophy was based on integrity, stewardship, and servant leadership. Their focus was on being a benefit to society and each other. God sent me to a Christian company to teach me some valuable lessons for what I was going to be walking through in the coming years.

When I first joined Lamplight, I thought it was a nuthouse. It was obvious that the right hand did not know what the left hand was doing, and the chaos made for some hectic days. After only two weeks on the job, I affectionately nicknamed my new place of employment the Funny Farm. It seemed as though it was a land of misfits, and I was now one of them.

I was finally starting to feel good about putting SC Johnson in my rearview mirror. The job at Lamplight was going to be a challenge, but that was fine because I liked a good challenge. Lamplight agreed to give me two weeks off, so as planned I headed to Florida to close on my townhome. The weather in Tampa was beautiful, and I was having a great time getting settled into my new neighborhood.

After a week in paradise, my phone rang. It was my youngest sister telling me I was not going to believe why she called. She asked if I was sitting down, and I knew that was not a good sign. There was a reason God had me out of the office during that specific time.

On April 8, 2005, I had made the headlines of the *Milwaukee Journal Sentinel* newspaper. Longtime SC Johnson executives investigated. Two suspected of fraud, money laundering, court records show. The article went on to say: "Former Transportation Director Milton E. Morris and his former deputy, Katherine M. Scheller, both of Racine, are suspected of overbilling the company by $1 million a month."[3]

She finished reading the entire article, and my only thought

<hr>

3 Gina Barton, "Longtime S.C. Johnson executives investigated," *Milwaukee Journal Sentinel* (April 8, 2005).

was, *This is absolutely insane.* I immediately called my civil attorney, Mike Penkwitz, and asked what was going to happen now. Mike told me I needed to call my new employer and explain things. "And what is it, Mike, you want me to say?" I asked.

I could not believe this was happening to me. My life appeared to be turning around and now this. Needless to say, I was angry and upset. I had absolutely no responsibility for domestic transportation. None. How could they say that about me? It was so unfair!

I made the phone call to my boss at Lamplight and explained the situation as best I could. He told me he would get back to me. Days went by without a call. I figured I was going to get fired and was an emotional wreck. I called again and he apologized, but he would still have to get back to me because they had not made a decision yet. Three days prior to my scheduled departure I got the dreaded call. But much to my surprise, I heard something I was not expecting: "We'll see you Monday morning."

~

Abbott Turner, the vice president of human resources at our parent company, wanted to meet with me. There was a lump in my throat so big that I could barely swallow the news. Abbott was one of the family members who owned the privately held WC Bradley Company in Columbus, Georgia, and he was flying up to Milwaukee for our Monday morning meeting.

I would have rather gone for a Pap smear, root canal, and walk across hot coals at the same time rather than walk back into that office on Monday morning. I was worried about what I had read in the newspaper and concerned about my future. Everyone knew I had a secret and why I was looking for work. I assumed the management team was having me come in because they would want to fire me in person rather than over the phone. Being in my shoes was not a fun place to be in that moment.

At eight o'clock on Monday morning, my boss escorted me into the conference room to meet with Abbott and the human resources manager from Lamplight. Heads were turning and the gossip had already begun as I was led past my fellow employees. It could only be described as the walk of shame.

Abbott led the meeting and I was about to find out whether or not his family practiced what they preached. Abbott would pass the test—his father William B. Turner taught him well. His dad authored a book entitled *The Learning of Love: A Journey toward Servant Leadership*. Servant leadership is about humility that comes from knowing yourself. His father goes on to say that love is a commitment to extend oneself for others. Leaders create a climate and are constantly asking:

> Are people growing, becoming more trusting and Spirit-filled, and becoming servants? Is there more creativity, more energy, and enthusiasm and more hope? If not, another dose of humility may be in order. Servant leadership is a circle of love in which a commitment to caring produces compassion that in turn, produces communication, creativity, and common vision—which ultimately produce a caring community.[4]

I was humbled and hopeful and about to receive a very special gift. Abbott looked at me and said the company was going to support me any way it could. What I was going through was a personal situation, and they were going to keep it that way. He brought my employees in after our meeting and told them the exact same thing. The owner of our company encouraged everyone to respect my situation as we had plenty of work to do.

I could not believe what had just happened. Both Bill and Abbott Turner knew it was the right thing to do. The most important thing a person will discover when they enter a circle of love and a caring community is God's infinite and undeserved love.

4 William B. Turner, *The Learning of Love: A Journey toward Servant Leadership* (Macon, GA: Smyth & Helwys Publishers, 1999), 152–153.

And once a person experiences God's love, that person will begin to change.

Unfortunately, given the circumstances, there were a small number of people who would never respect me. I was not able to tell my side of the story because of the pending legal proceedings, which was extremely difficult for me. It also impacted my ability to influence change to do what the company so desperately needed to do, which was to improve their operations.

~

Walking into the doors of Lamplight was like walking back in time. Lamplight was still hand packing and hand palletizing product. Everything was manual and there was paper everywhere. I even found typewriters. The employees' skill level was a far cry from what I was used to, and of the ten people who were reporting to me, none had a college degree. One man in particular did not even have his high school diploma, but it would be this young man, Charles, who would teach me more about life than you could ever imagine.

"You have to know it to live it, and understand it to survive it." Charles spoke with wisdom not found in any four-walled classroom. His lessons were learned on the streets. Existing. Surviving. But far from thriving.

Charles was one of my subordinates at Lamplight. I was managing customer service, transportation, and the onsite retail store; Charles was a customer service representative. He had spent time in the factory before his work ethic promoted him into the customer service area.

Charles and his young family lived in the toughest neighborhood in Milwaukee, a place you would not want to visit, much less live. When darkness fell, the crime rate rose. We often talked about how tough life was and how difficult it was to escape the unforgiving grip of the inner city. Based on his above-quoted definition of street life, Charles was surviving … but barely. He was a twenty-something African American man who was soft spoken and polite. He and his wife have two children and a cat named Skittles.

As a manager, one of the things I liked to do was fill my office with food. Pretzels, peanuts, candy, cookies—you name it, I had it. The warehouse clubs were happy to see me fill my cart with their oversized containers, and my employees seemed to appreciate the treats too. The snacks were the bait that lured unsuspecting workers into my office. I needed something to break the ice with my team. If the food is free and tasty, hungry people do not mind walking into the boss's office, even if they do not like or trust you.

I quickly realized that Charles was always hungry. Yet, somehow, puffed cheese balls for breakfast did not seem like a good way to start the day. Walking through the cafeteria one noon hour, I spied Charles sitting at a nearby table. God tugged on my heart when I saw him and a coworker having to share their lunch. Two gainfully employed men were not earning enough money to buy separate lunches.

I knew I had to help him. I would, however, have to be careful given that he directly reported to me. The food part was easy. I occasionally brought in leftovers or a sandwich, which he gladly accepted. A few McDonald's gift cards quietly found their way into his possession so he could treat his daughter to lunch over the weekend as well. On holidays, each employee received a grocery gift card from the company—Charles received his and mine.

Without grandeur, our family helped his when we could. My sister shared hand-me-downs from her girls, and my oldest son sent infant and toddler clothes when Charles' family welcomed a new baby into the world. As a family, we adopted Charles, much like we had done with others along the way. But this time it was different. I had an understanding and appreciation of how tough life can really be, even when a person is employed. Helping Charles and his family felt good—really good.

I learned that although people worked hard, many still faced excruciating decisions given their limited incomes. Even food was, at times, a luxury item. Each night I was safely tucked in my own bed, albeit at my parents' home, and each night Charles was having difficulty falling asleep because of gang wars and gunfire. That was a hard concept to wrap my head around. We lived twenty-five miles apart, but our lives were polar opposites. Compassion filled my heart for Charles and others like him.

To quote Charles, he told me, "It's hard."

My response was, "Charles, God will help you if you just ask him." Then I encouraged him to pray, which he did.

Charles had a great work ethic, a pleasant disposition, and a strong commitment to his family. But I was surprised to learn that he had not completed high school. As Charles and I were becoming friends, we talked about his lack of credentials. "Charles, if there is one thing I would like to see you do, it would be to get your General Education Diploma," I said as a manager and a friend. "It may not make a difference while you're working here, but it will make a difference if you ever leave."

I shared my sense of satisfaction having earned my college degree while working and raising a family. Although it was very difficult, it is something that no one can ever take away from me. Charles heeded my advice, worked hard, and we eventually celebrated with coffee and cake in his honor when he earned his GED.

~

I was hired at Lamplight as a change agent. Given that the majority of the employees had joined the company right out of high school and had never had any other work experience, formal education, or outside training, change was not going to be easy. Most employees only knew one way to do things, which was their way, and, unfortunately, that was not necessarily the best way.

A mentor of mine always encouraged us to make change our friend. I wish I had heeded that advice in my personal life. Change would come, but it was going to be on God's timetable, not mine.

As I hunkered down in my office trying to figure out where

to begin our improvement efforts, it was apparent the opportunities were endless. But because of my secret, I was challenged every step of the way. Some people would not talk to me while others were talking about me, and although the upper management team encouraged the staff to respect my situation, there were a number of employees who took delight in it. Unfortunately, some of these people were direct reports.

During the next few months, our company would be faced with numerous product recalls. Anyone who has ever been involved in a product recall knows how time consuming and expensive these efforts can be. Lamplight was spiraling out of control due to significant quality-control issues. These recalls were going to negate any progress we were making because our continuous improvement efforts had to be put on hold.

~

To make matters worse, in August of 2005 I was named as a defendant in SC Johnson's civil suit. Although my attorney was expecting it, I was not. When my lawyer called to tell me I was added to the lawsuit along with a number of other defendants, I asked what the company was alleging. Much to my shock and dismay, he told me my former employer was accusing me of being a co-conspirator in a racketeering scheme. The nightmare continued.

"So now what?" I asked Mike.

His response angered me: "Katie, you are along for the ride; you were too close to Milt."

On August 26, 2005, an article was published in the *Racine Journal Times*:

> In a lawsuit alleging large cash bribes at poker tables and golf courses, SC Johnson has widened that suit to include another former company employee who worked here.
>
> The amended lawsuit names Katherine M. Scheller of Racine as well as former SC Johnson Transportation

Director Milton E. Morris.

Both Morris and Scheller were fired after SC Johnson said it discovered an extensive corruption and racketeering scheme run by Morris with Scheller's help.

The lawsuit, filed last Oct. 18 in Racine County Circuit Court, also targets several trucking companies. ...

Over a period of years, the suit alleges, Morris channeled millions of dollars in transportation jobs to several companies in exchange for bribes of cash, gifts and trips.

In return, he became wealthy, according to the lawsuit. An ongoing investigation by the company indicated that Morris deposited more than $1.2 million, beyond his SC Johnson salary, into various bank accounts over the years of the scheme. He also reportedly had large amounts of cash in safe deposit boxes, as well as accepting lavish travel and expensive jewelry.

In exchange for the bribes and kickbacks, SC Johnson contends, Morris steered more and more business to his partners in the trucking industry. The Racine-based consumer product company contends Morris cost SC Johnson tens of millions of dollars in unwarranted trucking costs. ...

Morris is also under federal investigation, along with Scheller. ... The pair, both from the Racine area, are being investigated on suspicion of mail fraud, wire fraud and money laundering.

Morris had been SC Johnson transportation director since 1988. The lawsuit says the corruption was under way by at least 1998 and lasted until Morris was fired last Oct. 18.

The cash bribes were often paid during poker games with trucking company representatives. According to the lawsuit, Morris and those representatives often went to Las Vegas and other destinations to gamble, "wagering tens if not hundreds of thousands of dollars, the purpose of these trips was to convey cash and other goods and personal services to Morris and to develop a pretext for Morris' large inflow of cash."

The lawsuit states that Scheller joined the company's Transportation Department in June 1999 as import/export service manager, reporting directly to Morris. It says she joined the conspiracy with him in the last several years.

The suit says they had an "ongoing and long-standing personal relationship. Scheller often accompanied Morris on business trips and visits with some carrier defendants even though there was no business purpose for her travel."

"From her participation in the conspiracy, Scheller received nearly $195,000 or more in cash that she either deposited directly into her accounts or used to pay bills in cash," as well as expensive jewelry, the lawsuit alleges.

The pair also allegedly had plans to keep the scheme going even after Morris retired, and he had arranged for Scheller to succeed him as transportation director.[5]

~

I was in a tough position personally and professionally, yet regardless of the difficulty I had to roll up my sleeves and get to work. Lamplight was in deep financial trouble, and I wondered whether or not the company was going to make it.

Within a short period of time, the management team was forced to terminate over 75 percent of the workforce to save the company. This was hard on me and everyone else. As we entered the cafeteria to announce the downsizing, tears filled my eyes and compassion filled my heart. There were so many families that were going to be impacted by this change, and that was heartbreaking. This was an incredibly difficult time in the company's history and

5 Michael Burke, "SC Johnson adds another name to suit alleging cash bribes at poker games." August 26, 2005. *The Journal Times: http://journaltimes.com/news/local/sc-johnson-adds-another-name-to-suit-alleging-cash-bribes/article_0b4d4927-b74f-5ccd-bcbd-0d2c3afb8e6c.html* (October 21, 2015).

an agonizing time for me personally. God was using this moment to soften my heart.

Although the door was closing for the majority of our personnel, God was opening the door for some key replacements. When I least expected it, some of my prayers were about to be answered. I quickly found myself surrounded by a number of people who previously worked at SC Johnson. Lamplight's new president, vice president of sales (who would become my new boss), their marketing consultant, and director of finance had all spent considerable time at my former company, and I knew most of them quite well.

The arrival of these new employees made me feel much more confident about our chances for success and even more comfortable with my personal situation. They were all there to support me any way they could, which was good news because we had plenty of work to do.

3

My oldest son, Mike, was offered a chance for advancement in the Minneapolis/St. Paul area, so he and his wife, Kelly, moved into a beautiful home in Carver, Minnesota, on June 1, 2006. A few nights prior to their move, a horrific nightmare jolted me awake. In the dream Mike's youngest son, Colin, was in my care but wandered beyond my reach. Before I could grab him, he plummeted from the mezzanine of my former office. I could not get to him; I could not help him. He vanished from my sight and was gone. The terror jarred me from my sleep before I was able to look over the edge of the railing to see if he was dead or alive.

I called my daughter-in-law Kelly to share the details of my horrific nightmare, and my overnight recollection was greeted with dead silence. "Kelly, are you there?" I asked.

When she finally responded, I was speechless. "Katie, you are not going to believe this, but I had the exact same dream last night." Goosebumps covered me.

We agreed this was more than a coincidence, and she promised to keep her eighteen-month-old son on a figurative short leash. Dreams, even nightmares, have a strange way of coming true. Our nightmare unfolded into reality a few weeks later and, thank God, our premonition guided Kelly's attentiveness.

Answering my phone at work, Kelly's voice, barely audible, was full of distress. Her broken words were breaking my heart. Colin, my sweet little Colin, was in the intensive care unit at Children's Hospital in Minneapolis, breathing only with the aid of a respirator. "What happened?" I asked, but there was very little response from my terrified daughter-in-law. "I'll get there as fast as I can," I assured her.

Shock enveloped my very existence. *Hold it together,* I told myself. *Function. Book a flight. Tell my boss. Call my son with the arrival time. Key in ignition. Hurry home. Pack.* Quite frankly, time was a blur. I did not know what else to do, so I prayed. Right or wrong, I even began to negotiate with God.

My son picked me up at the airport after the hour flight and explained Colin had not been feeling well for weeks. Prior to their move, he even received intravenous fluids at the hospital in Green Bay because he was dehydrated and had a fever. After arriving in their new city, he was still not himself, still running a fever, and still not feeling well.

Late one afternoon, Kelly noticed his neck was beginning to swell. She knew something was wrong. Being a concerned mom, she took Colin to a nearby urgent care facility. The doctor thought he had an infection, wrote a prescription for antibiotics, and sent them home. Had Kelly put Colin to bed that evening he would not have survived. A few hours later, Kelly's motherly intuition kicked in, or perhaps our collective nightmare spurred her decision, and they headed to the hospital. The swelling continued to increase, and it was much worse than they had imagined.

Colin's condition was beyond the abilities of the local doctors. The healthcare professionals ordered the patient to be sent to Children's Hospital in Minneapolis immediately. With God as the copilot, a medical helicopter and team were at the hospital, as if waiting to transport my grandson. Colin was on the ride of his life as he and Kelly were airlifted to Minneapolis. It turned out that he had an infection in his lymph nodes, something doctors rarely see, and they needed to cut open his neck and leave it open to drain the poison from his sick little body. Still five months shy of his second birthday, Colin was in an induced coma on a respirator.

Mike and Kelly maintained a twenty-four/seven vigil at the hospital. I distracted and cared for my other two grandsons, Nicholas and Benjamin. And I greeted visitors. Lots of visitors. People who were strangers just weeks before cared for my son's family like life-long friends. The outpouring of love from their new neighbors was overwhelming. Dinners, cards of encouragement, and offers of help arrived each and every day. I was moved to tears by the kindness, generosity, and concern of their neighbors. Mike and Kelly had moved into Minnesota's version of Mayberry. How could we ever repay these people who exhibited God's love when we needed it so much?

Due to his condition, I was not able to see Colin for four days, and when I was finally able to visit, laying my eyes on Colin was as comforting as it was frightening. His breathing tube had been removed that morning and he cried throughout our visit, yet his painfully raspy voice was music to my ears. Late the following day he was released from the hospital.

Watching my son Mike, now a devoted father, carry his weak young son into their home was surreal. With gratitude, humility, and tears in my eyes, I thanked God for intervening on Colin's behalf and saving his life.

To this day I keep a picture of Colin on the respirator close at hand. One might ask why his mother would have taken a picture of him in that condition and why his grandmother would want it. It's because every day we need to be reminded that life is a precious gift and how quickly it can be taken from our grasp. God blessed us again, and Grandma Katie was finally starting to get it. My spiritual journey had officially begun.

～

Four months later, in November of 2006, I would be facing some health problems myself. I ruptured a cervical disc and was in excruciating pain. Quite frankly, the only thing I could compare the pain to was being in labor, and maybe in some ways I was.

We were making progress at work, but unfortunately the news of my injury was not well received. I attempted to work, but the commute was difficult and the pain was unbearable most of the time. Surgery was an option until I heard the neurologist say they would have to cut open my neck in order to fix the problem. I immediately had a flashback of Colin on the respirator and asked if there were any other alternatives. There was only one. Let the disc regenerate the cartilage itself, but that would take time and no one could tell me how long. Despite the pain, that was the method I chose.

The management team at Lamplight allowed me to work from home, yet I was not very productive. I was not sleeping and I refused to take anything other than ibuprofen. I needed to be patient, rest, and let my body heal. Part of me wondered if my ruptured disc was a result of God turning up the heat and trying to beat me into submission because, at the exact same time, the US attorney called my lawyer, Michael Cohn. The government's investigative team wanted to talk to me, live and in person.

As early as January of 2005, my lawyer talked to the US attorney, asking if I was the subject of a criminal investigation and in the line of fire. His response was that I was close to the line of fire. At that time we were uncertain whether or not I would become a target in the criminal investigation or if there would be charges filed against me.

Given this uncertainty and the fact that the civil and criminal cases were related yet different because of their burden of proof, we filed a motion for stay in the civil proceedings. Our motion was denied. I had no option but to exert my Fifth Amendment rights until we knew what was happening in the criminal investigation, because my testimony in the SC Johnson civil case could be self-incriminating.

Michael asked me to meet him at his office so we could prepare for this meeting, but he could see by the pained look on my face that I was in no condition to be interrogated. At the eleventh hour, our meeting with the federal government was postponed. They did not think I was ready.

~

While I was working in Wisconsin, I would use my Florida home to relax. At least twice a month, on a Friday night, I would fly to Tampa and stay there until the last flight departed for Milwaukee on Sunday evening. Holidays and vacation time were used to extend my stay, and I was on a first-name basis with stewardesses and rental car agents.

My townhome became my sanctuary. I quickly realized this house was a special blessing and helped me keep my sanity during a very difficult period of my life. Soaking in the garden tub was heavenly and absolutely one of my favorite things to do, so much so that it quickly became my Friday night, Saturday night, and Sunday morning ritual. The hot, steamy water and fragrant bath salts were just what the doctor ordered. My bathtub was the most relaxing, soothing, tranquil place in the world. It was the only place I could go to escape the truth of my predicament.

Given I was not in Florida on a full-time basis, it took a while to meet many of the neighbors. They were all very friendly, but my weekends were usually spent with Milt. Yes, the affair still continued.

One Friday night, I arrived about nine in the evening and opened the front door to an incredibly loud beeping sound. Great, the smoke detector needed a new battery. Did I even have an extra nine-volt lying around? I did, but the alarm was located higher than I could reach, so I went to the garage to retrieve the ladder, thankful I made that purchase. Given all of the smoke detectors were hardwired, I could get the device open, but for the life of me I could not figure out how to remove the battery. It was apparent I was not going to be able to sleep if I did not deal with this aggravating noise.

Now what? I wondered. *Well, the guy across the street looks pretty handy—he's always repairing something or doing woodworking in his garage.* I was positive he would know what to do. Although I did not even know his name, he was the only person I could come up with at this late hour. So I got up my courage, walked across the street, and rang his doorbell.

For the first time, I formally met my neighbors Joe and Julia. Joe was kind enough to come over and change the battery, and Julia tagged along. Little did we know at the time that this was the beginning of a very special friendship. God really did have me right where he wanted because, as you will eventually find out, Julia was going to be instrumental in guiding me on this journey.

∼

I returned to work three weeks after rupturing my disc, feeling much better. Since our downsizing, my team had been reduced to only a handful of employees. My subordinates covered the gamut of demographics. I had one employee as young as twenty and one who turned seventy while still employed at Lamplight. They came from all walks of life, which made my job interesting. You know there are going to be challenges when you are warned about personality conflicts in your interview and asked the question, "How do you deal with problem employees?"

Jane was my oldest employee and had many years of experience. She was quite good at her job as long as she could do it her way. We would often butt heads, and my personal situation did not help matters. Jane would be the first to greet a new employee and make sure they knew I was trouble. It was apparent that Jane did not respect me.

Deep down I believe there was a kind, compassionate woman, but she would not come out very often. When she did come out, work was wonderful and Jane was a joy to be around, but unfortunately most of the time she seemed terribly depressed. I tried everything I could to win Jane's confidence and trust, but the damage had been done. She was not going to change her opinion of me. Jane was a widow and never had children, yet I truly believed that somewhere beneath that grumpy facade, there was a sweet, lonely lady who just needed to be loved. I guess we were more alike than different.

One day Jane came into my office with some distressing news: she had breast cancer. It was the first time I ever saw her cry. I got up from behind my desk and gave Jane a big hug, and we were both crying. There was the woman I was hoping to meet; I just wish it had been under different circumstances. She was terrified and in for the fight of her life, and I was determined to do whatever I could to help her.

Each day I would walk during the lunch hour, and it almost became comical as to how many pennies I would find. I would walk the same route every day, yet each day I would find more coins. For some reason, the pennies were having a very positive impact on me. I began to hone in on my thoughts when I would find these little treasures, and I realized that every time I found a penny I was thinking of Jane. I told Jane that I believed these pennies were from heaven and it was God's way of telling both of us that everything was going to be okay. The good news was that these pennies were also having a very positive impact on Jane too.

I decided to write a poem entitled "Heaven Cent" and share it with my team. I gave each member a copy, attaching a penny that I had found along my walks.

This lucky penny was sent from above,
to let you know you are cared for and loved.
Treasure this blessing and keep this coin close,
to help you at times when you need it most.
A penny from heaven is truly a gift,
sent by the angels to give you a lift.
The angels are generous and will do their part,
if you promise to live with a grateful heart.
I found this penny while thinking of you,
may your prayers be answered
and your dreams come true.

Given the circumstances, my employees were finally starting to see me in a new light.

⌣

The meeting with the federal government was rescheduled for early February. It was time to tell the truth, the whole truth, and nothing but the truth.

I arrived at work ahead of schedule to ensure my calendar was still blocked—my boss didn't even know where I was going. The federal courthouse staff in downtown Milwaukee was awaiting my arrival, as were a few others. The investigative team included an Internal Revenue Service agent, the Postal Inspector, and a United States Attorney.

Michael Cohn accompanied me to the second-floor conference room, which was massive and intimidating. We seated ourselves at the long wooden table, and the government's team sat across from us. My lawyer and I were outnumbered, but that was the least of my worries.

Prior to arriving, I was asked to prepare one document, a summary of supplier gifts. We talked at length about the case, including SC Johnson's corporate culture and certain individuals. From there it was on to the gifts and cash Milt had given me. The team appeared to be particularly interested in my jewelry.

I shared that every time Milt gave me a necklace, bracelet, or earrings, I also received an appraisal that had his name on it. In addition, I was with Milt when he bought me earrings and a watch at a local jewelry store. By this time, I had a pretty good idea as to what transpired given my lawyers shared boatloads of discovery showing the extent of the corruption in this case.

As a result, I told the investigators that because it appeared the majority of the gifts I received had come from ill-gotten gains, I wanted to return everything. I even went so far as to suggest they send a truck down to Florida for my furniture. With regards to my travel expenses, I had no idea who paid for what. All I knew was that I did not pay for anything. I assumed Milt and his friends split the costs. One time I did question why a particular individual gave airline tickets to me, and I was told by Milt that his friend owned a travel agency.

There was only one significant piece of information I provided about myself that the government did not know. Other than that, I confirmed the evidence against me, and after a reasonable amount of time, much shorter than anticipated, the questioning came to an end. It felt as though the weight of the world had been lifted from my shoulders.

"That went well, Katie, really well!" Michael confidently said as we prepared to leave. My attorney was pleased and his demeanor lifted my spirits. Only one question remained, however: *Would the truth set me free?* That question would not be answered for quite some time, but that particular day it did not seem to matter. I had survived.

~

I did not know where I wanted to be, but it was not where I was. As a matter of fact, I did not want to be anywhere that even closely resembled what I had done or where I had worked for the last thirty years. My life was heading in a very different direction and I was finally going to make a change.

The civil case with SC Johnson was scheduled to begin on January 27, 2008, and I agreed with Lamplight's executive team that it would be best if I was gone by then. Our continuous improvement efforts made it clear that the company could combine customer service and sales management positions, so I offered up my job as a living sacrifice. Lamplight provided a severance package and kept me employed until the week before trial. I no longer wanted to be a distraction to their efforts, yet I was proud of my accomplishments and the results we achieved. My work there was done.

Although I knew leaving was the right thing to do, it was terribly difficult to say good-bye, so I asked my boss to make Thursday my last day instead of Friday without telling anyone. I could not bring myself to say good-bye to my very own team. I cried when I walked out, moved by the experience of the last three years. The Lord had brought me there to teach me some very valuable lessons and surrounded me with the right people to help me endure that difficult time. I hope someday each employee will recognize the significant life lessons that were taught beyond traditional class-room walls.

~

The civil case had a number of defendants, including Milt Morris and me, as well as Thomas Buske, Thomas Russell, and their respective companies. Additional defendants, Bay Darnell and Dave Eggleston and their company, were successful in securing a separate trial. The last defendant, Peter O'Malley and his company, reached a settlement before trial. As a result of this agreement, O'Malley would become a key witness for SC Johnson.

Given I had no money to defend myself, I had no choice but to let the jury decide my fate. I did not admit liability and, as much as I wanted to testify, I could not because of the criminal investigation. Attorneys for the plaintiff painted a picture of greed and corrup-tion with the defense team arguing SC Johnson was overstating the effect of the alleged wrongdoing. Buske's attorney said that much of the evidence that SC Johnson presented would go uncontested. He went on to say that the personal relationship between Morris and his client was not a secret and that it was not corruption. Instead, high-stakes poker and travel were part of the normal course of doing business.[1]

Buske's lawyer told the jury it must decide if SC Johnson was damaged by the situation. The jury needed to determine if the rates the carriers charged for their transportation services were out of line given the high level of service that was required.

Fewer than two weeks into the trial, Peter O'Malley took the stand and confirmed that Morris demanded kickbacks. The kick-backs were discussed in closed-door meetings in Morris' office. "'We sat down and he dictated (the kickbacks) to me,' O'Malley said.

---

1 This was reported in the *The Journal Times* on January 31, 2008.

'I didn't have much to say except to comply; otherwise I would not get the business.'"[2] O'Malley confirmed that he and Thomas Buske paid for Morris' travel to faraway destinations, including Hawaii, Spain, Scotland, and Mexico. O'Malley talked about the cash he had given Morris, yet stated he stopped payments and gave Morris the impression he would be paid after his retirement.

After close to four weeks of testimony, closing arguments began. SC Johnson's attorney asked the jury to award more than $100 million in damages given the breach of fiduciary duty, conspiracy to commit fraud, and the fact that the defendants violated the Wisconsin Organized Crime Act.

During the trial, both Buske's and Russell's attorneys admitted their clients provided payoffs to Morris in order to keep the SC Johnson business. They denied any culpability in an organized action to defraud the company and asked the panel of judges to award significantly lower damages. Buske's attorney asked the jury to award SC Johnson $8.2 million and Russell's lawyer requested the award to be $4.1 million given those numbers were based on the profits both companies made during the bribery scheme.

SC Johnson asked for $101.9 million in damages, and after a day and a half of deliberations the jury awarded the company $147 million. The jury set the following amounts of liability, which did not equal the $147 million cap in the case: Morris $58 million, Buske $52.9 million, and Russell $17.9 million. The jury verdict stated I was responsible for $2.2 million in damages.

The jury further set damages of $70.26 million for Morris and defendants Bay Darnell, David Eggleston, and their company, even though they were not involved in this trial. Additionally, the jury awarded damages of $61.7 million for Morris and Peter O'Malley even though O'Malley and his company had previously reached a settlement with SC Johnson.

2 Janine Anderson, "Witness: Morris demanded kickbacks," February 7, 2008. *The Journal Times*: http://journaltimes.com/news/local/witness-morris-demanded-kickbacks/article_40d5a6e5-6257-588b-b7f0-63553a365f6f.html (October 21, 2015).

I could not help but wonder if the jury understood their instructions. Bay Darnell, Dave Eggleston, Peter O'Malley, and their companies were not even involved in this trial. An appeal was filed, which the Wisconsin Supreme Court later denied.

In the meantime, the judge reduced the amount of damage to what SC Johnson was asking, to $101.9 million. That amount was doubled because of the Wisconsin Organized Crime Act, and this case quickly jumped to the top of the leaderboard as the largest civil verdict ever rendered in the state of Wisconsin. At the end of the day, my lawyer was right. I was along for the ride given I was too close to Milt. I was also on the hook for $203.8 million.

~

With the civil case over, I packed the car and headed to Florida. My neighbors Joe and Julia knew I was no longer working, and I told them to keep their ears open because I needed to sell my house. They did not know about my personal situation or what had just happened in court, and I was not ready to tell them.

A year earlier I had put my townhome on the market in anticipation of losing my job. Although my home was paid for and protected in Florida Bankruptcy Court, without a job I could not afford the taxes and maintenance fees. While listed, there was plenty of interest but no offers.

My attorney, Michael Cohn, suggested I sell the house and everything in it given I would most likely be asked to pay restitution. We had some preliminary discussions with the US attorney on potential criminal charges, and Michael thought it would help if I returned the money.

I took an unconventional approach in regard to the sale of my home, unconventional by the world's standards anyway. I prayed. My prayer was short and sweet. *God, if you want me to sell this house, then send me a buyer.* Well, guess what? He did.

While getting a pedicure, Julia mentioned to the technician that I wanted to sell my house. The nail technician had a male client who had recently come in and told her he was looking for a town-home in Palma Vista. She passed on his phone number to Julia, Julia provided the gentleman's contact information to me, and the rest is history.

Over the course of the next few months, this gentleman stopped by on numerous occasions to see my townhome and eventually gave me a verbal offer. When we first met, he told me he was not interested in buying the furniture or accessories. That was fine—I would cross that bridge when I got there. Well, guess what? There would be no bridge to cross. On his fourth visit, while we were casually talking, he said out of the clear blue, "I want to buy the house and everything in it with the exception of the loft furniture."

I almost fell out of my chair. "Excuse me?" I said.

He repeated, "I want to buy the house and everything in it." He wasn't kidding either. Not only did he buy everything except the loft furnishings, but I also recovered 100 percent of my investment. It is interesting that the loft furniture was the only furniture I had bought with money that I earned while working at Lamplight. Everything else was purchased with the proceeds from my condominium, and most of that money came from ill-gotten gains. I could not help but think of one of Dr. Charles Stanley's life principles: "Whatever you acquire outside of God's will eventually turns to ashes."

My house was in good shape, but I had another problem. What was I supposed to do with an estimated $100,000 worth of jewelry, most of which had never been worn? I was about to find out.

～

Julia had asked me if I wanted to attend a Bible study. After telling her I'd go, we entered the home where the Bible study was being held and I took my seat in the living room. As we were introducing ourselves, many of the ladies were already engaged in conversation.

There was a woman who was sharing how upset she was with

her husband who had just spent an excessive amount of money on a business suit. Although she admitted he needed the suit for his line of work, she felt the price was extravagant. I innocently asked what he did for a living, and, once again, I just about fell off my chair. Her husband sold jewelry.

What is the chance that I would attend my first Bible study with people I did not know and find someone who could help me sell my jewelry? It was a miracle. The woman gave me her husband's phone number, I called him the very next day, and he put me in touch with an estate jewelry company. I wish I could tell you I received 100 percent of its value, but I did not. I must say though, 40 percent was not too bad given the circumstances.

～

As Julia and I spent more time together, I began to meet other women in the neighborhood. One night we decided to head to South Tampa for dinner. It was the first time I met a neighbor by the name of Kim. The only thing I knew about her was that she lived a few doors down, was close to my age, owned an interior design studio, and drove a Mercedes. Of course, when she volunteered to drive, we took her up on the offer.

Kim was a Southern belle who was polite and soft spoken. She had recently divorced, which was why she bought a townhome in Palma Vista. As we were being seated at our table, I knew it was going to be a fun night. I had a captive audience and I may have missed my calling as a comedian. Kim and I had a lot in common, and it was obvious this was the beginning of another special friendship. I did not know it at the time, but Kim was also going to be very instrumental on my journey. God had just confirmed, without me knowing it, that he had me right where he wanted me.

Kim was a member of St. James United Methodist Church, located in Tampa Palms. She invited me to attend their eleven o'clock contemporary service and I was hooked. The music was fabulous and the messages uplifting. I was growing in scriptural knowledge and starting to apply biblical principles to my life. It felt really good to be back in church, and slowly but surely I was beginning to change.

The good news was that I sold my house and consigned my jewelry. The bad news was that it was time to pack up what few possessions remained and return to Wisconsin. My new friends were having a very positive influence on me, and they had no idea how difficult it was to say good-bye.

~

May through November was spent at my parents' home in Wisconsin. It was time for an overhaul of the family homestead. For the next five months I became a general contractor. I learned how to paint and varnish woodwork; we cleaned the entire house from top to bottom, replaced all of the carpeting, took many trips to donate old items, threw away a ton of stuff, and remodeled two bathrooms. Once finished, the house looked fantastic and the sweat equity I put into my great-grandfather's home where my parents have lived since I was born was well worth the time and effort.

In November I knew it was time for a change of scenery, and I found a small one-bedroom apartment just north of Tampa that became my home for the next seven months. At the same time, a media circus was getting ready to begin in Milwaukee. On December 9, 2008, the United States Court for the Eastern District of Wisconsin filed Case No. 08-CR-325 with the Clerk of Court. Unfortunately for me, it was not going to be the greatest show on earth.

Six months earlier, on June 24, I accepted and signed a plea deal with the federal government. Five individuals, including Milt Morris, Thomas Russell, Peter O'Malley, and two of his business associates, Michael Rivett and Patrick Kane, were each charged with two counts of mail fraud given their participation in the racketeering scheme. Milt Morris agreed to multiple counts of mail fraud and one count of violating federal tax laws.

I was charged with two crimes—misprision of a felony for failing to report my knowledge of the scheme and making a material false statement to a federal agent. As I looked at the combined criminal penalties for my two charges, I was facing a maximum term of imprisonment of eight years and a $500,000 fine, and I was responsible for $400,000 in restitution. Thomas Buske, another defendant in this case, would eventually be indicted, and former stockbroker John Burch had already pled guilty to money laundering charges and was sentenced to three years in prison.

We were all due in federal court the end of January to officially plead guilty to these charges. Fewer than twelve hours after this news was made public, only one Lamplight employee contacted me. Charles. I was delighted but not surprised. He learned the lesson. People come first.

Subject: My prayers are with you

I read the article in the *Journal* yesterday. That is a terrible thing to hear. Just know I am here and I still believe in you and if there is anything I could do, let me know. You never treated me different because of who I am and my walk of life and I will never forget that. You taught me to have faith and I do now. My feelings will never change and know that I am praying and thinking of you. Whatever happens, please never forget me and I will never forget you.

Charles, I will always remember your kindness. Although our streets and paths are different, you and I both know that "you have to know it to live it, and understand it to survive it."

Once the news of my criminal charges became public knowledge, it was important for me to tell my girlfriends in Florida. I wanted them to hear it from me, not see it on the news or read about it somewhere else. Julia, Kim, and another girlfriend named Eileen accepted my dinner invitation. As we were finishing our main entrée, I ordered each of them a second glass of wine. They looked at me a little confused, like, *Kate, why did you just do that? Are we celebrating something?*

With dismay, I took a deep breath, swallowed hard, and said, "Guys, I have to tell you something. It's important and it's serious."

Kim looked at me a little perplexed and asked, "Did you get arrested?"

"Well, kind of," I replied, and then I proceeded to share my story. Their acceptance of the situation was extraordinary. They had never met the "old" Kate and even had a hard time believing this could have happened to me. What I had dreaded for years, losing more friends over this situation, did not make one bit of difference to these special ladies. Their love was unconditional and I was thrilled that God had placed me in another caring community.

4

wenty-nine days had passed since the beginning of the new year. The month of well-intentioned resolutions and plans for self-improvement had all but slipped through my grasp. So I found a bit of irony in the timing of my appointment and the fact that I parked in the ramp of an athletic club. My life was in the process of a vast and vital makeover. I typically use the facility's ramp when I meet with my attorney, Michael Cohn. The only thing different about this day was that after I met with him, I was due in federal court to plead guilty to two felonies.

The slam of my car door reminded me of what I was preparing to face. Was I nervous? Yes. Was I scared? A little. Was I ready to get this mess behind me? Absolutely.

As I headed through the building and to the door, I found myself in synchronized steps with a man on the other side of the glass window. I looked out and my eyes connected with a younger African American man whom I had never seen before. Other than noticing his blue coat, stocking cap, and his general existence, I was too absorbed in my own thoughts to focus on any of his particular features.

My mind wondered about everything from whether or not I was wearing the right outfit and if the media would be in court, from hoping I would have the opportunity to fill in the gray area of this seemingly black-and-white case, to worrying if my antiperspirant would last through the afternoon's proceedings, and how I would pay my attorney's bill for his extended day at the courthouse. Fewer than thirty seconds later, as I stood on the corner waiting for the crosswalk to grant me permission to cross the street, the man I saw through the window stood next to me. The stranger greeted me with a hello and a plea for help.

You'll have to believe me when I tell you that in the Midwest, the January wind bites like an angry pit bull. The leaders of cities like Milwaukee, which flank the shores of the Great Lakes, should warn visitors that the unforgiving gusts of winter's wrath really do chill a person to the bone. I wanted to get moving, but he needed help, so I temporarily stalled.

He told me he was looking for a place to get some assistance. At this point, I was not sure if he was homeless, hungry, or going to steal my purse, but he did seem nice and was polite. And on that day particularly, who was I to judge another human being?

I told him I was not from the immediate area and, as a result, I was very sorry that I could not direct him. He explained his journey for assistance steered him to a shelter that someone recommended, but they could not help. He had tried the Salvation Army and a number of other places without any luck. He shared his frustration: "I must have talked to one hundred people, and no one can help me." Shaking his head and half laughing, he continued, "I'm starting to feel like a dolphin; I've had to drink so much water over the last two days."

I asked him if he was hungry, and he said that he was. Before I could say anything more, he resigned to what he believed was yet another rejection. He said he was heading back to the Greyhound bus station, but I stopped him. I told him that I would like to help him, but he would need to walk one more block with me until we reached the lobby of my attorney's office. I knew security personnel stood guard over the building's main entrance for all who entered, whether alone or with a hungry stranger.

As we continued our walk, I asked him where he was from. He stated, "I'm from St. Paul." I casually mentioned that my son lived in Minnesota, not far from St. Paul. We were both shivering as we reached the building, victims of Wisconsin's frigid temperatures and winter winds. As we stepped inside, he told me he was in town for a funeral, and that while he was there someone had stolen his suit. I found that comment strange—*Why would someone steal his suit?* I thought.

Within the safety of the building, I retrieved two $50 bills from my purse and handed the money to the gentleman. "I can't buy you a new suit," I said, "but I can help you get home and get something to eat." His eyes stretched to the size of saucers as he stared at the money in the palm of his thawing hand. His expression was that of disbelief and gratitude, and he simply and softly thanked me. "No booze and only healthy food," I firmly stated while pointing my finger at him, as if I had any control over what he chose to do with his newfound wealth.

As I gathered my belongings and prepared to walk away from him and toward Michael's office, he asked my name. When I told him, he then approached me, his right hand extended. As our hands touched, he said, "God bless you." I was convinced, at that moment, he was an angel. Warm tears filled my eyes as we parted ways. Here I was, facing one of the most difficult days of my life, and God wanted me to know that he was with me.

~

Exhausted after my day in court, I looked like I'd aged ten years during the last week. Dark circles encased my eyes and I looked like I had just gone ten rounds with a championship fighter. In some ways I had. I was beat up, worn out, and humbled beyond words. *How in the world can this be happening?* Every time I relived the events, I would break down and cry. *Did I do the right thing by pleading guilty?*

Judge Clevert's passionate questions were still ringing in my ears: *Are you pleading guilty just to get this behind you? Are you doing this for your family? Are you pleading guilty because you are guilty? Is this what you want to do?* Although I wanted to scream, *Yes, I want to get this behind me; yes, I am doing this for my family;*

yes, I took gifts; but no, this is not what I want to do. I sat alone in the courtroom, broken beyond measure.

Through tears, I uttered a barely audible yes. I was guilty on count eight: misprision of a felony, because "I was aware of kickbacks in the Transportation Department at SC Johnson and I encouraged a coworker to not talk to authorities as they lacked evidence." I was also guilty on count nine: making a false statement. "I made a false statement regarding the company's gift policy. I stated that I had not accepted gifts, when indeed I had accepted gifts in excess of $100."

Judge Clevert's final question caused me to take pause. "So, Ms. Scheller, how is it that you find yourself in this situation?"

Feeling a tremendous amount of shame and humiliation, I sat in silence searching for the right words. After close to a minute, I composed myself, took a deep breath, and as my voice cracked, I said, "I slept with the boss." I stated my guilt and the reason why. Somehow, though, the punishment did not seem to fit the crime. I was facing a total of eight years in prison, and my sentencing date was set for June, on my wedding anniversary of all days.

Having just pled guilty to two felonies, the judge ordered another drug test. I once again was led into the basement of the federal courthouse to pee in a cup in front of a probation officer. My bodily functions now required a witness. Judge Clevert also limited my travel. If I wanted to go see my grandkids in Minnesota, I would have to get the court's permission. I thought to myself, *You have got to be kidding me. I'm not a criminal.* As if it were any comfort, I was right: I wasn't a criminal. That morning I became a convicted felon.

As the probation officer led me to the elevator and we headed downstairs, a warped sense of familiarity washed over me. I had been in the same area earlier in the morning for my booking. During the booking process, a federal marshal led me past the three holding cells that held seven men—the stench of perspiration and desperation was overpowering.

Half kiddingly, I said to the US marshal, "I must be in the wrong place." He assured me I was not. "What did those men do?" I asked.

He replied, "You don't want to know." I was definitely in the wrong place.

The first order of business was answering questions about my life. My family, my financial situation, and who I could trust with my belongings if I was ever put in jail. I laughed and wondered who would want all of my worldly possessions: a blow-up mattress, television, and lawn chair.

Then it was on to the mug shot. The picture showed a person I did not recognize. I had not aged ten years; I aged twenty. It was so bad I begged the marshal to retake the picture. He graciously agreed and encouraged me to smile. The second photo was not much better.

Next it was on to the fingerprints. Since my mundane life had yet to include the need for fingerprinting, I envisioned three-by-five index cards and a metal tin of ink like teachers use to stamp "Good job" on their students' papers. Not so. The fingerprints of this generation are digitally preserved for the ease of tracking people. The process was interesting but not one I would recommend as something you need to experience.

As I drove back to my parents' house to regroup, I knew I had to be strong given how difficult this entire situation had been on them. Pulling into the driveway, I adjusted the rearview mirror and put on my game face. My mom and dad were in their seventies now, and even with six very different kids and a slew of grandchildren, they did not plan on having a convicted felon in the family. They hated the newspaper articles, they hated the blogs, and they hated the gossip, and I hated the fact that I had put them in this situation.

My lawyer arranged a meeting with my probation officer for the next day so I could finish everything while I was still in town. From an emotional standpoint, I figured the worst was behind me. But I could not have been more wrong.

~

Friday found me, once again, in the basement of the federal courthouse where my probation officer led me to her office that was filled with stacks and stacks of paperwork. Surely she was overworked and underpaid. Her office, however, was not a cold, bureaucratic nerve center. A lamp softly illuminated the room; her demeanor was gentle and welcoming. I hoped we would get along due to the fact that we would probably be seeing each other for years to come. After answering the standard list of questions, we began to talk—or more accurately stated, my probation officer began to listen.

For the first time since all of this began, someone was finally willing to listen to my side of the story. No judging. No questions. She just let me get it all out. I cried and cried until my tear ducts went on strike. Years of pent-up emotion flowed from my lips. This woman who exuded compassion expressed genuine concern about my mental health. In response, I retrieved from my wallet pictures of my kids and grandkids. Placing their smiling faces on her desk, I assured her she need not worry. I would never harm myself. Nothing was worth taking my own life.

During the time I battled my former company, two of my relatives lost their wars with mental illness. They committed suicide and I saw what it did to their survivors. That was why Milt's mental stability was of great concern to me and one of the reasons I felt moved to help rather than abandon him over the past five years given he twice threatened suicide.

My probation officer got an earful. Maybe more than she expected, maybe less. I told her everything relating to me personally, my relationship with Milt, and many more things. I told her it was always about love and never about the gifts or the job or the trips. But it was not until I stated aloud that I was still friends with Milt that it hit me. And it hit me like a ton of bricks.

I told her that I walked and talked with Milt each day but his wife did not know this. It sounded so dirty and wrong in the safety of her tranquil office. It wasn't until I heard myself say it that I knew I still had some unfinished business to take care of. I was continuing to live a lie, and although it was killing me on the inside, I did not know what to do on the outside. Milt needed me and I needed help. A devil was perched on one shoulder, an angel on the other. They sparred back and forth, each continuing to entice me as I argued with myself. No wonder my probation officer questioned my state of mind.

Milt and I did need help. When a codependent person like me met a sexually addicted person like Milt, we did not recognize our incompatibility and we somehow convinced ourselves we would live happily ever after. Due to the fact that I was hopelessly devoted to Milt, the basic bargain was struck. The addict plays the role of the wise and dominant parent, and the codependent woman is in the role of the needy child who is too insecure to leave.

At some level I was able to hook Milt's inner child by promising to love him as he has never been loved before without Milt having to give me anything other than sex. Codependents are notorious for promising a mother's love, which was exactly what Milt was missing. Milt got sex anytime he wanted with no emotional cost, and I got what I wanted in return. It was the hope that Milt would never leave me and the fact he would also provide the security I so desperately craved.

The addict is hooked, gets the care he unconsciously needs, and maintains his power without having to admit and take responsibility for his own neediness and insecurity. Partners in addictive relationships truly believe that they have found the one person who will make them happy. Just like I said earlier, I was convinced I had found my soul mate.

What I really needed to do was to learn how to love myself. It was time to deal with the emptiness in my own heart. Given my inability to do this alone, God was going to have to help me break the chains of addiction.

~

That same afternoon my car pulled into the once-familiar driveway and my arrival was not a surprise. My girlfriend said it was all right to stop by and drop off a copy of *The Shack* for her husband. This book is a story about one man's journey and attempt to come to grips with his emotions. The main character's struggles had a profound impact on me and prompted me to purchase a copy for Milt's former best friend.

With book in hand, I rang the doorbell. I was not sure what I was going to say. The massive front door was all that stood between me and Milt's best buddy, his partner in crime, and another defendant in this case. This man had pled guilty to his charges two days earlier. The door slowly opened and his wife invited me in. I had not seen the two of them since October of 2004.

As she escorted me to the kitchen, I caught a glimpse of Tom Russell sitting in the den, casually dressed. He looked so depleted, and I may have been the only one who could relate to just how beat up he was. I placed the book on the table, he greeted me with a big hug, and I couldn't help but begin to cry.

We had all been through hell—neither his family nor mine was immune to the torment. This ripple effect may have been what bothered us the most during this ordeal. We could handle it, but our poor families suffered day in and day out through the civil and criminal proceedings. If only we could turn back time. If only we had made better decisions.

We eventually slipped into leather chairs and friendly conversation. I admitted I was unemployed, flat broke, without money to defend myself, and sleeping on a blow-up mattress. Somehow I managed to laugh. My sense of humor could not be taken from me.

He did not ask about Milt, but I shared that I knew Milt had written him a letter of apology. I told him I did not know what the note contained, but I felt it was part of the healing process for these former best friends. He made it clear that he did not want to hear from Milt, and I told him to call me if he changed his mind. We visited for another hour, and the conversation volleyed from news about grandchildren to plans for the future and from legal frustrations to spiritual truths. As I was getting ready to leave, Tom not only took my number but also shared his address in Florida. He asked me to give his address to Milt.

This was huge. Neither one of them could move forward until they could forgive each other—and themselves. I hoped and prayed this would eventually happen. I was lucky. I was able to forgive fairly early in the process. I hated who I was when I was angry. It consumed and changed me. So it was up to me to decide that each day would be a good day. It was the one thing I could control.

In spite of the whirlwind of emotion during the previous few days, overall I had remained pretty stable during the last four and a half years. Even my attorneys were surprised and impressed with how well I held up during the civil and criminal proceedings. The credit goes to my sense of humor and positive attitude, but the glory goes to God. Without my faith I would be nothing. If a person does not turn to God during a time like this, he or she may never turn to him. I read books written by many Christian authors and surrounded myself with anyone and anything that could provide answers as to why this was God's plan for my life—when it certainly was not the life I had expected.

The battle I endured over the last few days, however, was obvious. My eyes remained swollen, and my lack of sleep churned my nausea. Bananas and Triscuits sustained me. I am not sure if this was better or worse than the McDonald's breakfast burritos that nourished me after I got fired. The truth is that stress plays funny tricks on a person's body.

Saturday morning arrived and I was ready for my return flight to Florida. I could not wait to get out of Wisconsin. My girlfriends had arranged dinner when I returned so I did not have to be alone. As I drove into my old neighborhood in Palma Vista, I wondered how I was going to be received. It was about four o'clock in the afternoon when my friend Julia, dressed in her bathrobe, met me at her front door.

~

I sat at Julia's kitchen table and tried to put a positive spin on my situation. We talked briefly about the trip, but she could see the pain in my face. My eyes didn't lie. It was a tough few days.

When I arrived, Julia actually seemed a little bit anxious but I did not know why. She was still in her bathrobe, which was somewhat unusual given it was four o'clock in the afternoon. She told me she had a special gift for me that I could not say no to or it would hurt her feelings. She put a lot of thought into her plan.

Julia led me into her master bathroom, where candles burned peacefully on the garden tub's edge, bath gels and other fragrant products lined the counter, plush towels rested near the sink, and a fresh robe hung from the closet door. Her gift to me was a much-needed soak in the tub, a treat she knew I needed, one I would greatly appreciate and a gift I could not resist.

Julia knew me well. This was one of the few ways I liked to relax and yet I had not soaked in a luxurious tub like this since I sold my house eight months earlier. I hugged her and completely lost it. Sobbing, I said, "Julia, I have just had the worst three days of my life."

She whispered, "I know." Julia held me tighter than anyone had ever held me before—anyone. She did not say another word. No words were needed. Her love spoke for itself.

I struggled to regain my composure. I was almost half naked, or "necked" as she called it, before she closed the bathroom door. Water filled the garden tub at a fairly fast pace—I was ready. My soak required emptying the hot water tank and she encouraged me to do so. I told her I might not come out for days. "Take your time," she said. "I'll be waiting. Come out when you're done."

I eagerly picked out my bath salts. The sweet smell of jasmine wafted through the steamy air. The water was as hot as I could stand and the dimmed lights lured me into a deep relaxation. For a brief moment all of my problems seemed washed away. It was a calming and peaceful experience and the most precious, thoughtful gift I had ever received.

Reluctantly I crawled out of the tub, knowing my other girl-friends would soon be arriving. It was so kind of Julia, Kim, and Eileen to see that I had company when I returned. Kim and Eileen did not press me for details; they just allowed me to talk and share the experiences I had just had. That's what girlfriends do. They are there for you when you need them and are great listeners. Yet because they love and care about you, every once in a while they speak their minds. Because you love them in return, you listen. Honest conversations are not always easy, but they are necessary.

Julia had taken her dog out for a walk, so Kim, Eileen, and I continued our conversation. I was sharing the story of meeting my probation officer and mentioned to them that I told her I was still exercising and talking to Milt on a regular basis, but his wife did not know we were still friends. This was the second time in two days I had said this out loud, so I knew deep in my heart it was bothering me.

Kim, who was normally soft spoken, looked at me, turned her head as if to muster up enough courage to say something, and told me what I needed to hear. "Kate, I have wanted to say this for two weeks," she admitted. "I am not sure if you are ready to hear it, but I need to say it. This has got to stop!" There, she had said it. And you know what? I was finally ready to hear it. She came over and gave me a hug and continued, "You need to give his wife that gift—she deserves to have her husband."

Her words were more impactful than imaginable, as Kim was terribly hurt when her husband cheated on her. I had finally met someone who was willing to tell me what it was like to be hurt by an affair. It was hard for her to say, because she was still hurting from it. It was hard for me to hear because I immediately thought of Milt's wife and the hurt I had caused her. I appreciated Kim's straightfor-wardness. It was not going to be easy, but she was right. This had to stop. I had to give Milt's wife the gift she deserved, her husband.

At that point, Julia walked in, saw that I was upset, and asked what was wrong. "Just group therapy," I replied.

We reiterated our conversation, then Julia plunked down in the chair and began to speak. "You guys are not going to believe this. Early this afternoon God laid the exact same thing on my heart. So loudly and strongly, in fact, that I had to pull the car into a parking lot. There was only one other time that God spoke to me this way and that was after my mother died."

Bewildered, none of us could believe what was happening. I shared a couple other small signs that had appeared over the last few weeks, including the fact that I was praying for a successful separation from Milt. God was trying to get my attention, I was trying to get his, and it was working. He was sending out reinforcements. A full-court press. I was finally open to the change I so desperately needed, and God was providing strength and guidance through my friends.

Well, we all knew what I needed to do, so I asked them, "When do you think I should do this?"

"Better sooner than later," Kim responded in a direct voice. Why did I know she was going to say that? I reflected on the fact that I was in the process of a six-week Bible study at St. James called *Discerning the Voice of God* by Priscilla Shirer. The course was intended to teach us how to recognize when God speaks.

We had finished our third week of study, which was titled "The Voice of the Holy Spirit." As part of our homework we were asked to write what the Holy Spirit had taught us. As I looked back on my notes, I smiled. Here is what I had written one week earlier.

What has the Holy Spirit taught you as you studied today?

That God will be persistent in guiding me toward total obedience and will be with me every step of the way. He may also use others to help me.

What is God asking you to do as a result of today's study?

Be receptive to every prompting and look for messages everywhere. Remain obedient knowing God is guiding my specific steps and direction.

And finally,

Write a prayer responding to God's commands to you.

Dear God, thank you for purposefully and persistently working in me to be obedient. Please remove all strongholds in my life so that I may walk in your light. God, help me hear your voice and guide me with authority. Give me the strength to endure the trials of next week and help me be a shining example of love, joy, peace, patience, kindness, goodness, faithfulness, gentleness, and self-control.

Little did I know that in fewer than eight hours God was going to answer that prayer. He had already laid some heavy stuff on my heart and was ready to help me remove the stronghold in my life. Given God is an awesome God, he was also going to be nice enough to tell me exactly what I needed to do. Now it was up to me to listen.

~

As I made the drive up I-75 toward my apartment, I turned on The JOY FM and contemporary Christian music filled the car. I sang along, glad that no one could hear the notes I missed, comforted by the lyrics of the songs. The melodies were familiar as they were part of the Sunday morning worship services at St. James, my home church. My home church and my home apartment. Either way, I was home.

Apartment living was interesting. This was my first experience in a rental. My other homes were all big and beautiful, so this was new to me. I quickly realized that living in an apartment was like having a disposable life. Tenants would come and tenants would go. When they left, most of what they owned was deposited into the Dumpster. Their cars were packed with whatever remained, and they headed off to their next destination. I was now one of the drifters.

As I turned into the complex, I stopped at the mailbox to retrieve my much-needed unemployment check. Opening the door of my apartment, I found it exactly as I had left it. The lawn chair, which served as my recliner, was waiting for me, and so were my television and blow-up mattress. That was it. Home sweet home. My material possessions were reduced to a few items: the clothes on my back and not much else.

Exhaustion consumed me as I stepped over the threshold. I could not wait to crawl onto my AeroBed and let the low humming of the television lull me to sleep. My emotions were fried, and I desperately needed new strength. I had some unfinished business to take care of. Thankfully, I do not remember too much after my head hit the pillow at eleven o'clock at night.

It seemed like mere minutes, but five hours later I was jolted from a deep slumber. I found myself sitting on the edge of the mattress, my head cradled in my hands. Cries escaped my throat. "I can't live like this anymore!" I bellowed in a voice I hardly recognized as my own. Over and over again, this plea bounced off the surrounding walls. My desperation escalated. "God, please help me! I can't do this alone. I can't live like this anymore."

My emotions were on the brink of disaster. Tears and groans spilled from me in a way I had never experienced before. I was completely broken. With one final appeal, I begged in total surrender, "God, please help me." Suddenly, peace enveloped me.

Quiet tears continued as I heard God speak: *Tell him to love her like he's never loved her before, and he will get his miracle.* Humility drenched me as I ran into the kitchen, grabbed a piece of paper, and transcribed these words. God had just told me exactly what I needed to do.

I had to give Milt's wife the gift she deserved, and I needed to give Milt God's gift of direction for his life. Milt had been praying the impossible prayer for months. He told me that each day he was praying for a miracle, that somehow his life would be spared, that he would not get any prison time, or if he did, it would be reasonable so he would not die in jail. It appeared that God was putting the ball squarely in his court and the rest would be up to him. And me.

I had to let him go. Not for today. Not for ten days. But forever. No deals, no weak moments, no manipulations. He was a married man and he needed "to love his wife like he's never loved her before," and then he would get his miracle. I knew in a few short hours I would release him; I would have to say good-bye.

Needless to say, I did not fall back to sleep. For three days, I had not slept but a few hours each night. Neither was I eating, and the mirror confirmed it had been a rough week. But somehow I knew I had to pull it together because the place I needed to be on Sunday morning was church. I had to continue to pray for God's strength, and I needed the support of my girlfriends. I hopped into the shower, got dressed, and headed to St. James.

Many of the congregation's members were outside serving as greeters and visiting with one another, which is our Sunday tradition. Two women, whom I had met while working in the Metropolitan Ministry tent at Christmas and who could both see something was wrong, welcomed me. I received a big hug from Paula, who asked me if I was okay. "Not really. It's personal," I said.

"Well," she responded, "you are in the right place, and I will pray for you. I hope things get better."

~

Home. My home church. That was what was so special about this place. I always felt welcomed, accepted, and loved. During the three months I had been in Florida, I did not miss one service. I enjoyed the format, the music, the sermons, and the people. I was growing in my faith, and these folks provided opportunities for me to serve. I was willingly becoming one of God's disciples.

Pastor Steve knew my story. Three weeks earlier, I had bared my soul and my past to him. Pastor Steve was a calm but happy gentleman, several years younger than me who exuded compassion. He helped me begin my volunteer service through the church. He was the closest thing to God I could find, a godly man no doubt, and he was the person in whom I confided. God knows the truth, but I did not want Pastor Steve to be hit with any surprises down the road, should someone find out I was a convicted felon. It was hard to tell him the truth and risk his judgment or rejection, but it was important to my healing process. Steve encouraged me to continue to walk in faith, making God-honoring decisions.

It was Super Bowl Sunday, a day earmarked across the country by parties and festivities. Pastor Steve's morning message shared stories of biblical feasts and celebrations. He encouraged those in attendance to take time out of our busy schedules to uphold traditions like Super Bowl parties and embrace the fellowship opportunities these celebrations provide.

Steve explained that as we walk with God, we are inspired to show up each week and worship. Following the inspiration, God prepares us to do his work. We surround ourselves with the things and people who can help us become the person God intended us to be. Finally, we reach the point of celebration and thanksgiving for our journey and the end result.

The words inspired Kim to lean over to me and say, "Kate, he's given you the framework. This is how you need to serve it up, in a positive way. Celebrate that you have finally gotten to this day."

How true. I had survived so many struggles. This was not a day for sadness or gloom. This was a day of celebration. Pastor Steve and Kim's words sealed the deal. By twelve thirty my journey was taking me to Milt to say good-bye so he could love his wife like he'd never loved her before.

5

I pulled into the cul-de-sac where we routinely parked our cars—the dashboard blinked 1:15 p.m. The warm sun drenched the undeveloped subdivision near Milt's house. Homes had yet to be built but the paved roads provided a safe, quiet place for us to walk and talk. This place was a pseudo therapist's office where we pounded the pavement and talked about anything and everything.

Conversations ranged from growing in our faith to how we felt about what was happening to us, and from how this experience had changed both of us for the better to openly admitting we were ready to get on with our lives. The walks provided an escape from the stress of each day and also kept us in great shape. On this path, we clocked more than hundred miles each month, steps that hopefully led us away from dysfunction. We had agreed to meet at one thirty, and, as usual, I was early. Milt knew this was one of my habits, so it was not a surprise to see him pull up a few minutes later.

I grabbed a box of Kleenex and bottle of water before I exited the car. "Let's sit and talk," I said after I greeted Milt.

"Nah, let's walk," he responded. A part of me figured he knew what was coming. Our steps soon synchronized as we traced the familiar path. Our faces, still chiseled with the emotions of the past week, relaxed when we were back in one another's company.

As we walked under the blue Florida sky, a handwritten note peeked out of my pocket. Milt did not know I had gone to visit his estranged best friend. My excitement rose as I presented him with a piece of paper that resembled and symbolized a white flag of surrender. For a long time, Milt's anguish was fueled by a need to be forgiven by his longtime friend. His eyes fixated on the scribbled address, recognizing the handwriting of his "partner," a name they affectionately called one another. Relief washed over Milt's face as he realized he could send his letter of apology and it would be openly received by this person he loved like a brother.

I was so happy for Milt. He was finally going to be able to release the burden he had carried for years. He was finally able to tell his best friend he was sorry. My efforts were rewarded because this was one of the last things I needed to help facilitate. I could give Milt that precious gift as a going-away present, the gift of forgiveness.

The moment of gladness soon turned to sadness. It was my turn to talk about how I was feeling and Milt was listening: "Milt, I cannot live like this anymore. Let me tell you what's been happening to me over the last few days." I then shared the story of my angel encounter on Thursday, the meeting with my probation officer on Friday, what God laid on my heart on Saturday, and the fact that God spoke to me that very morning. The promptings could not be ignored. I continued, "Our strength has to lie in the Lord, not in ourselves. We have to remind ourselves that the dark moments of our life will last only as long as necessary for God to accomplish his purpose in us."

We needed to celebrate the fact that we were starting to see the light. From my other pocket, I retrieved the note I had written during the night, the first-class heavenly mail. I read the note aloud documenting what God instructed me to tell him. "Milt, God told me to tell you to love her like you have never loved her before and you will get your miracle. Milt, you need to give your wife of forty-nine years that gift, and you cannot do that while I am in your life," I said while handing him the note.

Through this trial we had to realize that our heavenly Father was not punishing us, but merely opening our hearts and hands to receive something better. Milt was heartbroken. I was his only close friend, his rock. Unfortunately, sometimes I was also his crutch. I was the one who helped him hold it together through this whole ordeal. When everyone else walked out of his life, I stayed. A true friend really does walk in when the rest of the world walks out. But what Milt failed to realize was the fact that his wife stayed too.

I provided strength, a listening ear, and companionship to Milt for close to five years, and he did the same for me. But I needed to give him the space God instructed, which was the hardest thing I have ever had to do as a friend. My work was ending and God was gently shutting the door.

Milt pleaded with me to reconsider, but I countered with a request for him to keep an open mind and heart to God's prompting: "Milt, I do not know what God wants you to do. I have an idea, but I think you have to figure it out for yourself. It may be your wife, it may be your family, I do not know what it is. But I do know with one hundred percent certainty that you cannot do it while I am in your life. Pray about it, call your pastor, do whatever you need to do, because you have less than 150 days to get it right because our sentencing date is set for June 26. God has given you a special gift. He told me to tell you what you need to do to get your miracle."

We hugged, we cried, and I thanked him for his love. Tears spilled onto my T-shirt as I gratefully acknowledged his friendship and told him I would pray for him each and every day. Milt told me he loved me. More importantly, he once again apologized for the situation he had put me in. He had already apologized years earlier and I had forgiven him, but he needed to articulate it again—it was part of the healing process and part of his miracle. We agreed that our friendship was not fair to me, not fair to him, and certainly not fair to his wife.

With a broken heart, puffy eyes, and a runny nose, I said goodbye to my old boss, my love, one of my best friends, and my exercise buddy. Although I was truly celebrating how God was working in our lives, it hurt to breathe. I felt like I had just been tackled by the front line of the Green Bay Packers and the wind had been knocked out of me.

We parted ways on Super Bowl Sunday.

~

Partial obedience is disobedience. You cannot negotiate with God. Due to the fact that I was attempting to walk away from a lengthy codependent relationship, it should not have been a surprise when a familiar number showed up on my caller ID Sunday night. My girlfriends predicted this would happen and they told me not to answer the phone, but I did anyhow. Milt asked me to meet him for a cup of coffee on Monday morning, and little codependent me agreed.

The Golden Arches greeted us, and I was steadfast with my position. Over and over again I told Milt I refused to live like this any longer. We replayed Sunday afternoon's conversations, but this time it was a little bit different. The core of my being was gouged and bleeding, and the hurt was obvious. Why had I agreed to come?

Milt's hand reached across the table to take mine and he asked me to look at him in his eyes. Reluctantly, I did. He tenderly apologized for all the hurt he has caused. As he continued, I just wanted to scream. I wanted to jerk my hand from his grasp, to shed his control from my life once and for all. In his delusion, he thought we could still be friends. He offered to come over and walk near my house if I preferred. Why was he not getting what I was saying?

I struggled to find a way to get this crucial message through his thick skull. "Okay, Milt, I'll make you a deal," I said. "I'll come over to your house, and we will sit down with your wife. If she gives me permission to walk and talk to you, then I can still be your friend."

It took less than a second for him to retort, "You know I can't do that."

"I know you can't," I said smugly. "That is why I know we are doing the right thing." He walked me to my car and made one more futile attempt to change my mind. His image finally got smaller in my rearview mirror as I drove away. This was so hard.

~

I reflected on the painful memories Milt had shared as we walked and talked over the past two years. As a child, he experienced things that were hard to comprehend. The physical abuse he suffered at the hands of his stepfather was horrific and, as a result, he left home when he was fifteen. He was emotionally abandoned by his family and never felt good enough. Through all his searching and despair, he too began looking for love in all of the wrong places. The ongoing affairs, the lustful thoughts, the sex addiction, and narcissistic behavior were all trying to fill a void.

Eventually Milt became addicted to me. I represented the love and nurturing he was missing. Unfortunately, our relationship was still being used as an attempt to locate this elusive love. Milt found great comfort in our friendship, and I believe our time together helped him escape the truth of his excruciating childhood pain that he had yet to deal with.

All of his life Milt believed people would like him if he had enough money, expensive clothes, a beautiful house, a luxurious car, and a powerful job. The success he enjoyed throughout his career was not enough, however; he continually wanted more. The accomplishments did not satisfy him, which is why I believe he got into the trouble he did—it was never enough. Millions of dollars could not fill the emptiness in his heart. He had yet to realize that a person cannot buy love.

I was trying to help Milt end this vicious, addictive cycle, and although the adult in him agreed, the wounded child remained petrified. We both needed to take an inward journey into the chaos and fear, deal with the pain from our past, and learn how to fill our hearts with God's love. The good news was that we were beginning to see the light. It was time to take responsibility for our actions. We were developing confidence and knew that something needed to change.

Neither one of us wanted to live like this anymore. And that is where God came in. He was surrounding us with the right people and circumstances to begin our healing. God was also making it clear that our recovery had to include sexual abstinence, which is exactly why he was trying to distance me from the object of my affection.

~

That same morning, I was back at St. James volunteering as a member of their prayer committee. Prayer requests were made to the church, and our committee typed and shared them with the congregation. I took my seat at the desk to begin my work when Pastor Steve came into the office and welcomed me back. I told him I had survived my ordeal in court, and I think we were both glad I could actually share what happened without crying. My excitement could not be contained, however, when I told him about meeting an angel. He just looked at me and smiled. Steve had a calming effect on me. His body language spoke of the pleasure he found in watching my transformation. We talked for a few more minutes before I returned to the task at hand.

While plugging along on the keyboard, one of the ministry leaders stopped by and introduced herself. I mentioned I was unemployed and had additional time to volunteer if they needed me. We discussed my interests, and I shared that I had a knack for getting along with older people. The Homebound Ministry team sounded like a good fit, and she promised someone would contact me.

Turning back to the computer, I paused as I read the next prayer. It simply stated: "My dear, dear friend. Please shower her with prayers, strength, and God's grace." I did not even have to look at the name on the card. It was my girlfriend Kim. I immediately felt her love, and her precious gift of prayer touched my heart. Kim's concern had landed me on the official prayer list. I needed all of the help I could get. I was now going to have more than a thousand people praying for me.

The woman who led the Homebound Ministry team called when I returned home. She told me about two opportunities that were available, but one of them was slightly more pressing than the other. There was an elderly couple who lived in an assisted-living facility and their family was hoping someone could visit. The names were familiar. Just hours earlier, I had typed prayer requests for them. I informed her that the husband was in a local hospital's intensive care unit. She provided me with the address and directions to the facility, their room number, and permission to head over on Tuesday and see how I could help.

Only a handful of days had passed since my encounter with that cold, hungry angel, and somehow I had survived. The previous days left me emotionally spent, so uninterrupted sleep was what my mind and body desperately needed. But as Monday's moon began to make way for Tuesday's sun, I was prematurely wrenched from my dreams.

The realization hit me over the head like a ton of bricks. As I circled my sparsely furnished apartment in the mystical pre-dawn hours, I was filled with total amazement. I could hardly believe what I experienced. "He was from St. Paul. From St. Paul," I repeated aloud to no one. "It was St. Paul who had a role in this—it had nothing to do with Minnesota!"

St. Paul sent me my angel, and we met on the corner of Broadway and Mason in Milwaukee, Wisconsin. All of a sudden, the funeral and the missing suit made sense. For it was Paul who wrote 2 Corinthians 5:17: "This means that anyone who belongs to Christ has become a new person. The old life is gone; a new life has begun!"

The angel stated he was in town to attend a funeral—it was my funeral: the end of my previous life. My old ways, my past sins, were gone. Thank goodness someone stole his suit. My angel symbolized and delivered the message that my Christ-filled new birth, my new life, had begun.

Christians are brand-new people on the inside. The Holy Spirit gives us new life when we are born again, and that happened to me on Super Bowl Sunday. Do you remember when my angel told me he had to drink so much water he was starting to feel like a dolphin? Bet you didn't know dolphins symbolize rebirth, did you?

What makes this encounter even more extraordinary is the fact that Paul is the person I have most admired on this journey. St. Paul—the guy to whom I can truly relate, the apostle who was applauded for his perseverance and deep faith, the author of my favorite books in the Bible, and the guy who did his best work in prison. As unbelievable as it sounds, an angel really touched me.

~

Tuesday morning I checked in with the director of first impressions at the assisted-living facility and told her I was part of St. James' ministry team. She was happy to see that someone was here to visit Helen, commenting, "She is so lonely."

The facility seemed really nice and did not smell too bad. I was ready to brighten someone's day, but the spring in my step quickly deflated. As I turned the corner and entered Helen's room, I was not ready for what I found. Helen was slumped over in her wheelchair drooling on her shoes. I did not know if she was dead or alive.

"Helen? Helen!" I practically shouted. She could barely lift her head, and I helped her sit up. I grabbed some Kleenex and tried to wipe her face. My stomach churned. The woman at the front desk failed to prepare me for this initial scene. She told me that Helen was not always able to verbalize her thoughts due to her Parkinson's disease. That particular day was a day she could not talk. So here I was in a room with a woman I did not know, and she was not feeling real well and not able to communicate. She began to rub her stomach. *Uh-oh.*

"Helen, do you have to use the restroom?" I asked. She managed to nod in affirmation, and I quickly left to get some assistance. When the aide arrived, she asked me to help her get Helen in the bathroom. It was too late, and we had a mess. Poor Helen. I apologized that I had to excuse myself. I was not trained to handle a situation like this and, obviously, neither was my stomach.

It took quite a while to clean her up. The clock's hands signaled the start of the lunch hour, so we needed to head down to the cafeteria. I did not bring anything to eat either, which was a very good decision.

Helen was able to point to her table, and I pushed her in and took the spot normally reserved for her husband. I helped her with her food. Helen was having a difficult time eating, and I was having a difficult time watching and wondered what I had gotten myself into. It took Helen almost two hours to eat her lunch. I said good-bye four hours after arriving, promising I would be back the next day.

~

On Wednesday, my journey down the familiar hallway appeared to end at a different destination. Helen was sitting straight up in her wheelchair, anxiously awaiting my arrival. Much to my surprise she could talk! It was a good day as I learned many things about her—when she was born, where she grew up, where she used to work, and when she got married. She shared the names of all of her family members and coyly admitted she had married a younger man.

I asked, "If you could watch anything on television, what would it be?"

"Comedy," she replied. Helen and I had something in common: we both loved to laugh. We also had similar interests in books and loved to read the Bible.

Helen was starved for companionship. As we sat in the living area of her small apartment, a woman from a few doors down named Margaret walked by. I immediately knew Margaret was a character and invited her in for a visit. She looked at me a little perplexed, like no one had ever done that before. The three of us sat and talked and laughed together, although Margaret did most of the talking. I told Margaret that Helen's husband was in the hospital and that I was there to help.

Margaret looked sad. She understood. She had lost her husband, a Baptist minister, years ago. She looked deep in Helen's eyes and held her hand and told her that she knew what she was feeling. "I know what it feels like when you begin to lose the man you love," Margaret said. "It's very, very hard. It tears your heart out, doesn't it?"

Helen nodded.

"I know you miss him, don't you?"

Helen nodded again, and I was beginning to wonder if she was talking to Helen or to me.

"But it will be okay, sweetie. God will take good care of him, and you know what? He will also take good care of you. It will all work out the way it's supposed to—it always does, it's God's plan," stated my wise new friend.

The conversation flowed as we shared other facets of our life, including special memories. Margaret was an honor student, she sang a song to us in Latin to prove just how smart she was, and Miss Stout—God bless you wherever you are—you were her favorite teacher. We even visited Margaret's room, where she gave us a bird's-eye view of her cardinal collection.

It was official—we were girlfriends. Lunch duty was much easier to digest the second day, and I was hungry to make the most out of my volunteer opportunity. As I headed out the door, the receptionist thanked me for my time. "People don't do what you're doing, and you will be blessed for this," she said.

I turned, looked at her, and smiled, "I already have been!"

～

Within twenty-four hours, a frantic message pleading for my prayers was left on my voicemail. Milt's grandson had reportedly suffered a medical emergency and was in the hospital. I did not know what to believe and, once again, like a good codependent, I called out of care and concern. Surprise. Everything was fine.

Then Thursday rolled around, and I was gone most of the day. As I was heading home from Bible study, the phone rang. Like Pavlov's dog, I answered. "I'm not supposed to be answering your calls," I said to Milt on the other end.

I responded to his inquiry as to where I was, and he told me he had visited my front door. When I got home, it looked like Christmas minus the sleigh and eight tiny reindeer. Tons of goodies lined the threshold of my rented abode. Tucked along the juvenile tidings of bribery was a handwritten note. Apparently, in my absence, Milt had made multiple trips to my apartment that day. He asked me to reconsider my decision and listed numerous reasons why he felt our friendship could and should continue. Touching Bible verses peppered his message. Yet again, he claimed he would respect my decision to sever the friendship if that was what I wanted.

We were speeding along on a roller coaster of emotion and yet by doing the right thing Milt was terrified of losing me. He needed to read and reflect upon the words he had written. He needed to listen to God. It was bigger than us. Milt needed to understand his behavior without losing sight of God's point of view. He needed to dig down deep into his soul and live these biblical principles.

Friday arrived and so did another call. Again he wanted to meet for breakfast. Again I told him that was not a good idea. And again he argued the point. I told him we could agree to disagree, but without his wife's permission I could no longer see him. He was starting to get mad, which was good. I was making progress.

"Well, if that's the way it's going to be, then I guess this is good-bye," he said.

"I guess it is," I replied as the line disconnected.

Seven silent days passed before Milt showed up on the eve of Valentine's Day. Finally after a cordial talk, he understood why I felt so disrespected by his resistance to change. He apologized and we once again talked about God's plan for our lives and the need for both of us to be obedient.

Slowly, Milt was learning to look to his pastor for support and guidance. I encouraged this relationship and even offered, on a limited basis, to accompany him to sessions with his pastor. I was too closely involved to realize my offer continued the codependent cycle. Letting go was hard.

Milt was involved in a program that helps people overcome hurts, hang-ups, and habits. Celebrate Recovery is a Christ-centered ministry, and Milt was a trained and certified facilitator. Each week, he would help a small group of recovering addicts get back on the right path. Through his volunteer efforts, Milt was touching hearts and changing lives, yet he was unable to recognize his own needs.

Although Milt had made great strides in his spiritual journey, and as hard as he was trying to be obedient and follow God's will for his life, his fear of abandonment had a stranglehold on him. The thought of losing me left him gasping for breath.

~

It had been a month since God had spoken to me about my relationship with Milt. With the exception of the anxiety I was feeling relative to my finances, my attitude was good. I was broke and living paycheck to paycheck. There was not much left over once I got done paying my attorney, and at my lowest point I was down to $34.42 in my checking account.

On February 28, I got up at midnight for a potty break and much to my surprise once again heard God's voice: *Hebrews 13:5.* I was groggy and thought, *Okay Lord, Hebrews 13:5,* and went back to bed. Well, about four o'clock in the morning I got up a second time and I heard him again, but this time it was much louder and more direct: *Hebrews 13:5.*

I was now having a conversation with God in the wee hours of the morning. "Yeah, I know, this is the second time you told me. I'm really tired; when I get up in the morning, I'll go read Hebrews 13:5," I said. I could not have even told you if Hebrews had thirteen chapters, but I kept my promise and first thing in the morning I stumbled to my lawn chair, sat down, grabbed my Bible, and opened it to the book of Hebrews. Well, guess what?

Hebrews does have thirteen chapters, and I could not believe what I found:

> Don't love money; be satisfied with what you have. For God has said, "I will never fail you, I will never abandon you." (Hebrews 13:5)

I was shocked and speechless. God knew I had a great deal of concern regarding my finances, but, more importantly, he also knew I had a love of money. This was one of the reasons I had found myself in the position I was in during that time. God had to empty me so I could get to know him a little bit better. And although we were in the very early stages of our courtship, with a promise like that, I knew he was one man I could trust.

When I told the associate pastor at my church what happened, he asked, "Katie, when God spoke to you, did you hit your knees?"

I sheepishly admitted, "I didn't know I was supposed to."

~

As I continued my Homebound Ministry volunteer efforts, I realized I had found my calling. I was amazed at how much Helen was eating after a short while. The first few times I visited it was like watching a baby bird struggle with a worm. I chalked some of it up to her condition and some to the fact that she missed her husband. Within a week, however, I had commented on what a great job she was doing as she cleaned her plate, which was a far cry from our first lunch. She looked at me, smiled, and said, "You are good for my appetite!"

I will also treasure the kind words of Margaret, who reminded me that because she had been married to a Baptist minister, she knew I was a Christian. When I asked her how she knew that, she simply looked at me and said, "You have a Christian smile!" *Wow, this has been a great day.*

Well, unfortunately not every day can be a good day. When I arrived on Monday, Helen was sick. We did not even go to lunch.

So while she sat with a bucket in her lap, I provided some company. Her husband was not doing well, and it looked as though her family was beginning to pack up his belongings. I wondered if this had something to do with the way Helen was feeling—I'm sure it did. As much as everyone hated to admit it, it was only a matter of time before Helen would be alone on a full-time basis.

A few weeks later, a new lady named Grace joined our dining room table. Grace was a small, robust Italian woman with a lot of spunk. I could hardly believe it when she told us she was ninety-three years old! Grace loved to cook and apologized that she could not invite me over because she did not have a stove in her room. Her favorite recipes included stuffed green peppers and her spaghetti sauce with meatballs. The secret ingredient in both was the potato, but not until the sauce came to a boil.

Well, given Grace's love of food and cooking, I shared that I had a girlfriend who loved to eat. As a matter of fact, I told Grace she would start wondering what's for dinner before we even finished lunch. Grace looked at me and said, "You know what she needs?"

"No, Grace, what?" I asked.

"A good man!"

I almost died laughing. If she only knew the rest of the story.

About a month later, while having dinner, Grace was upset and asked me what she should do. Apparently some of the aides were teasing her, claiming she broke her wheelchair. In her thick Italian accent, gesturing with her hands, she asked, "How could I break a wheelchair?"

"Grace, they're teasing you," I responded. "They know you didn't break the chair. Just remember, they wouldn't tease you if they didn't love you." When Grace asked what she should do, I said, "Tease them right back! They really do love you, Grace. Catch them off guard, show them your spunk, and make them laugh."

So she looked at me and asked, "Like this?" Grace proceeded to pick up her crocheted afghan to reveal her naked bottom. I could not believe it! She came to dinner without any pants on! Shaking my head in disbelief, I proceeded to push Grace back to her room and found her shorts on the back of the wheelchair.

That's what I loved about this experience and why I had spent virtually every day for four months volunteering. I got to hear great stories, create some of my own, assist the residents with their day-to-day needs, and share God's love. One thing was certain: this assignment brought a tremendous amount of joy into my life. Unfortunately, it also provided a fair amount of heartache.

6

race was hospitalized a short time later. When she returned, her hands and arms were bruised from the intravenous feedings she endured during her weeklong hospital stay. Grace was slowly regaining her strength, but she still looked really tired and was extremely weak. She was not very talkative and did not have much of an appetite, which was understandable. After eating only a few salted crackers, she asked me to take her back to her room.

As I pushed Grace down the hallway, she glanced back at me with a concerned look on her face and in a serious tone asked if I would help her with her black shoes. She was wearing only a pair of socks that day because her legs and feet were so swollen. Once in her room, and with Grace seated in her wheelchair, I took off her socks and grabbed the oldest, most worn-out pair of black-laced shoes I had ever seen. The style of the shoe reminded me of a pair my grandpa used to wear, but these had seen better days. Grace wanted to see if her shoes would fit on her feet.

I tried to get the right shoe on her foot, but given the significant swelling of her lower extremities, it was extremely difficult. After quite a struggle, the shoe was finally on. It appeared much too tight, so I asked, "Are you sure you want to put on your shoes today?" She said that she did.

I was down on the floor, trying to get the second shoe on, and, unfortunately, not having much luck. At one point when I was just about ready to give up, Grace encouraged me to "try again." I stretched the black woven material as far as I could, slightly ripping the seam, and loosened the laces until they almost fell off the shoe.

Lo and behold, and much to my surprise, it took just one more push and a firm tug on the back of the heel—we did it.

Both shoes were now on her feet and Grace had a huge smile on her face. With a sense of relief and delight, she joyfully proclaimed, "They fit!" The happiness that had been missing earlier in the day quickly returned as Grace held out both feet, admiring her old black shoes.

Any one of us would have thrown those shoes out long ago, but they were Grace's only pair of shoes and one of the few things that still signaled a sense of normalcy for her. When she wore her shoes, she was able to stand and walk a step or two. Without them she did not have the confidence to steady herself.

Grace had always been an active woman and took care of herself at home up until a few months before that. She reminded me of my grandma. Her mind was sharp, she led a very simple life, and she was always willing to help others. Residing in an assisted-living facility, however, was quite an adjustment for Grace. Her social life was virtually nonexistent and she was no longer able to take care of her basic needs.

It was getting close to the time when I normally left, and now that we had her shoes on, I asked Grace if she needed to use the bathroom. "No, I just want to sit in my recliner," she said. I helped Grace out of her wheelchair and held her hand while she took three steps to the cream-colored leather chair that sat next to her bed. Once seated, I assisted Grace with her oxygen and covered her with her afghan.

Grace thanked me and wanted to know, "What's next?" I did not want to answer that question. I was thinking, *What's next, Grace? Nothing! Absolutely nothing. You just sit here hoping and praying that someone comes to visit.* Then I said, "Grace, it's one o'clock. The next time you eat is at five."

Grace looked at me like she did not believe what I had just said. "So I sit here for four hours until supper?"

Once again, I did not want to answer the question but had to tell her the truth. "Yes, Grace, that's what you have to do. There are no activities planned this afternoon."

"Then I don't need my teeth?"

I just smiled. "No, Grace, you don't need your teeth. Would you like me to get the container?" I grabbed the yellow plastic container that held her teeth, and she deposited her dentures into the water. I left them on her side table. They were ready and waiting for her next trip to the dining room.

"Grace, your television is on and you can take a nap and rest, and I'll see you tomorrow." I gave Grace a kiss on her cheek and headed out the door, feeling very sad about her situation. I was doing everything I could to help, but somehow it did not seem like enough. As I walked down the hallway, my heart was breaking and I began to cry.

I knew that Grace was not used to being alone and that she missed spending time with her family and friends. Her health had declined to the point where she could no longer care for herself, which was extremely difficult for her to accept. I also knew that virtually every bit of independence had been taken from her and for the first time in her life she was totally dependent on others.

As I walked down the hallway with tears in my eyes, I asked God, *Why? Why does it have to be this way? Why does Grace have to bear this burden?* And do you know what I heard in my spirit?

God said, *Grace is simply fulfilling my purpose for her life. You may have noticed that although Grace's health is declining and she is facing numerous challenges, she never complains. And even today, on a day when she is not feeling well, Grace found a way to be happy. She was grateful that her old black shoes fit on her feet and together we were able to teach you a very valuable lesson.*

~

My time in Florida was winding down, and Helen's husband died one week prior to my departure. It was an emotional week and my heart was hurting over the sadness she was experiencing.

The hardest thing I had to do was walk into her room only a few hours after his death. What do you say to a woman you have grown to love, a lady you admire given her struggles with Parkinson's disease, and a wife and mother who is hurting to the core of her being? You don't say anything. You just hug her, hold her, and begin to cry.

When you do finally speak, you tell her how sorry you are, hold her hands, look deep into her eyes, and focus on the fact that her husband is no longer suffering. You then promise that you will be with her every step of the way. Within a short time, the family leaves to begin making arrangements and you are left with a woman who just lost her husband of forty-seven years.

It was getting close to lunch, and Helen wanted to stay in her room. Seeing Helen cry was heartbreaking, and before the afternoon was over we had gone through an entire box of Kleenex. As dinner approached I insisted we go to the dining room. I felt it was important to get Helen back into a normal routine as quickly as possible, which ended up being a very good decision.

We shared the news with our dining room table, and the women were all supportive. Grace had been widowed a number of times. So I asked, "Grace, how did you do it? How did you survive having to bury three husbands?"

Grace responded, "You just do it. They died." Helen was listening intently.

"Wow, Grace, you must be strong," I said. "As hard as it is for Helen losing one husband, you've lost three."

Grace then said, shrugging her shoulders, "It happens. You have no choice. But I did tell the fourth one, 'Don't get too close, they all die.' He didn't believe me—he got close. And guess what? He died!" Boy, did we laugh.

Helen then looked at me with a big smile on her face and said, "You know how Grace survived?"

"No, Helen, how?" I inquired.

"She has a sense of humor."

Well, that did it. I could see Helen was coming around. We

actually stayed in the dining room until almost seven o'clock, and when we got back to her room Helen thanked me for making her go to dinner.

"It always works out the way it's supposed to, doesn't it, Helen?" I asked. "I'm glad we went to dinner too." I stayed a little bit longer, kissed her good night, and told her I would be back in the morning.

I spent an incredible amount of time with Helen during the week, and our godly discussions were not only meaningful but also uplifting. It is so apparent God had a hand in this. Quite frankly, it was a miracle that brought us together. At the most vulnerable time of my life, when I was lost and trying to find my way, and during the most difficult time of Helen's life, losing her husband, there we were together, all a result of God's plan.

~

The day after Helen's husband's funeral was my last day volunteering at Hearthstone, and I was thrilled that Grace decided to attend her first happy hour event. For the last four months, Helen and I would routinely attend the Friday afternoon festivities, and I loved to dance with the residents. Let's just say, Grace was about to find out what she had been missing.

It didn't take long to see that Grace was thoroughly enjoying the live entertainment as she was tapping her feet, snapping her fingers, and singing along with the music. When the moment was just right, I snuck up behind Grace and pushed her wheelchair out onto the dance floor. And boy was she surprised. Although a little reluctant at first, she decided to make the most out of our spotlight dance. I was amazed at Grace's dance moves; it was apparent she used to be the life of the party. Grace's smile was as big as ever, even though I was not sure who was having more fun.

As the song ended, I pushed Grace back to her spot, but she had a surprise for me. Even though I was sweating and out of breath, we were not done. The next song was one of her favorites and she insisted we dance even more. Ninety-three-year-old Grace, who had difficulty standing, let alone walking, was adamant about getting out of her wheelchair for our last dance together. I helped Grace stand up and supported her as best I could, which was no easy task.

With Grace leading, we held hands and began to sing the 1956 classic "Que Sera, Sera." We sang about wondering if we'll be pretty or rich, and a mother's response that whatever will be, will be.

While singing the last chorus, I had tears in my eyes. As I continued to search for the answer as to why this was God's plan for my life, I thought that maybe this should become my theme song. The last few weeks had been emotionally tough, and although I was ready for a change of scenery, it was difficult to say good-bye.

~

As a drifter of the Willow Creek apartment complex, the departure tradition stayed intact. I deposited my lawn chair and blow-up mattress into the Dumpster, loaded my car with what few items remained, and headed off toward my next destination—Wisconsin.

After arriving home, I found a card tucked in the front passenger seat that one of my friends deposited without my knowledge. Opening it, I found the following written:

It's been said that life is like a garden. Every small work of kindness and every thoughtful gesture is like a tiny seed, and when you plant these seeds, wonderful things happen. Smiles appear, dreams blossom and love takes root and grows. Before you know it, happiness is all around you. It takes a lot of care and effort to tend to the garden of life, but you're one of those people who have a special gift for it. Hold on to that gift, because people like you make the world a more beautiful place.

As I stood in the driveway reflecting on these words, I knew God had a hand in this. Over the last seven months, these ladies, both young and old, had a profound impact on me, and it was apparent we were making a difference in each other's lives. I really liked the person I had become and was grateful for the unsolicited feedback regarding my ability to minister to others.

~

As I brought the last of my belongings into the house, my mom handed me some newspaper articles. Four of the defendants in the criminal case had been sentenced within the last two weeks. Thomas Russell received two years in prison and three years probation. Peter O'Malley was sentenced to twenty-eight months in prison, two years of supervised release with thirty hours community service each year, and a $7,500 fine. Michael Rivett received three years probation with sixty days of home confinement and a $1,000 fine, while Patrick Kane received three years of probation with a $1,000 fine.

Three months earlier, Thomas Buske had been indicted on six charges of mail fraud, six charges of interstate transportation of stolen property, and ten counts of money laundering. Mr. Buske pled not guilty, and as a result both my sentencing and Milt's were delayed. The government wanted us to testify at trial, and our sentencing was delayed until October.

~

Prior to heading back to Wisconsin, we had discussed Grace's upcoming ninety-fourth birthday, which would take place on August 12. We agreed it would be a perfect time for a return trip to Florida. Grace was excited that I was coming down for her birthday, and I promised it would be a special day.

In mid-July, I talked to Helen and asked how everyone was doing. She said Grace was not feeling well. That broke my heart. As a result, I decided to send her something to lift her spirits. The middle of August could not get here quick enough—my girls needed me.

While checking e-mails one day at the end of July, I found a message from Helen's daughter with the subject line "Sad news." Grace had passed away in her sleep. I could not believe it. I stared at the computer screen hoping there was a mistake. It couldn't be our Grace; we had a birthday party planned. Sadly, the facility confirmed the news.

The receptionist told me the envelope I had sent arrived that very day. There was a special gift inside, a devotional book called *Grace for the Moment* by Max Lucado.[1] I included a card to let Grace know I was thinking of her and looking forward to celebrating her birthday.

Her birthday gift, a bouquet of red silk roses, was already wrapped as I was going to carry it on the airplane. As I took it out of the gift bag and placed it on my dresser, I was heartbroken. I called Helen that evening, and her daughter said she was equally impacted by the loss. I explained how instrumental Grace had been in helping her mother cope with her dad's death. Grace was able to comfort Helen with her sense of humor, and it was Grace's quick wit and matter-of-fact approach to life that helped turn Helen's attitude around and begin her healing.

How often have people come into my life for only a few short months yet had the impact of a lifetime? Not many, and I am eternally grateful for Grace's friendship and love. Her life lessons are impacting far more people than she could have ever imagined.

~

After a wonderful summer with my family, I was ready to head back to Florida. My October sentencing was delayed until February, and just happened to be on my SC Johnson work anniversary of all days. An extended-stay hotel would be my home until I could find a place to live. It was a Sunday and I had just finished packing when the phone began to ring.

It was my friend Paula calling from Tampa. She was at church

---

1 Max Lucado, *Grace for the Moment: Inspirational Thoughts for Each Day of the Year* (Nashville: Thomas Nelson, 2000).

and could hardly contain her excitement. An acquaintance of hers, a woman by the name of Diana, walked up to her just prior to the eleven o'clock service and calmly but directly said, "Paula, I need a roommate. Now!" Paula told Diana she knew the perfect person, and before the end of the day, I had a permanent place to live.

Something interesting happened when I spoke to Diana. Given I would be living in her home, I had to be upfront about my legal situation, yet when I began to tell her I became pretty emotional. It was not because I was upset or sad; rather, I was completely overcome by the presence of God.

Diana admitted that she too had a "power surge," and we knew it could only be one thing, the presence of the Holy Spirit. We could not deny God's hand in this, including the fact he gave me something I always wanted; Diana's house was on a golf course. We agreed I would begin my month-to-month lease on November 1, 2009, and I arrived on Friday, October 30. There was an instant bond that formed between us, and I moved in the very next day.

Diana was a widow, having lost her husband two years prior. Her husband had been an absolutely wonderful partner and father. High school sweethearts, they never fell out of love during their forty years of marriage. They had moved to Florida ten years earlier to enjoy the sunshine and warm weather and began planning their retirement. Unfortunately, her husband passed away in November of 2007, and given the state of her finances, Diana had no choice but to take in a roommate.

Diana was a clone of the Energizer Bunny—she kept on going and going and going. To know her was to love her. She loved to laugh, loved to dance, and had a wonderful sense of humor. She was ten years older than I, so I had to wonder where she got all of her energy. Diana did not require much sleep and was always active. To be honest, I wondered why she even had a house because she was never home.

I quickly realized that Diana kept herself busy so she would not have to come to terms with her husband's death. Even though it had been two years since he passed away, Diana had not fully grieved the loss. God knew what he was doing when he put the two us together, because slowly but surely Diana was going to have to deal with this pain and I was going to help her through the grieving process.

～

Diana knew I was writing a book because I would routinely work on my computer at the kitchen table. I could not wait to get the following story on paper and spent three full days writing about my latest God encounter. This story, which also served as my Christmas letter, is one of my favorites and I have entitled it "The Christmas Miracle."

On Wednesday I finished reading the book *You Were Born for This* by Bruce Wilkinson. As the book's subtitle says it contains *Seven Keys to a Life of Predictable Miracles*. A miracle in this case is defined as "an extraordinary event manifesting divine intervention in human affairs."[2] All God needs for a miracle is a willing servant through whom to work.

It was a pretty easy decision to tell God I would be more than happy to be one of his delivery agents, and I was excited to see what would happen. I took the challenge that very same day: "I want to partner with heaven to deliver a miracle to someone in need."

On Thursday I came across an article in *Good Housekeeping* on forgiveness. I found it interesting that in just two days I had read some significant information on this subject. A chapter near the end of the book in *You Were Born for This* also focused on forgiveness, as forgiveness was one of the three keys to special delivery miracles. I wondered if this was a coincidence. I should have known better when I finished reading the book *The Christmas Sweater* by Glenn Beck on Saturday. Forgiveness was definitely the theme of

2 Bruce Wilkinson, *You Were Born for This* (Sisters, OR: Multnomah Books, 2011), 83–88.

the week, so I wondered what message God had in store for me.

Here's what I learned. If we lived in a perfect world, no one would need to forgive. But we don't live in a perfect world. Despite our best efforts, we hurt the people we love. That's why forgiveness is so important. Without it we live with regret, anger, pain, and bitterness. Carrying unforgiveness in our heart will never allow the healing process to begin and give us the opportunity to experience peace. Hurting people hurt others and will continue to do so until they learn how to forgive.

Forgiveness is the gift you give yourself. It is absolutely one of the most precious gifts you can give or receive. "Why?" you may ask. Because it is a gift filled with love. Forgiveness turns negative emotions into positive ones. Burdens are lifted, grudges disappear, and emotional and psychological well-being is restored. Forgiveness is a choice, and once you realize that you are able to forgive, your heart can begin to heal. When your heart heals, your spirit can be lifted and life takes on incredible new meaning.

Late Saturday morning I decided to go out and enjoy the weather and take a long bike ride. I used my exercise time to reflect on life and pray, and I was still a little overwhelmed by all of the reading material that had been put in my path that particular week. What was God really trying to tell me? Did I have some unresolved conflict I needed to address? Despite my best efforts to believe I had forgiven everyone relative to my personal situation and they had forgiven me, I knew better—there was still some work to do.

About ten miles into my ride, my son Mike sent me a text message to let me know that the Marquette/Wisconsin basketball game was on at five that evening. Given I am a die-hard basketball fan, he knew that I would be interested in the matchup. I was not aware they were playing and responded to his text by telling him it sounded like fun, but I would have to find someplace to watch the game because I did not have cable.

Ahh … the little things in life … like basketball on ESPN. I was happy to have something to do. I immediately thought about going over to Lee Roy Selmon's restaurant to watch the big rivalry. The sports bar was close to home, and I could already taste the barbecued pork sandwich and coleslaw.

It was two hours before game time so I decided to take a quick drive up to Wesley Chapel to do a little Christmas shopping. After I bummed around Dick's and TJ Maxx, it was getting close to five and I thought instead of barbecued pork, I'd just have a hamburger. So I headed over to Winner's Grill, which was right around the corner from the mall. I had been to Winner's a number of times before. The food was good, and I knew they would be broadcasting the game.

I walked in and sat next to a guy at the bar. I'm not sure why I chose the seat right next to him, as there were twenty-five other empty stools to pick from, but I sat down anyway. I even debated about moving after a few minutes, but something kept me in my seat. I told him I was there to watch the Wisconsin game, which was not something that someone from Florida was accustomed to hearing. He mentioned he was originally from Chicago, and we had a nice conversation. We talked about a lot of things, including the fact that I was unemployed and everything I owned fit in my car, and the fact that he had been in an accident with a semi six months earlier, sustained a serious back injury, and was unable to work.

If I had to guess, this guy was in his early forties and was fairly good looking, if you like men who shave their heads and are casually dressed. He seemed to have a good sense of humor and an outgoing personality. He laughed when I told him about some of my life experiences (like attending the Women's Final Four in Tampa). And I laughed when he told me he was looking for a quick settlement in his legal matter (good luck with that one, as I was headed into year number six) and he commented that I had a "glow" about me.

That was an interesting pickup line. Actually I had to admit that "glow" could be attributed to an unusual streak of hot flashes that had now reached day number eighteen. Menopause is not much fun.

I shared some of my spiritual experiences with him, including my favorite story about when God spoke to me not once but twice during the night and told me to read Hebrews 13:5. He found my spiritual journey and stories to be quite incredible, and after I quoted the Scripture above and shared a few other things that had happened to me, he told me if he had any hair on his head or the back of his neck it would be standing on end.

We both loved to talk. He even commented at one point that I sounded a lot like his wife. He told me that he was married and had four daughters. I was kind of wondering what a guy with a wife and four kids was doing in the bar, but I did not think it was any of my business, so I didn't ask.

I told him that some of the ladies at the nursing home where I volunteered thought I was an angel—maybe that explained the "glow"—but I always kept my wings tucked in my sweatshirt. We were gaining each other's trust when I asked him, "Is there anything I can do for you?" (That is one of the steps in Wilkinson's book.)

It was at this point that we finally got around to introducing ourselves. His name was Pete, and given the Ultimate Fighting Championship was on at the same time as the game, he mentioned that as a young man he had gotten into plenty of fights and that getting beat up "really hurt." At one point during our conversation I thought Pete was going to leave when he closed out his tab, but for some reason he decided to stay and order another beer. We continued to talk and got into a pretty deep discussion about forgiveness. It was now becoming apparent why God made sure I had those resources.

Pete was hurting. This time it wasn't because of a fistfight; he was hurting to the core of his being—his eyes didn't lie. I suddenly realized why I was eating a hamburger instead of a barbecued pork sandwich and why I was at Winner's Grill instead of Lee Roy Selmon's. The Holy Spirit had led me to the exact place where I needed to be and put me in the seat next to Pete.

I had arrived as a Wisconsin basketball fan, but in less than an hour I had become one of God's delivery agents. I shared that forgiveness was one of the greatest gifts a person could give him- or herself, and he wondered out loud, "How do you do that? How do you forgive?"

I told him I had to forgive myself before I could forgive others, and, quite frankly, I chose to forgive because I didn't like who I was when I was angry. It took me a long time to face the pain and disappointment of losing my job and the fact I had lost many dear friends because of my poor decisions.

As we talked, I felt a little bit of pressure to select the right words. I was only going to have one chance to get this right and make a difference in Pete's life. Ministering to others is hard work when it's a relatively new calling. I quickly remembered many of the things I had learned during the week and shared some of those lessons, but I decided to let my heart do most of the talking. Sharing my hurt, heartache, and pain, and letting someone know how beneficial the healing process can be validated that forgiveness is an awesome gift.

I was now looking at a man with tears in his eyes as he bit his lower lip and tried not to cry. It was almost like he knew the answer to the question before he asked me: "So why is it that you came in here and sat next to me? Why didn't you go to Lee Roy Selmon's like you had planned?"

And I responded exactly how the Holy Spirit told me to. "I came in here tonight to give someone a miracle."

He began crying and told me, "You just did." I could not believe this was happening. I was now crying because once again I felt God's presence and was overwhelmed by the circumstances and the realization of what was taking place. He said, "You kept me from doing something really stupid tonight."

I reached over and gave him a napkin, grabbed one for myself, and there we were, two grown adults in a bar with tears streaming down our faces. He said he never cried, and I told him that it was okay to show his emotions, because I did it all the time. I gave Pete a pat on the back, told him everything was going to be okay, and asked him, "What were you going to do?"

Pete was reluctant to tell me, but he finally did. He said he had seen a woman he had a history with earlier in the afternoon and they both smiled and waved to one another. He was going to have a couple of beers before heading over to her place, given he had a few hours to kill prior to picking up his wife at work. Well, we both knew what would have happened if he would have showed up at her house, and he thanked me for sitting down and talking to him.

I told him I was the "other woman" and I was proud of him. I reminded him that every day is a struggle and that life is hard, but if we are willing to turn our problems over to the Lord and trust him, then he will guide our steps, help us remain obedient, and teach us how to forgive. God had a little bit of divine intervention in there for me as well.

"Well, I can only give you one more bit of advice, Pete. Do not let anyone steal your joy, because the joy is in the journey and forgiveness is a choice." The ball was clearly in Pete's court. He could forgive himself and his wife for their differences and return peace, joy, and love to their relationship, or he could return to his old habits of dragging others into the situation and not resolve his issues. Based on Pete's reaction, I'm pretty sure he made the right decision.

I was "glowing" as Pete headed out the door to pick up his wife. "Thank you so much for everything," he said. I did not finish watching the game. Given what had just happened, the game did not seem to matter anymore. I chose to head home to begin writing about my latest miracle.

～

I finished journaling late Saturday night and decided that

because my son Mike was instrumental in making this happen, I would share my story with him. God really does work in mysterious ways. Mike, did you have any idea that God was working in your life when the Holy Spirit prompted you to tell me about the game? Makes you pause and think, doesn't it?

I fired off the e-mail to Mike on Sunday morning before heading to St. James for their eleven o'clock service, where we were in the third week of our sermon series on the King of Kings. That day's talk was going to be on the King of Conflict. Another coincidence? Not when God is involved.

The underlying theme of the message was, you guessed it, forgiveness. I didn't know if I should laugh or cry. I looked back into the church to try and find my friend Paula because I had called her Saturday night to tell her what had happened. Although our eyes did not connect, our hearts did, and we knew it was the Lord at work. Four times in five days. Simply unbelievable.

I immediately thought of Pete and wished he was in church. I shook my head and chuckled again when minutes later, Scripture was quoted, and it was the story of Peter. Jesus accepted Peter even though he was the guy who stumbled many times. And in spite of Peter's failures, he went on to do many great things for God. "Then Peter came to him and asked, 'Lord, how often should I forgive someone who sins against me? Seven times?' 'No, not seven times,' Jesus replied, 'but seventy times seven!'" (Matthew 18:21–22). And Jesus told us in another place, "If you forgive those who sin against you, your heavenly Father will forgive you. But if you refuse to forgive others, your Father will not forgive your sins" (Matthew 6:14–15).

We were challenged during the service to let go of any bitterness we may have carried into church and lay our conflict at the feet of Jesus. It was at that point that I knew I had to take care of some unfinished business. I took a deep breath and laid down the last little bit of anger I was carrying over my legal issues. I sat back, wiped away my tears, listened to the soft piano music, and experienced a wonderful feeling of peace and contentment. The burden had finally been lifted.

I have learned that you can do great things for God, yourself, and others if you are willing to make allowances for those who are hurting. I hope and pray that anyone I have hurt along the way can find it in his or her heart to forgive me. I can tell you from my personal experience that it's not always easy to forgive and it may take some time, but forgiveness is the most precious gift you can give or receive. It is a gift that is found deep within your heart and it is a gift that is filled with love. Are you ready to give it away?

Will this season be filled with love, joy, peace, and contentment, or will it be another year filled with unresolved conflict and anger? You get to choose. I trust that you will make the right decision, and, when you do, please remember to thank God for your Christmas miracle.

~

I lived with Diana for two winters. Little did I know when I moved in that I would be spending every bit of that time helping Diana's heart heal. Diana could not afford to stay in her home and was forced into a short sale, which meant I was busy doing what I do best—helping her clean, organize, donate, or sell virtually everything she owned.

When it was all over, I was able to support Diana and help her grieve the loss of her husband while God prepared her heart for the next season of her life. The devotional that hung on the refrigerator spoke volumes: "There is a time and season for everything. There is a season to mourn, and a season to move forward. Failure to move forward will prevent you from fulfilling God's destiny for your life." I was encouraging Diana to move forward with her life, and she did, even though I was not practicing what I preached. I failed to move forward. I still had a secret.

~

I tried to break the chains of addiction—I really did. I did not want to live like that anymore. But more than a year after telling Milt I could not see him without his wife's permission, I was right back where I started—sleeping with the boss. I was such a hypocrite. I was honoring God by attending church, participating in Bible studies, growing in my faith, and serving others, yet I was still violating God's commandment: "You must not commit adultery" (Exodus 20:14).

Why can't I let Milt go? Why can't I walk away? What is wrong with me? Once again, there was only one answer to all three of these questions. It was a matter of my heart. If there was any consolation at all, I learned that even the apostle Paul had a hard time pleasing God. He wrote:

> So the trouble is not with the law, for it is spiritual and good. The trouble is with me, for I am all too human, a slave to sin. I don't really understand myself, for I want to do what is right, but I don't do it. Instead, I do what I hate. But if I know that what I am doing is wrong, this shows that I agree that the law is good. So I am not the one doing wrong; it is sin living in me that does it. (Romans 7:14–17)

I knew that what I was doing was wrong, and as much as I wanted to do what was right, the sin living inside of me controlled my behavior. There is a reason why the Bible says, "Run from sexual sin!" First Corinthians 6:18–20 goes on to say:

> No other sin so clearly affects the body as this one does. For sexual immorality is a sin against your own body. Don't you realize your body is the temple of the Holy Spirit, who lives in you and was given to you by God? You do not belong to yourself, for God bought you with a high price. So you must honor God with your body.

The only time I was able to honor God with my body was when we were twelve hundred miles apart. We continued to talk every day. Why? Because my fear of not wanting to be alone and Milt's fear of abandonment kept us trapped in that vicious cycle. We found security in each other, not in the Lord.

I continued to lie to my friends during this time as well. My family knew better than to ask. The exact thing that got me into trouble in the first place, which was not being honest with myself or others, was slowly killing me. And believe it or not, that was a very good thing. It wasn't until I could die to my fleshy desires and resist the Devil that he would flee and things would finally change.

It was time to push through the fear, learn how to trust God, and let the Holy Spirit guide me. Paul wrote to Timothy, "For God has not given us a spirit of fear and timidity, but of power, love, and self-discipline" (2 Timothy 1:7). Until we learn how to walk in step with the Spirit, we will continue in sin.

Although my behavior was far from perfect, I was making progress. I enjoyed six months of sexual sobriety at a time. I was doing what I needed to do to grow in my faith. I surrounded myself with the right people and circumstances to learn the truth about God's Word, and I even went so far as to hang a rather large picture of Jesus in my bedroom. Guess what? It kept us out of there.

It was time to accept my shortcomings and realize that I was a sinner, a sinner saved by God's grace. God had given me everything I need to live a godly life. The guilt and shame had to go. I needed to embrace the words found in Romans 8:1: "There is no condemnation for those who belong to Christ Jesus."

It took me a while to figure out my spiritual journey should not be dictated by rules and regulations; rather, it should focus on developing an intimate relationship with Christ. This journey is not about laws and perfection; it has always been about my heart: "The LORD doesn't see things the way you see them. People judge by outward appearance, but the LORD looks at the heart" (1 Samuel 16:7).

In order to change our heart, spiritual growth has to occur, and spiritual growth takes time. It is a slow and delicate process that requires much patience. While we worry about how fast we grow,

God is more concerned about our strength and character as we grow. He wants us to have the mind of Christ through the process.

Jesus is the only person who walked in human flesh and was still perfect. Our failures are teaching tools and are a part of God's plan. The only discipline God will give you is discipline to heal you. God is all-knowing and all-loving and is never shocked or surprised when we sin. He stands ready to forgive us the moment we repent, which I did every time I was disobedient. We cannot grow and begin to change until we realize we cannot reach the life we desire by ourselves. We need to be empowered by God's love and let the Holy Spirit guide our hearts.

One of my favorite definitions of obedience is found in Beth Moore's *Breaking Free Workbook*. This definition helped me realized that an obedient life is not a perfect life.

Obedience does not mean sinlessness, but confession and repentance when we sin. Obedience is not arriving at a perpetual state of godliness but perpetually following hard after God. Obedience is not living miserably by a set of laws but inviting the Spirit of God to flow freely through us so the power to be victorious comes from God and not from us. Obedience is learning to love and treasure God's Word and see it as our safety. Walking with God in the pursuit of daily obedience is the sure way to fulfill God's plan for your life.[3]

I was on the right track.

On the last night of our Breaking Free class, I held hands and looked into the eyes of my accountability partner, a beautiful young woman by the name of Jonie. Quite honestly, it was like looking into the eyes of an angel. Through tears, I promised Jonie that I would allow the truth of God's Word to set me free.

Not only did I feel different, but my behavior was starting to

---

3 Beth Moore, *Breaking Free Workbook* (Nashville: Lifeway Christian Resources, 1999), 91–92.

reflect a change of heart. Small steps showed I was making progress because, for the first time in my relationship with Milt, I was able to set appropriate boundaries with him, say no, and actually mean it. I wasn't where I needed to be, and although I would occasionally stumble, I had stepped onto God's path of righteousness and was walking with the Spirit toward a life of obedience.

It was only a matter of time before God had my heart right where he wanted it.

1

I returned to Wisconsin in April and made an appointment with my insurance agent, Julie, to discuss health care coverage. Julie was also a high school friend and former coworker, and she was one of the few friends who stuck by me throughout this whole ordeal.

We talked about the case and the fact that my son Brian was getting married in July. I confided that I was struggling with the expenses for the wedding and upset that my sentencing now coincided with the date of the rehearsal dinner. Julie looked at me and said, "Come work for Nick. I don't care that you are a convicted felon. I will pay you eleven dollars an hour to babysit." She quickly added, "Katie, I think God sent you back early to help our family."

The truth was that I had not seen Nick in years. Nick started having epileptic seizures when he was about two years old, and these episodes caused extensive brain damage. Despite their efforts to get to the root of the problem, Nick's condition worsened, and by the time he was twelve Julie had no choice but to put him in a facility that cared for the disabled. That decision tormented her. Although we lost touch for a number of years, I always felt I let Julie down by not being more supportive during that time in her life.

Julie decided to bring Nick home eighteen months before I met with her. Their house had to be remodeled to accommodate his needs, and things like a wheelchair-accessible shower and bedroom had to be added to the first floor.

While volunteering at the nursing home, I was complimented many times on my caregiving abilities. I would feed the residents, spend time visiting with them, and, on rare occasions, even assist with bathroom duty. One day I was approached by one of the employees and asked if I ever considered becoming a certified nursing assistant: "You're so good at it, Katie. The ladies love you and we love you. It is a perfect match for your skill set."

I quickly replied, shaking my head, "I couldn't do that. If it was work I wouldn't be as effective. And besides, my famous last words: 'I don't do dirty diapers.'" Not only was I going to learn how to do dirty diapers, but I was also going to learn how to do dirty diapers with a smile on my face. Don't ever say you can't or you won't, because God will show you that you can and you will.

God opened the door and I walked through it. I agreed to help Julie with Nick's care during the summer of 2010. I was clueless about what I was getting myself into, but God knew he had me right where he wanted me.

At the time, Nick was eighteen years old, and at five foot eight and one hundred and fifty pounds, he was not huge but far bigger than me, and boy was he strong. Nick could not speak, could not feed himself, and was incontinent. He suffered from epileptic seizures, sometimes on a daily basis. Nick also liked to walk, and, if there was any good news, it was that I would stay in shape since trying to keep Nick in the house was a challenge.

The summer was interesting for a number of reasons. First, God really did show me that I was capable of doing just about anything I set my heart to. Although at times being a home health aide was frustrating, the experience humbled me. Second, God arranged my circumstances so that I could be there to help Julie as caregivers would come and go. And last but certainly not least, God knew how much money I needed for my son's wedding and I earned the exact amount to cover expenses.

The summer breezed by. I had put in over three hundred hours with Nick and had a new appreciation for Julie and the challenges she and her family face on a daily basis. My heart goes out to everyone who cares for children with special needs. My assignment was also part of God's plan to give Julie strength to make some tough decisions. There were two aides who needed to go. Julie was far too patient given the circumstances surrounding Nick's care. Nick's safety was of utmost importance, so I had more than one "tough love" conversation with Julie regarding the termination of these individuals.

This experience also exposed me to another side of life. I was shocked at the day-to-day challenges with Nick's care. The thing that was most stressful was not knowing if Nick was going to seize, which meant I always had to come prepared to expect the worst. While visiting with Nick's neurologist, I learned the seriousness of these seizures—when the doctor said a seizure could signal the end for Nick, I wanted to take off running.

This was one time I was happy that I was finally trusting God. When Julie and I prayed asking God to send stable, dependable workers, he did. But what I found interesting was that these ladies, although they were great with Nick, had personal struggles they openly shared with me. Three aides were facing the same challenge: they were all struggling with unforgiveness. God was nice enough to deal with that issue in my life and put me in a position to share my testimony and provide resources to help their wounded hearts heal. I was able to minister to these women about God's wonderful gifts of grace and forgiveness.

Nick's nineteenth birthday arrived, so we planned a very special day. Julie purchased a cake and Nick's stepdad was busy fixing his favorite meal, which was steak on the grill with potatoes and vegetables. We were anxiously waiting for dinner, given we all had presents for the birthday boy.

As dinner was being served, Nick's brother went into the living room to get him. As they stepped into the dining area, Nick went into a grand mal seizure, and I went running for the oxygen tank. Julie just kept on crying, "Not on his birthday, God, not on his birthday." For the next minute, as Nick did when he had a seizure, he turned blue and we encouraged him to breathe.

When he finally recovered, Nick remained on the floor with

the oxygen mask on his face, and you could hear a pin drop. It was heartbreaking. *Why, God, why does it have to be like this?* And once again, like my experience with Grace, God told me it was so that people like me can learn what true love and compassion are all about.

It was not until I was able to look at Nick as Jesus did that I could be joyful about his care, and his diapers. I remember telling my mom one afternoon before heading to work, "If Nick poops his pants today, I am going to have a nervous breakdown." It was still about me, and God was not going to release me from this assignment until I started to learn what he had for me in this season of life. Well, Nick filled his pants, and that was the day I saw Jesus lying on that floor with a dirty diaper instead of Nick. If I could do it for Jesus, then I could do it for Nick.

Julie thought I was sent to help her family; in actuality, however, I believe God sent her family to help me. One of the things that I did not tell you was that Nick did not cry. On my last day of work, as I pulled away from their home, I was crying for Nick and thanking God for this experience of getting to serve him in this way. Feeling God's presence as the tears flowed, I heard the voice of God: *Well done, my good and faithful servant.* Another lesson learned, which meant I was one step closer to becoming the person God intended me to be.

The summer was everything I expected it to be. My sentencing was once again delayed, and I was able to relax and enjoy my son's wedding. The night of the rehearsal dinner God provided a double rainbow, and I knew Brian and Ellie's marriage was blessed.

~

Labor Day weekend was spent in Minnesota visiting my grandchildren. I returned to Wisconsin, recharged my batteries, loaded the car, and spent two days traveling to Florida as my road trip continued.

In the fall of 2010, I jumped into a thirty-week discipleship study with both feet. If I was going to take this journey seriously and really get to know God's Word, then I had to be willing to dedicate the necessary time to learn everything I possibly could. Up until that point I had only attended women's studies, so this would be my first coed class. It did not take long to discover I did not like the format or the pace of the study. I stuck with it for about six weeks before becoming a "Bible school dropout."

Now what? I wondered. Well, remember Paula? Although I was not a close friend of hers, God reminded me that she hosted a women's small group in her home. I called asking if there was any way I could attend. "Sure," she replied. "Come on over next week. We are studying Joyce Meyer's *Battlefield of the Mind*, and I even have one extra book." It sounded good to me, so off I went the following Tuesday, not realizing that Paula's house was exactly where God wanted me during that season of my life.

Paula had a beautiful home in Tampa Palms. She had hosted this group of ladies for years, and many were members of our church. The group was very diverse, most were Spirit filled, and we were all close to the same age. The group welcomed me with open arms, and it was time to get to work. I had previously read *Battlefield of the Mind* but never completed the workbook.

One of Joyce Meyer's favorite lines is, "You need to think about what you are thinking about."[1] Thank goodness there were no mind readers in that assembly that day. Getting to know this group of ladies was both interesting and entertaining. It was fun to try to figure them out, listen to their stories, observe their various personalities, and wonder if their lives have been as challenging as mine. For the first few weeks, I secretly wished there were name tags because I could not keep everyone straight.

In my mind I was questioning, *Is that one Laura or Lorrie? Who knows.* I could remember Josie, because she had just been diagnosed with breast cancer and much of the conversation centered

1 Joyce Meyer, *Battlefield of the Mind: Winning the Battle in Your Mind* (New York: Warner Faith, 2002), 96.

on her treatment. Of course I knew Paula, having previously met her while volunteering. Then in came another woman named Ruth Ann, who had a ministry and a master's degree in theology. No wonder she knew so much about the Bible.

Mary walked in slowly with the aid of a cane; she was recovering from a stroke. Deanne, who I think was Jamaican, was always late because of work; Patrice, who lived in South Tampa, was hit or miss as she was frequently flying to St. Louis to care for her aunt; and Ann, Sheila, Shana, Gloria, Debbie, and Gina rounded out the group, although their attendance was sporadic. Then there was me, still trying to figure out God's plan for my life.

As we delved into the study, I was learning that our actions are a direct result of our thoughts. "Those who are dominated by the sinful nature think about sinful things, but those who are controlled by the Holy Spirit think about things that please the Spirit" (Romans 8:5). Boy, is that ever true. Our minds have the capacity to create entire conversations and experiences out of absolutely nothing. Through fantasy we can enjoy things that do not even exist in the real world.

If I thought about Milt long enough, I would eventually find myself in a place I did not want to be. My mind was being held captive by my desires, and because the process of temptation starts with our thinking, it can be difficult to escape. That is why we must rely on God's power, not our own. Our sinful nature is always hostile to God. We must remember that Jesus has freed us from the power of sin that leads to death, but letting the Spirit of God guide our minds and hearts leads to a life of peace.

An intimate relationship with Christ comes only from spending time in his presence and his Word. There are no shortcuts to a life of intimacy. Discipleship is more than knowing who Jesus is; it is also about understanding the truth of his Word and obeying his teachings. God will provide the insight you need to put his Word into action, and sometimes the Holy Spirit will even reveal God's thoughts and plans.

I was really enjoying my small group and was thrilled to be part of another caring community. God opened the door so I could meet some new friends. And I would eventually find out that when these women said, "We do life together," they really meant it.

~

Do you believe that everything that happens in life has spiritual significance? I do. Every problem we encounter, every trial we endure, and every temptation we face is an opportunity to build character if we are committed to living righteous lives. Our challenge, however, is to walk with God in the pursuit of daily obedience so he can execute his perfect plan in our lives. We have to believe that God loves us enough to provide the right situations and circumstances to ensure our success.

Not a big surprise, but one of my struggles continues to be in the area of sexual temptation. God makes it very clear in his Word that sex is reserved for marriage and sexual intercourse outside of marriage is a sin. With the help of God, I have been able to resist these temptations and change how I am feeling or what I am doing when I feel most vulnerable. One word of advice though: don't ever assume God does not know what you are thinking or feeling, because God knows everything.

While I was in Tampa, I chose to worship most of the time at St. James United Methodist Church. However, on a few occasions, I attended a slightly more charismatic place of worship called River of Life. The messages delivered at River of Life have been nothing short of miraculous and always took place in God's perfect timing. I would like to share one story that I believe serves as a testimony as to how God can work in your life if you are willing to listen and obey what he speaks.

I was experiencing some significant sexual temptations in my mind and praying for God's help to resist acting these thoughts out in the reality of my life. On three occasions during the week of March 27, 2011, the Holy Spirit rose up inside of me and began telling me to attend River of Life Church on Sunday, April 3. Finally, after the third prompting, I told God, *Okay, I'll go.*

I could hardly believe my ears as the pastor began his sermon on the authority of Jesus. There were a number of Bible verses that were shared that day, and I am going to list them in paragraph form as they tell a very interesting story, one that was very appropriate given my struggles during that time:

> God blesses those who patiently endure testing and temptation. Afterward they will receive the crown of life that God has promised to those who love him. And remember, when you are being tempted, do not say, "God is tempting me." God is never tempted to do wrong, and he never tempts anyone else. Temptation comes from our own desires, which entice us and drag us away. These desires give birth to sinful actions. And when sin is allowed to grow, it gives birth to death. (James 1:12–15)

> The temptations in your life are no different from what others experience. And God is faithful. He will not allow the temptation to be more than you can stand. When you are tempted, he will show you a way out so that you can endure. (1 Corinthians 10:13)

> God's will is for you to be holy, so stay away from all sexual sin. Then each of you will control his own body and live in holiness and honor—not in lustful passion like the pagans who do not know God and his ways. Never harm or cheat a fellow believer in this matter by violating his wife, for the Lord avenges all such sins, as we have solemnly warned you before. God has called us to live holy lives, not impure lives. Therefore, anyone who refuses to live by these rules is not disobeying human teaching but is rejecting God, who gives his Holy Spirit to you. (1 Thessalonians 4:3–8)

> If you fully obey the LORD your God and carefully keep all his commands that I am giving you today, the LORD your

God will set you high above all the nations of the world. (Deuteronomy 28:1)

After receiving this message, I obviously thanked the Lord and shared my testimony with a few others. Don't ever underestimate why God puts you where he does and how quickly you can become one of his agents of delivery.

When I told Milt the story, he was intrigued. Milt did not always fully understand how I hear from God. I have often explained it this way: if random thoughts come to you that are so "out of the blue," something that you could not have come up with on your own, it is usually the Holy Spirit trying to bring something to your attention. The Holy Spirit will keep at it until you hear him loud and clear. Although Milt believed me, he said he never heard from God like I did. Well, that was about to change.

The next week I agreed to meet Milt for breakfast. On the drive over, I was listening to The JOY FM radio station and they were interviewing Mandisa. I could not believe it when the first thing I heard during the interview was 1 Corinthians 10:13, which was one of the Scriptures from the sermon I heard the week before. Was this a coincidence given I was having breakfast with Milt?

As I entered the restaurant and joined Milt, I told him about the radio message that happened to be one of the same Bible verses God had given me the previous week. I told him, "See how God works in my life? I can't make this up."

After a delicious breakfast, I walked Milt to his car and hopped inside to say good-bye. Not a good move for someone who is trying to resist temptation. To make a long story short, the second Milt touched me—the very second—I received a text message. I immediately said out loud, "Uh-oh, it's God." I pulled my phone out of my pocket and could not believe what I read: "This is a test." I showed the phone to Milt and neither of us could believe our eyes.

"There you have it," I said. "Now do you believe God is working in our lives?" Then I went on, "This is as much for you as it is for me, and I don't think God could have made it any clearer. How in the world could I receive this text message at the exact same time you touched me—the very second? Only God could arrange that. And you know what? This is one test I am going to pass." I thanked Milt for breakfast and made a beeline for my car.

The moral of this story is that God will not release us from anything that enslaves us until we have come to the mind of Christ in the matter. God wants us to think the thoughts of Christ toward the situation so we can begin to heal and move on. We need to reprogram our thinking with the Word of God, because if we can change the way we think, we can change the way we feel. And the better we feel about ourselves, the more we will trust God, love him, and obey his commands.

~

In May of 2011, my son Mike and daughter-in-law Kelly were faced with a dilemma. Daycare costs were exorbitant, so Mike asked if I would be interested in babysitting. Sounded like fun, but it would not be my decision; it would be up to Judge Clevert.

My attorney petitioned the court, asking for permission to spend the summer in Victoria, Minnesota. After waiting close to a month, another door opened for me to walk through. The car was packed, but this time I was heading north to spend some quality time with my grandsons.

The kids were involved in many activities, and Grandma Katie was their chauffeur to and from various sporting events, birthday parties, and Vacation Bible School. Grace Church in Eden Prairie would become their home away from home for an entire week in June.

On Wednesday of that particular week, my youngest grandson, Colin, who was in the kindergarten/first-grade classroom, ran up and asked, "Grandma, do you want to see my worksheet?"

"Of course, Colin," I replied. As I looked down at the yellow sheet of paper, I stood in awe as I read the key verse of the day— 1 Corinthians 10:13: "God is faithful; when you are tempted, he will also provide a way out …" I could not believe it. God was now using my grandson to keep me on the right path.

Colin's worksheet went on to say that sometimes obedience costs us something. We know that no matter the cost, however, obedience to God is always the right and best choice. The worksheet also mentioned Joseph, stating that they were going to see that God was always with Joseph, in the good and bad, through the ups and the downs, and in the pits and in the palaces and prisons. I had to pause and just shake my head.

Over the years I could relate to so many Bible characters. Queen Esther was asked, "Who knows if perhaps you were made queen for just such a time as this?" (Esther 4:14). And I wondered the same. The apostle Paul moved around a lot, but I prefer not to be reminded that he did his best work in prison, and then there was Joseph. I love the story of Joseph.

God does not ask for talent, intelligence, or uniqueness as prerequisites for serving him; rather, he seeks obedience and availability. God handpicks ordinary people to make a difference in this world, and Joseph was chosen to ensure the greater good of God's kingdom. He was the kid with the fancy coat who was sold into slavery by his brothers. He was also the guy who was falsely accused and thrown into prison.

For those of you who do not know, Joseph was his father's favorite child, but he was also self-righteous. He made three mistakes as a teenager. First, he was a tattletale; second, he was a show-off, always flaunting his coat of many colors; and third, he abused one of his God-given gifts, the ability to interpret dreams. At the end of the day, Joseph was a pretty arrogant kid, telling his brothers they would one day bow down to him. Although God did give Joseph this dream, Joseph chose to rub this revelation in his brothers' faces.[2]

What Joseph did not realize, similar to our experiences from time to time, is that we do not have to brag about how good we are

---

2 I enjoy the writings of R. T. Kendall, and two of his books have really blessed me on this journey. The first is *Total Forgiveness* and the second is *God Meant It for Good.*

or what God has planned for our lives, even if God has told us what is going to take place before it actually does. God will exalt us in due time.[3]

God had given Joseph many spiritual gifts, and one was interpreting dreams. His gifts were in good shape, but unfortunately Joseph was not. He was young and sometimes foolish. That can be true regardless of our age. Our arrogance and pride can get in the way of serving others, as can our insecurity and refusal to trust God.

God had a plan for Joseph and he was going to make sure Joseph was properly prepared for that plan. God also has a plan for us, and we too must go through a preparation phase as God conforms us into his image. What we have to realize is that even though God is working in our life, we need to be patient with the way he works. It took Moses forty years before he was ready, and Joseph waited twenty-two years to be vindicated. During this time we need to remain deeply rooted in our faith, because we cannot always see what God is up to.

When God taps you on the shoulder, be encouraged. Wonderful things will begin to happen as God readies you for his work in his kingdom. Unfortunately, as wonderful as it can be, it can be equally difficult. Many times for God's will to be done, things may get worse before they get better. Sound familiar?

When God works in our lives, just like he did when he began to work in Joseph's life, he usually does so without any advance warning. In my particular case, I went to work on the morning of October 18, 2004, anticipating boarding a flight around noon for a business trip to Dallas. At about ten that morning, God's plan began to play out and my life would be forever changed. God tends to draw attention to our "sore spots" when he intervenes, targeting areas that need to change. In Joseph's case it was his coat of many colors. In my case it was sexual sin.

---

3 Much of what I am going to share is adapted from Kendall's book *God Meant It for Good: A Fresh Look at the Life of Joseph* (Moravian Falls, NC: Morningstar Publishers, 2008), 102–104.

When God prepares us, he also tends to shock us. He does this not to scare us, but to point out how sinful and frail we are and how we need to depend on him for strength. That is why when you hit rock bottom like I did, the only person who can help is God. At my lowest moment, when I was humbled, broken, and feeling hopeless, there was no place to go but up. There was going to be a lot of work to do in me, but God made me a promise, a promise he would keep: "I will never fail you. I will never abandon you" (Hebrews 13:5).

The other good news is that once we are ready, willing, and able to submit to God's authority, there is no turning back. When you are ready to start a new life, you are sometimes placed in situations that are not easy to handle. You have to learn to cope with change, which can be difficult. Sometimes you are uprooted from your family, and sometimes friends walk away. But if you put your faith in God, you will see that he really does work all things together for good. Doors start to open, new friends appear, and for a while you can even be on the top of the world while experiencing the worst of circumstances. God does us an enormous favor when we finally head down his path for our life. It's not always easy and the journey may take some twists and turns, but when God wants us to break from our past, he puts people, places, and things into our lives that are more bearable and many times much more enjoyable.

How did God do this for Joseph? He gave him rest from his enemies and made his presence known to Joseph, and Joseph prospered in his new career. One indication that the Lord was with Joseph was the way he adjusted to his new surroundings.

One of the things that happened while Joseph was in Egypt was that he was tempted sexually by Potiphar's wife. Although Joseph resisted the temptation, Potiphar's wife told a lie and Joseph found himself in prison. What is interesting about the sexual temptation is the fact that Joseph did not realize that God was testing him to see if he could be trusted with even greater responsibility. Joseph passed the test and was obedient, yet despite Joseph's faithfulness and self-control, he was thrown into jail.

God did Joseph a favor, however. While he was incarcerated, he had to keep his mouth shut. God says that if we will be quiet, say nothing, and do not try to manipulate the situation, then he will be moved to act on our behalf. God loves to step in and help us, but he wants to do it himself, so that he gets the glory. One of the most precious blessings we can receive is when God tells us to be quiet. Would it surprise you to know that is exactly what God told me on the morning of October 18, 2004?

God did Joseph a great favor when he could not defend himself. It meant God would take over. Thus, when you realize you have no defense, just shut your mouth so God can begin to work on your behalf.

The most important test that a person may have to pass before they are greatly used by God is to be punished for doing well and then to keep quiet about it. That is exactly what happened to Joseph. He was put into prison because he did everything right. When God chastens you because you have done right and you take it well, then you can be trusted. And when you can be trusted, God will do amazing things in and through your life.

~

During the summer, when I was not babysitting, you could find me at Carver Park Reserve. Because I have always loved to exercise outdoors, I enjoyed many late afternoons and early evenings on the walking trails there. The park was also my sanctuary on the weekends. I mentioned to my family and friends that I was working out alone, and they warned me that I should be careful. I assured them there was nothing to worry about—the park was safe.

The six-mile course reminded me of an enchanted forest, and the trails were hilly in spots, which made for a great workout. One day as I walked up the largest hill, there was a woman sitting on the ground with Rollerblades on, who appeared to be injured. As I approached, I heard her say, "Oh good. Here comes my top-of-the-hill angel."

When I asked if she was hurt, she responded, "No, I'm just tired." We talked for a few minutes before I encouraged her to keep up the good work—she had three miles left to go. She thanked me for cheering her on before skating away.

About two weeks later, walking the same loop, I was almost to the top of the hill when my family's words were ringing in my ears. I could see an older man coming toward me. He was scruffy, his clothes tattered, and he looked somewhat unkempt. I would be less than honest if I did not tell you I was a bit concerned. I was in the middle of the park, all alone, and I was not sure anyone could hear me if I screamed.

My fears were quickly dashed as our paths crossed. We exchanged pleasantries, and as we talked I learned this man was an ordained minister. We met on the top of the hill, at the exact same spot where the woman called me her "top-of-the-hill angel." This was more than mere coincidence—God had just sent me another angel.

This gentleman joined me on my walk, and I was now exercising with one of God's delivery agents. Given that he was older, he needed to rest after a mile, so we found ourselves sitting on a park bench enjoying the sunshine and warm weather. Our friendly conversation continued.

For whatever reason, I shared my circumstances, wondering out loud why Milt and his wife stayed together. His next question was quite direct: "Did you ever think that maybe you are in God's way and that is why he cannot work in Milt's life?" This teacher's godly wisdom forced me to reflect on my behavior and, as we finished our walk, I thanked him for giving me a different perspective, one from God's point of view.

You cannot make progress with God as long as you are holding on to pieces of your old life. It was time to completely let go. God was finally going to give me the power and desire to do what pleased him. I had known it for years, but this angel's friendly reminder confirmed that there were big changes coming. I was going to get out of God's way whether I liked it or not.

~

In July, the boys went camping and I decided to fly down to Tampa to surprise Paula. She was in the process of moving, and I found it interesting that another friend was downsizing. Unfortunately, Paula found herself in this situation because of her divorce. As we helped Paula box up belongings and determine what was to be moved and what should be donated or tossed, she became visibly upset as we unloaded items from the attic.

This area held memories of happier times. Baby items, toys, stuffed animals, children's books, Christmas decorations, and photo albums moved Paula to tears. Her heart was broken and the divorce was difficult for her to accept. Needless to say, she was feeling a compilation of emotions, grieving the fact that her kids were grown and she was beginning the next season of her life all alone.

As I was working up a sweat lending a helping hand, I could not help but think about this situation and situations just like it. *Why do we walk away? Why aren't more couples fighting to save their marriages? Why do we look outside of marriage for love, and why are so many husbands and wives afraid to protect the sanctity of marriage?*

Divorce breaks hearts, destroys relationships, damages children's well-being, and puts futures in jeopardy. It creates anxiety, anger, bitterness, and resentment, which is exactly why the Bible clearly tells us in the book of Malachi that God hates divorce. Divorce has impacted my family and several of my friends' families, and it breaks my heart to see how divorce impacts children too. It is my belief that many marriages could be saved if couples would put Christ at the center of their relationship, for a triple cord is not easily broken.

Unfortunately, in many marriages, Christ is nowhere to be found. A lack of spiritual, emotional, and intellectual intimacy usually precedes a breakdown in physical intimacy. It's easier to walk away and find someone else to meet your needs than it is to fight for your marriage and uphold the covenant you made before God.

What does the Bible say about marriage? Marriage is God's idea (Genesis 2:18–24), and commitment is critical to a successful marriage (Genesis 24:58–60). Romance is essential if a marriage is to flourish (Genesis 29:10–11), as marriage is supposed to be a time of great joy (Jeremiah 7:34). It creates the best environment for raising children (Malachi 2:14–15), and unfaithfulness destroys trust, which is the foundation of all relationships (Matthew 5:32). Marriage is permanent (Matthew 19:6), and, ideally, only death should dissolve a marriage (Romans 7:2–3) because marriage is a symbol of Christ and his church (Ephesians 5:21–33). God's Word is very clear about this: "Give honor to marriage, and remain faithful to one another in marriage. God will surely judge people who are immoral and those who commit adultery" (Hebrews 13:4).

The week flew by, Paula's move was complete, and I returned to Minneapolis, thrilled to be reunited with my grandsons. Early September was fast approaching, and it was almost time for the boys to head back to school once again. Babysitting was hard work, but we created a lifetime of memories and the summer was a special blessing in my life.

My sentencing was set for November 23, and I wondered if this was the reason God allowed my summer getaway. The preparation phase continued, and with my future in God's hands, I knew that no matter what happened the day before Thanksgiving, I had to continue to trust him. My heart was getting closer and closer to where it needed to be.

~

In September I returned to Tampa and decided to stay with my girlfriend Kim. Kim was a veteran negotiator, and it was actually a great deal for both of us when she said, "You help me pack and move to St. Petersburg and you can live here rent-free." Another move, another girlfriend downsizing, and another opportunity for me to do what I do best. For the next six weeks, we sold furniture, got the entire house packed up and cleaned, had an estate sale, and moved Kim's remaining belongings over to her new place.

On Thursday mornings during this time, I was attending a Bible study, learning all about divine interruptions. In the middle of October I found myself in downtown Tampa, attending my third Women of Faith Conference with my friend Bonnie. Even though I chose to attend this event with a group of ladies from church, I found myself sitting alone most of the time, reflecting on my journey.

In four weeks, I would be heading to Wisconsin for a much-anticipated and long-awaited judgment and sentencing day. Although I had a tremendous amount of peace regarding my situation, knowing that God was in control, I was still trying to figure out what I was supposed to be doing with my life.

A new speaker named Angie Smith had joined the Women of Faith team and was sharing a story about her fourth pregnancy. She had undergone an ultrasound after learning she had become pregnant and the news was not good. The baby's heart chamber was not developing properly, nor did the baby have a bladder. The doctors encouraged Angie to terminate the pregnancy, but she and her husband prayed for a miracle. It appeared their prayers had been answered when, to the amazement of nurses, the third trimester ultrasound showed the heart with four chambers and the baby had a bladder. Their fourth daughter, Audrey, was born prematurely, weighing a little over three pounds.

The crowd absolutely loved the picture of Audrey on the scale in the delivery room—she was perfect in every way. Unfortunately, Angie went on to share that they only had their little bundle of joy for two and a half hours. Audrey's lungs had not fully developed, and she passed away shortly after birth. Tears began to stream down many faces in the arena as we thought we were going to hear about their miracle.

Angie said she could not explain why this had happened, but she had to trust God with the outcome. Well, little Audrey's short life did prove to be miraculous and a special blessing for thousands of women that day. Her two and a half hours of life provided hope and encouragement to all who listened to her mother share her testimony of faith.

Angie mentioned that particular day happened to be the day to recognize women who had lost children to either miscarriage or an unexpected death. She asked anyone who had lost a child to stand so they could be recognized. What happened next drew a collective gasp from the audience. Although I cannot be sure how many women were standing, I would estimate that it was well over a thousand, some even in my own group. Even Angie could not believe the number of ladies standing, as Women of Faith had never done this before. All she could say, and what we heard over and over again, is, "You are not alone. You are not alone."

I have never been so moved by a single moment in my entire life. Even though I had never lost a child, when I realized how many women had, I wept. Tears were flowing, women hugged one another, and my heart could not help but be touched by this poignant moment. What became very clear was that it does not matter what you are going through; you can take comfort in knowing that you are not alone. Even when you feel alone, God is always with you—always.

～

I came home from the Saturday session emotionally exhausted. Lying on my bed, I asked God to reveal what he wanted me to do with my life. His answer came early Sunday morning when I heard, *Write the book.* I had begun writing three years before that point, and when I was filled with the Spirit, the words would flow quickly and effortlessly. I had completed many chapters but had not written a single word in months. Between helping friends move and babysitting, there had not been a lot of extra time to write. I submitted a special prayer that Sunday: *God, please give me wisdom and guidance to continue to follow your will for my life and complete my book.*

Tuesday night I headed over to Bible study. We got through the first chapter of a new study when God changed the agenda. The other women were not aware of my personal challenges, and although I had shared my legal situation with Paula months earlier, we decided to wait before telling the group the rest of my story. We both knew the time was right, so I grabbed my computer and began to read some of the completed parts of my book.

I quickly realized why small groups are so important. I was blessed to have friends who would listen and not judge me, and it was apparent that my testimony was touching their hearts. We laughed, we cried, and I received the inspiration I needed to sit down, continue to write, and trust God with the rest of the story.

Prior to leaving, we all stood up, formed a circle, held hands, and prayed. We shared what was on our hearts, yet when I heard Patrice say, "Oh, Lord, thank you. Who better to send to prison than our dear sister Katie—what a wonderful servant she would be," I could not help but open my eyes, look at her, and say, "Really, Patrice? You are praying that I go to prison?"

My coming-out party gave me a renewed sense of confidence to finish what I had started. I simply smiled, realizing this get-together took place on the seventh anniversary of the day this journey had begun. Maybe I really was made for such a time as this.

~

Thursday, November 10, 2011. I got up early knowing the morning would fly by as I had to be at St. James by ten o'clock in the morning for my Jonah study. Although most of us know the story about Jonah and the whale, the purpose of this story was not to teach us about Jonah but to teach us about God. Through Jonah's experience, God reveals that although he will pour out his wrath on the wicked, he is also a God who eagerly pours out his grace and mercy on those who repent. Jonah is a story about second chances.

As that day's class came to a close, I wrote down my prayer concerns. When it came time for me to pray, I could hardly speak.

Through tears I shared I was facing one of the most difficult days of my life on November 23, and I asked the women to continue to lift me up in prayer. As I regained my composure and gathered my belongings, my phone rang. It was a familiar number—it belonged to my attorney, Michael Cohn. I quickly exited the classroom to have some privacy, and we discussed my upcoming sentencing.

I became extremely frustrated as we reviewed the protocol and fine-tuned my statement, yet I had to remind myself that just a few minutes earlier, God's presence filled the room. Who was I going to trust? Our conversation ended and I hopped in the car and headed toward Land O'Lakes, Florida.

8

For the past two weeks, I had spent many hours volunteering at Really Good News Ministry. Ruth Ann, a friend from our small group, founded the ministry, which, among other things, provides Bible reading plans called Just One Word. Just One Word is a calendar that encourages "students of the Word" to spend time in the Bible each day and write down what they hear from God. I was providing assistance in the development of the 2012 calendar and was also busy writing a press release for Ruth Ann's new book, *The Radical Power of God.*

On the ride up, Ruth Ann called, inviting me to lunch. It was a nice break, but she sensed I was not myself. When we finally arrived at the ministry, Ruth Ann asked what was wrong and I told her. As she always does, we immediately began to pray, asking God to take away my frustration. Then I began to relax.

Over the course of the next few hours, I was making progress on our priorities but still having a hard time concentrating. We talked again and did an impromptu Bible study on being filled with the Holy Spirit. We discussed the importance of being filled with God's power, especially given my upcoming challenges.

In Ruth Ann's book, there is a chapter titled "Setting Your Anchor in Christ with God's Power." The chapter describes being baptized in the Holy Spirit, which goes beyond receiving the Holy Spirit when we are born again. There are three points to consider: God the Father did not allow Jesus to begin his earthly ministry until after baptism with water and the Holy Spirit; Jesus said we would receive the power before we go out into ministry; and Jesus said that anyone who has faith in him would accomplish even greater things than he did.

Okay, that seemed to make sense me, but then she writes that a spiritual language comes with the power. Ruth Ann described the moment she was baptized in the Holy Spirit and even went so far as to tell me how to be filled with the Spirit, including a special prayer to be prayed.

"Well, I tried that a few weeks back and it didn't work," I said. So we talked about my experience and she asked if I wanted to pray for the power. "Sure, what do I have to lose?" I responded. We held hands and she questioned whether or not I wanted her to pray on my behalf. "Why not?" I commented. "You've been at this a lot longer than I have."

Ruth Ann's prayer went something like this:

Dear heavenly Father, we humbly come to you now with our heart, soul, and body, and we yield them all to you. Lord, your Word says that you will give the Holy Spirit to those who ask. So we are asking for you to fill Katie with your Holy Spirit and give her evidence of your filling with a prayer language in another tongue. We thank you, Lord, for this special gift, and we receive it now by faith, in the mighty name of Jesus.[1]

It was now my turn to pray. Through tears I prayed a similar prayer. I began to feel God's presence in a very tangible way; I was crying and knew with certainty God was up to something. We could feel his power in our hands, and it was as though I was hanging on for dear life. I asked to receive evidence of the filling of the Holy Spirit with a prayer language in another tongue, telling the Lord I received it by faith, and we ended with a resounding *amen*. It was an exhausting and uplifting experience.

So what happened? Absolutely nothing. But it was my expec-

---

1 Ruth Ann Nylen, *The Radical Power of God* (Mobilize Press, 2011), 65.

tation to receive my prayer language that kept me focused. I finished up my work. As we parted ways, Ruth Ann assured me it was going to happen that day. I got in the car and thanked God for an incredible day. I felt his presence a number of times and was finally at peace. I was confident due to the fact of what I had just experienced, that God had taken me to the next level and the rest was up to me.

As I drove in the driveway when I arrived home, I knew I needed to have some quiet time with the Lord. The house was empty and I headed upstairs to my bedroom, which consisted of a mattress topper on the floor and a television. I never replaced the lawn chair. But it did not matter what was in that space; God was going to do a mighty work in that upper room.

In the dark and on my knees, I lifted up every care and concern that was in my heart to the Lord. It took only a short time to feel God's presence, and this was the fourth time that day I was overcome with emotion. I thanked God for his love and confessed every one of my sins, asking for his forgiveness. Although I was on my knees, I felt a bit unsteady. I told the Lord I was grateful for all the people he put in my life and asked him to shower each of them with extravagant blessings.

I had been praying for close to twenty minutes when I found myself crying out for God's help. It was similar to what I experienced on February 1, 2009, the day I was born again. *God, I cannot do this alone*, I pleaded, *please take me by my hand and help me*. I lifted my right hand into the air, and, at that very moment, my body arched upward and an unrecognizable prayer language was spoken out of my lips. I had officially spoken in tongues. My tears were gone and I experienced incredible joy.

The only thing I could do was grab my head and with the biggest smile, walk around my bedroom repeating, "That was awesome! That was so cool! Incredible! Thank you, Lord. Unbelievable!" Words could not describe the moment. I immediately texted Ruth

Ann: "Oh my God! I just spoke in tongues! It was awesome! Thank you, thank you, thank you!"

Ruth Ann: "Oh, he is God … keep speaking and the miraculous will flow."

"I can't even begin to describe the moment! It was incredible!"

Ruth Ann: "If you are driving, pull over!"

I texted back, "No, I was in my bedroom on my knees in the dark! I would have crashed the car if I was driving! He knew that! ☺"

~

Jesus promised his disciples, "And now I will send the Holy Spirit, just as my Father promised. But stay here in the city until the Holy Spirit comes and fills you with power from heaven" (Luke 24:49). It's surprising how little the average Christian knows about the Spirit of God, and I was no exception. Most people can tell you a little bit about the life of Jesus and can give you a pretty good idea about God the Father, but when it comes to the Holy Spirit they are not quite sure what to think.

In John 14:15–17, Jesus promises us the Holy Spirit:

> "If you love me, obey my commandments. And I will ask the Father, and he will give you another Advocate, who will never leave you. He is the Holy Spirit, who leads into all truth. The world cannot receive him, because it isn't looking for him and doesn't recognize him. But you know him, because he lives with you now and later will be in you."

The regenerating power of the Holy Spirit came on the disciples just before Jesus' ascension, and the Holy Spirit was poured out on all the believers at Pentecost shortly after Jesus ascended into heaven. The Holy Spirit is the very presence of God within us. The indwelling and empowering ministries of the Holy Spirit operate in different ways and have different purposes; however, it is God's will for both of these tasks to be performed in each of our lives.

Robert Heidler's book *Experiencing the Spirit* gave me wonderful insight into what I had just experienced.[2] The key words are *indwelling* and *empowering*. The *indwelling* of the Holy Spirit is automatic and we receive it when we are saved or born again. But the *empowering* of the Holy Spirit, or the baptism of the Holy Spirit, is the ministry by which the Spirit of God "comes upon" us with power to equip us for supernatural ministry. It gives us the power of God, which we need if we are to be effective doing the work of God.

The Spirit's indwelling is designed to mature us, causing us to grow in the Lord. The Spirit's empowering is designed to equip us, enabling us to serve the Lord. To put it another way, the Spirit indwells us to give us victory over sin, making us holy; but the Spirit empowers us to give us tools for ministry, making us effective.

The indwelling of the Holy Spirit is when the Spirit lives within us to give us the character of Christ, and empowering of the Spirit comes upon us in power to give us the ministry of Christ. The whole purpose of the Spirit's empowering is to equip us to minister to others and to change individual lives through the power of God.

Our spiritual prayer language is to be private and used for intense communication between our spirit and the Lord. This prayer language will edify us and will also help us stand up against the Enemy. This is one of the reasons why Paul wrote:

> And the Holy Spirit helps us in our weakness. For example, we don't know what God wants us to pray for. But the Holy Spirit prays for us with groanings that cannot be expressed in words. And the Father who knows all hearts knows what the Spirit is saying, for the Spirit pleads for us believers in harmony with God's own will. (Romans 8:26–27)

The Bible tells us in the book of Acts that every one of the apostles spoke in tongues on the day of Pentecost: "And everyone present was filled with the Holy Spirit and began speaking in other languages, as the Holy Spirit gave them this ability" (Acts 2:4).

---

2 Robert Heidler, *Experiencing the Spirit: Developing a Living Relationship with the Holy Spirit* (Ventura, CA: Renew Books, 1998), 48.

And in 1 Corinthians, the apostle Paul thanks God that he speaks in tongues and expresses his desire for every Christian to receive their prayer language. He goes on to say that a person who speaks in tongues is strengthened personally. Then in another place, he writes, "Pray in the Spirit at all times and on every occasion. Stay alert and be persistent in your prayers for all believers everywhere" (Ephesians 6:18).

I was so thrilled to be baptized in the Holy Spirit. Although I was exhausted, I asked God to continue to fill me with his power and allow me to feel his presence again. I was lying on my back and my body seemed to be frozen in time. I could not move and total peace enveloped me. The only way I can describe what I was feeling was that it felt like I was getting a Jesus massage from the inside out. I prayed for close to an hour, and as I whispered my prayers, I asked over and over again to be filled with the fruit of the Spirit, the very essence of God: love, joy, peace, patience, kindness, goodness, faithfulness, gentleness, and self-control.

I needed to exhibit these godly qualities in my life. I wanted to be a virtuous woman, and I was determined to become a woman after God's own heart. "For we know how dearly God loves us, because he has given us the Holy Spirit to fill our hearts with His love" (Romans 5:5). Our heavenly Father had another surprise for me, however, and as you are about to find out, November 11, 2011, was going to be another very special day.

~

When I woke up on November 11, I was still on cloud nine. My plan was to spend the day with my girlfriend Kim. I arrived in St. Petersburg midafternoon, hardly able to wait to share what had happened to me. As I reflected on what God had done, I was all smiles knowing God had orchestrated my living arrangements. He knew I needed to be alone and without distraction to take my faith to the next level. Where better to do it than in an empty house.

I was like a little kid at Christmas sharing details about the awesome gift I had just received. Kim was so kind. She listened and reinforced how wonderful God is. We had a great day, but I decided to return to Tampa rather than spend the night. Kim had arranged a date first thing in the morning and I preferred to sleep at home anyway. I had no idea why God arranged that date or why he wanted me home alone, but I was about to find out.

When I got back to Tampa, I hopped in the shower, put on my pajamas, crawled under my comforter, and turned on the television. I remember checking the time—8:40 p.m.—when I decided to turn off the lights and call it a night.

Lying on my back on the floor in the dark, I began to pray. Within five minutes I began to feel God's presence, and I continued to ask him to take me to another level. It is very hard to explain the feeling when God's Spirit aligns with yours. As I said before, it's like being massaged from the inside out and you almost feel like you are floating.

Here is what happened between 8:40 p.m. and 11:17 p.m., and during the night. As you know, I had struggled with sexual sin throughout my life. It was driven by loneliness, insecurity, and the fact that I did not feel loved. Although I could say that the majority of my problems had been fixed, the temptation to sin had not been completely removed at this point in my life—in fact, I wondered if it ever would. I had enjoyed significant periods of sexual sobriety, but I continued to stumble from time to time. I knew that God is patient with our progress and we need to focus on how far we have come, but I still needed his help in this area.

As I was praying, I pleaded with God to remove my lustful thoughts, take away my sexual immorality, and get rid of the demons that had held me captive my entire life: *Take the guilt, Lord, take my codependency, take my shame—please take it all,* I begged. After I shared every prayer I needed God to answer, I told him I was ready to be transformed.

I prayed over and over and over again, asking God to allow me to speak in my prayer language, and I eventually began speaking in tongues. The inflection of my prayer language bordered on angry and direct, to quiet and peaceful. As the intensity of my voice increased, I sensed the anger of God directed toward my body. At times, when it seemed like God was really mad, my body would tense and jerk.

Although I could not control what was happening with my physical movements or my speech, I did have the capacity to think. What was I thinking? That God was casting out my sexual demon. As the Holy Spirit continued to speak through me, I was breathing, yet I wasn't. How hours of prayer could escape my lips was unexplainable. There were a few moments when I remember swallowing and catching my breath, but after I received a two- or three-second break, the language and body movements continued once again.

Again, I was not scared because I knew that whatever God was up to was necessary to transform me into a new creature in Christ. It was up to me to continue to let God use me as his vessel. So I decided to go with the flow. As the purification and cleansing process continued, the pace and authority of my prayer language demonstrated God was serious about what he was doing, and it was not easy.

What happened next was wonderful. It felt as though I was surrounded by angels and they were holding and guiding my arms. Over what seemed to be a three- to five-minute duration, my arms were moving in slow motion into the shape of wings. My arms felt like they were fully extended over my head. I had an incredible peace come over me and I stopped speaking and smiled, convinced I had received my wings. As magical as the moment was, and wanting to savor the feeling forever, I returned to my prayer language knowing God was in complete control.

After a prolonged period of intense prayer, the stronghold of sexual addiction was broken when the spirit of immorality that was within me was forced from my body. Completely exhausted, I laid there for an extended period of time being bathed in the Spirit. I was at total peace. I did not want this feeling to end. I knew I had to get up, but I couldn't. When I finally could, I rolled off the bed, stumbled downstairs to check the clock, and it was 11:17 p.m. That's when I went into the bathroom to clean up and change my clothes, being completely exhausted.

When I climbed back into bed, I asked God for more. I wanted to be back in the Spirit. Once again, I was flat on my back with my arms opened to receive God's anointing. I prayed, *God, cleanse me and make me pure.* My prayer was short and sweet. Within seconds I began to pray in my spiritual language. This time, though, it was much more peaceful as my prayers were whispered the majority of the time. There were periods when the inflection and intensity of my voice increased, and there were also periods of time when I lost control of my body. Once again it felt as though I was being carried by angels, and the wing formation repeated itself.

I cannot be sure how long this lasted. I remember singing "Amazing Grace," and, quite frankly, I did not care how long it was taking. I was along for this incredible ride of transformation, and words cannot describe this miraculous moment. It was apparent God was leading me in prayer. As the strength of the anointing subsided, I was again bathed in his Spirit.

As I returned to a more conscious state, I knew God was not done with me. I continued to pray, keeping my prayer simple and specific: *Clothe me in your righteousness, Lord.* I then went back to what seemed to work very well and continued speaking in tongues. God answered that prayer quickly, I prayed an Our Father, and very peacefully and confidently, it was on to my next request: *Fill my heart with your desires, Lord. Fill my heart with your love. Fill my heart with what hurts yours.* Once again I was used as God's vessel in prayer and a special peace enveloped me. I was now whispering and calm, knowing God was in complete control as he answered each and every prayer.

By purifying and cleansing me, God has made me righteousness, which means to be in right standing with him. This is one of the most vital areas of our Christian walk. Some people confuse righteousness with holiness, but righteousness has nothing to do with the way you act or the way you live your life. Holiness is your conduct, but righteousness is who you are, the nature of God that resides within you.

You do not come into right standing with God by being good or acting right. It is faith in Jesus Christ and his redemptive work at Calvary that brings you into right standing with God. Righteous character cannot be produced by human effort; it only comes by the Spirit of Christ working in people's hearts. It is love that can only come from God.

The next morning, I woke up feeling like a completely new person. You know why? Because I was. I had been writing for hours when my phone rang. It was Milt. I told him he was not going to believe what happened, and I began reading what I had written. Little did I know that while I was sharing the miracle of my transformation, Milt had to pull his car off the road because he could not believe what he was hearing.

Milt invited me to a late lunch, and when I arrived, he could see something was different. I was still in awe of my miraculous moment, and Milt was convinced I had lost my mind. We finished lunch and drove over to see the progress on my apartment. I had put a reservation on a cute little place on the north side of Tampa that was under construction, hoping and praying come sentencing time I would be given probation.

As I turned left into the complex, I knew God had given me the strength to finally end my relationship with Milt. I even think Milt knew something was about to happen without me having to say too much of anything. After inspecting the second-floor corner unit, we walked toward our cars and Milt seemed to be self-absorbed and quite introspective. Very few words were spoken—he could see there was a definite change in me.

As we parted ways, the last thing Milt said was, "You will never find someone who loves you as much as I do." I did not have the heart to tell him I just had.

~

With my sentencing date fast approaching, it was time to head back to Wisconsin, so I decided to fly home rather than drive. I got to the airport two hours early, relieved that I allowed adequate check-in time.

As I weaved my way through the maze of weary passengers, I found myself behind a woman who had just lost a loved one. She was carrying a picture of a young man that was inscribed with his date of birth and date of death. As we approached the X-ray machine, one of the TSA agents whispered to the other that his ashes were being scanned. My heart hurt for this woman, assuming this young man was her son, yet I said nothing. As I put my bag on the conveyor, I knew I should have extended my sympathy. Gathering my belongings, I felt terrible about not showing any compassion.

Well, God is a gentleman. He reminded me about ten minutes later that I did indeed miss a wonderful opportunity to bless someone. *How could I be so stupid?* I asked. God gently assured me that I would have many more opportunities—I wasn't to miss the next one.

I boarded the plane and settled into seat 12A. I picked the window seat because I wanted to sleep. I closed my eyes and was determined to be asleep before we pushed back from the gate. About five minutes later, the passenger in 12B arrived. She accidently hit me with her bag and apologized for waking me up. "Wasn't sleeping," I responded. "No big deal." Given there was no room in the overhead, she had no choice but to visit the back of the plane with her carry-on luggage. I was so tired. The week's events left me exhausted, and I desperately needed to get caught up on some much-needed sleep because in one week I would find myself back in federal court.

As we leveled off, I heard God speak: *1 Thessalonians 5:11.* I was wondering why he was bringing that verse up in my spirit? "Come on, God, I'm tired," I quietly said. Then I heard two more times: *1 Thessalonians 5:11*. God was not going to let me sleep until I looked up that Scripture.

I asked the woman seated next to me to please excuse me as I needed to get something from the overhead. My Bible was tucked away in my knapsack, so I pulled it out, sat back down, and read 1 Thessalonians 5:11: "So encourage each other and build each other up, just as you are already doing." I just smiled. God was giving me a do-over and I was not going to miss this opportunity.

So I turned to the woman seated next to me and asked, "Do you need to be encouraged?"

She looked at me very sadly and said, "Yes, I do." She did not say anything for a few minutes, and then she turned toward me as if to muster up enough courage and strength to speak.

Her name was Mary Ann and she was seventy-six years old. I was kind of surprised. Although she appeared to be physically and emotionally drained, she looked younger than that. What she was about to share broke my heart. Her husband of more than fifty years had just left her, her son Daniel was serving a twenty-year prison term, and she was estranged from her grandchildren. For the next two hours, I showered her with compassion and encouraged her with God's love.

We discussed our lives, laughing about some of the similarities yet saddened by the struggles we each faced. The best thing I could do for Mary Ann was ask for God's help. We prayed for strength, for patience, for her son, for her husband, and for her grandkids. I also went right to the throne, speaking in tongues, asking God to give Mary Ann some peace and a good night's sleep. She laughed when I told her she was not even going to get up for a potty break, and that if she wet the bed she couldn't blame me.

God sure does direct our steps and arrange our circumstances, doesn't he? He made sure Mary Ann and I sat together, led me to the appropriate Scripture, and allowed us to have some special time together. When you are empowered by God, amazing things really do happen. God was guiding my words and my heart, and I knew I had just made the most out of this opportunity.

Just prior to landing in Milwaukee, Mary Ann asked me if I would do her a favor. "Could you please send some encouraging words to my son in prison?" she asked. How could I say no to that? She gave me his address at a correctional institution in central Wisconsin, and I promised to send him a Christmas card.

At the same time I remembered what my best friend from high school said in her letter to the judge. Jane wrote: "Katie wants to move forward in her life and what would make more sense in this situation would be to have her somehow work as an encourager in prisons where so many women who have no hope need a word of hope. She would be an inspiration to them." *A prison ministry? Seriously, God? You must have me mixed up with someone else.*

~

It was my long-awaited judgment and sentencing day. My sister Susie drove and we arrived at the federal courthouse right on schedule. I intentionally picked this time so I would not have to see Milt. Although my sentencing was not scheduled for an hour, the hearing could be moved up so we needed to arrive early. We took our seats on the bench outside of Judge Clevert's courtroom and waited. My attorney, Michael Cohn, was in the courtroom—he wanted to see how Milt's sentencing played out.

Within a short time, the rest of my support team arrived. My son Brian and daughter Jenny were first, followed by my friends Mari and Julie, and my civil attorney, Mike Penkwitz. We sat outside the courtroom and waited, and waited, and waited.

A little before eleven in the morning, Michael bolted from the courtroom to tell me Milt just got hammered, receiving ninety-seven months in prison. "You need to change something in your sentencing statement," he insisted. Apparently the judge was not in a very good mood. I pulled out my statement, noted the changes, and took one last potty break. I again asked God to direct my steps given I did not want to see Milt. Well, guess who came out looking for me when I was in the bathroom? Prior to entering the court-room and because of what just happened to Milt, I told my kids to expect the worst—I was most likely going to prison.

I took my seat at the wooden table near the back of the room, adjusted my microphone, and opened my portfolio. I had waited three years for this day, and, as strange as this may sound, I was happy to finally be in a position to put this part of the journey behind me.

While waiting for the sentencing to begin, the US attorney turned around and shared some kind words regarding the letters that were submitted on my behalf. These letters touched my heart. Family members, friends, coworkers, and former business asso-ciates wrote some amazing letters to Judge Clevert. I hoped and prayed they would help.

Judge Clevert's reputation preceded him. One of four fed-eral judges in the Eastern District of Wisconsin, he was by far the toughest. He was known to always take the government's side, but I was hopeful he would show compassion toward me. He had been merciful to the other defendants. Peter O'Malley received twenty-eight months, Thomas Russell received twenty-four months, Michael Rivett received sixty days of house arrest, and Patrick Kane received probation. These individuals were involved in the racketeering scheme, but I was not. I hoped my sentencing state-ment would clear up a few things relative to this case; however, my attorney told me he thought Judge Clevert had made up his mind long ago.

"All rise." As protocol had it, the US attorney spoke first, then SC Johnson, then my lawyer, then me. The US attorney stuck to the sentencing guidelines. "Being bright and highly able, Ms. Scheller should have seen this for what it was," he said. Even though Judge Clevert questioned whether the punishment fit the crime, the US attorney would not waver. It was almost as if the judge was pleading with him to say I deserved less time, but he stood with his hands behind his back, his head in the air, and for a rather long period of time did not speak. I was convinced God held his tongue.

Up next was SC Johnson. Only one problem: they were a no-show.

My lawyer began to speak, having prepared four pages of notes, which included excellent arguments as to why I deserved a downward departure along with supporting documentation, most which had come from the US attorney. We had another problem though: the judge cut Michael off before he even finished the first page. This was not good.

It was my turn and I was able to get through my entire sentencing statement. I apologized to my family, Mrs. Morris, and SC Johnson, and I tried to clear up the confusion relative to my job responsibilities, telling Judge Clevert I had absolutely no responsibility for domestic transportation. I reminded him that at no time during this entire investigation did anyone uncover any criminal activity or irregularities in the area in which I had direct control.

There was some discussion back and forth, and the judge seemed to be all over the place. At one point I thought I was going to get probation, yet at another point I thought he was going to lock me up and throw away the key.

Although Judge Clevert believed the genesis of my problem was a matter of my heart, I was still involved in a crime and not truthful when investigators confronted me. "For the most part, the women I see here are victims themselves," Clevert said. He went on to say I was manipulated by men. Taking everything into consideration, Judge Clevert thought a sentence below the guidelines was appropriate. I closed my eyes, waiting for his judgment to be rendered, and heard "thirty-six months and one year of supervised release."

I took a deep breath, my attorney put his arm around me and told me he was sorry, and I heard someone behind me begin to cry. Judge Clevert asked if I had any preference on where I wanted to serve my time. I turned and looked at my kids and did not have the heart to say Florida.

I took the news in stride, and although I knew the kids were hurting because of their tears, I was not able to show much emotion. My sister thought maybe I was in shock. It didn't feel that way. I really believe it was because of my faith. I may not have always understood why God does things the way he does, but I did know he works all things for good. God had told me two years ago that he would take care of the injustice in my life. The rest was up to me. Was I going to trust him, accept my punishment, and be obedient? I had no choice.

Before leaving the courthouse, I sent a text to my friends in Tampa telling them I was sentenced to three years in prison. Within minutes, I received the following three messages from Paula:

God sees your acceptance and obedience. Expect a miracle! Keep this to yourself. May he get the GLORY!

Humility, my friend, is to be studied in Scripture.

Wow, the Spirit is speakin!

Think back to the story about Joseph for a moment. Although Joseph appeared to be ready, he was not. God still had some work to do in his heart. Joseph was trying to manipulate his future, and God was continuing to prepare his heart. There was still a fair degree of self-pity and self-righteousness that God needed to remove from Joseph. I believed prison was necessary for God to continue to prepare my heart for supernatural ministry, and God was nice enough to tell me what I needed to do: "Humility is to be studied in Scripture."

On the way home, I made a number of phone calls to let everyone know what happened, and I was still in a very good frame of mind. It was tough, however, to walk into my parents' house. They were struggling. I tried to tell them many times that everything was going to be fine, but, unfortunately, they were my parents and their oldest child had just been sentenced to thirty-six months in prison.

As I headed upstairs to change my clothes, I began to think about my decision to not request Florida. I decided it was time to do what was best for Katie, so I picked up the phone and called both my probation officer and attorney and told them I wanted to request Coleman, which is a federal prison camp just north of Tampa.

The first week in December I received an e-mail telling me that was exactly where I was designated to serve my time and that I needed to surrender on January 4, 2012, by two o'clock in the afternoon. I cannot begin to tell you how happy I was. My prayers had been answered. God knew the desires of my heart and he knew I needed sunshine and warm weather along with my spiritual support team to survive. I ran downstairs to tell my parents, and they could see my excitement as I could not get the smile off of my face.

I spent a few days researching the Federal Correctional Complex at Coleman, and it's a good thing I am a creature of habit and love structure, because I was going to get it. With a check-in date less than a month away, I booked my return flight to Tampa. Everything was falling into place just like God had planned.

9

I had to fly back down to Tampa after Thanksgiving to pick up my car and decided to stay for a few days before heading back home. During the night of December 2, God gave me a vision. I saw something not once, not twice, but three times. Each time I would see it, I would wake up. Then I'd fall back asleep again, then when I saw it again, I'd wake back up. There in capital letters, written in white on a dark background was the title of the book: VIVIAN. It was as though God was telling me this story is about a real-life *Pretty Woman* and it will be God who climbs up the fire escape with my bouquet of roses.

I called my sister Susie, who had helped me with much of the editing, and shared my latest God encounter. The only thing she could say was, "No way."

"Yes way," I confidently replied. "It's God's decision. Shoot, he is the one helping me write this crazy book and who better to rescue me." The title *Vivian* made sense given what I was feeling when I saw Julia Roberts. As I thought about this sequence of events, I smiled. You know what this means? It means that God also had to direct Julia Roberts' steps so that she was sitting next to me at the pool.

It should not come as a surprise that when God reveals things, he also confirms them. I called Paula to tell her that the Lord revealed the name of the book, and, although she was excited, she could not talk because she had just arrived at work. But what was about to happen sealed the deal for me. Paula called back about ten minutes later—in fact, I was surprised to hear from her. "Katie," she said with a fair amount of excitement in her voice, "you are not going to believe what just happened. I turned on the television in the workout room and Anderson Cooper was on." I thought she was going to tell me something about gray hair when she said, "You know, the guy with the gray hair?"

"Yep. I know who you are talking about," I replied.

"He was just telling a story about a woman who had dressed her daughter up as Julia Roberts in *Pretty Woman*, and Anderson then said, 'The prostitute … what was her name? Vivian.'" Paula was now beside herself. "Katie, that is your confirmation," she said. It was fun to hear her excitement and how God was working in all of our lives.

When I shared this story with my daughter Jenny not five minutes later, she started to chuckle. "Mom, I dressed up as Vivian for Halloween." Then I burst out laughing.

On the drive back to Wisconsin, God spoke these words to me: *This book is dedicated to all those who struggle with codependency. The security you crave can only be found in the Lord.* As I wrote down this message, I realized that God had big plans for this book.

~

I returned to Racine and started getting things checked off my to-do list. I promised Mary Ann on the airplane that I would send a Christmas card with some encouraging words to her son in prison. Check. That task was complete. I was surprised when I received the following letter in the mail, dated on December 14, 2011.

Katie,

Wow, God really does work in our lives at all times. Mail call is the highlight of each and every day. They put up a list of names at 3:30 p.m. and if your name is checked you are one of the men who will have a smile on his face because he is getting a letter from family and friends. It had been four days since my name had been checked.

This past Saturday my mom came up to visit me with a

family friend. It was great to see her so happy after the past couple of years she has had. For one hour and 59 minutes I had a smile from ear to ear, and then it was time for her to leave. I have a smile on my face as she leaves out the door as my heart is in pain. I don't want her to see me hurting. I don't believe any parent wants to see their children hurting.

Okay, back to the "mail list." They put the mail list up at 3:30 p.m., again no check. I headed back to my room and waited for dinner. At 7:00 p.m. that night they called me to the officer's station. I got up there and a staff member handed me an envelope. He said it got stuck in the mailbag. It was a greeting card from someone in Racine. I don't know anyone from Racine. I had to look at the name on the envelope again, yep it was me. I got back to my room and opened up the card. I read "airplane, Tampa and your mother"; I knew exactly who you were. I just smiled and shook my head. Here I was just having a crummy couple of days and I receive a Christmas card from a woman I don't know who met my mother on an airplane, let my mom talk about our painful times in our lives, listened and prayed.

Katie, you should know I called my mom the following day you guys arrived in Milwaukee to make sure she got in all right. The phone calls I make are 20-minute timed calls. Katie, my mom talked for 19 minutes and 30 seconds about meeting you and your conversation. Her spirits were high and she sounded great. So thank you for taking the time to talk and pray with my mom.

Katie, first of all, thank you for reaching out to my mother on that flight and sharing Scripture with her. Then I want to thank you for taking the time to write me.

After my arrest in March of 2007, I have been on an emotional roller coaster. I have been angry with God, wondering how or why he would want to see me hurt so bad. I go to chapel weekly and have come a long way since 2007. I was very, very depressed in 2007; I snuck in pills to the jail and took over 75 pills. I was out for three days and woke up handcuffed to a hospital bed. Through talking to our chaplain and other Christians here, I believe I found my sticking point. I believe my ex-wife has forgiven me, my family and even God, because I asked, but I can't forgive myself. My two children don't have a father to love and care and be there for them. I can't get past that. I pray on it and some days I feel as though I have taken ten steps forward then I see a TV commercial of a father and his son, and I'm back to square one.

Sorry if I went on here, don't want to dump all my problems on you. I wanted to say thank you and get this in the mail. So thank you, Katie. I hope you didn't mind me writing you back.

God bless and thank you,
Daniel

As I read this letter my heart hurt. There are so many innocent victims of crime. Many are young, many will never know their parents, and many children will be forced to grow up in broken homes while other kids will become familiar with social services. God knows how much this hurt my heart. And I believe it also hurts his heart. God also understands that we struggle with unforgiveness, particularly with forgiving ourselves, which may be why he prompted me to print out my Christmas miracle story, address another envelope to Daniel, and head to the mailbox.

I realized that day something very special was going to happen as a result of my incarceration and obedience. Interestingly enough, I did not tell Daniel or his mother why I was flying to Milwaukee. Mary Ann had no idea about my plea agreement and sentencing, yet through this meeting God revealed some of the challenges I would encounter as I began my ministry.

One thing was certain: this was going to be the toughest, most heart-wrenching assignment I would ever have.

~

The next two weeks flew by. Milt had tried to contact me numerous times, and knowing him like I did, I fully expected him to reach out over the holidays. As a result, I was not surprised when I received a voicemail from him on Christmas Day. The next day there was an e-mail from him.

> Katie, my intent in sending this note to you is not to try and convince you of anything but rather to offer my two cents on a couple of items.
>
> First, I do not believe for a second that God told you to not have further contact with me. The Bible is clear on what God tells us. For him to give you an order like this would be in complete violation of him allowing us to make our own choices, thus destroying one's own will. God does things for us but again that would destroy the free will that he gives us. He desires that we make choices that will please him.
>
> Secondly, I would encourage you to stop telling people that you can speak in tongues. You are scaring your friends. The Bible is clear on tongues; they are a spiritual gift given to believers who accept Jesus Christ as their personal savior. All believers have at least one spiritual gift and many have multiple gifts. The Bible is also clear that we are not to brag about our gift but rather use the gift to edify the Lord. When we brag about having this gift we are edifying ourselves and not God.
>
> Thirdly, I believe God intervened on your behalf to keep you from taking that job at the ministry for whatever reason. He only wants the best for his children and will protect us if he feels it is necessary. In your case you have changed in ways that truly worry me. Please do not get me wrong, I am not judging anyone but rather walking a fine line and pointing out my observations.

In any event, I truly do not expect a reply but this has been on my heart for some time. I wish only the best for you and pray that God will pour out his many blessings on you every day.

Just for the record, you now owe me one Diet Coke as you may recall our bet that one day you too would find that back door that so many of my friends have found. I would not be honest if I did not tell you that I miss our friendship, but like you I am dedicated to pleasing and serving my God.

I prayed about responding to this note because God had been revealing many things to me over the previous two days, especially when it came to obeying his commandments. I was almost certain God was giving me permission to reply, and, if I was wrong, I was going to have to ask to be forgiven. I decided I was going to reply and then ask God for forgiveness. So I wrote an e-mail back to Milt:

First and foremost, I will always be your friend ... and I do not owe you a Diet Coke. I will never owe you a Diet Coke! I am simply following God's will for my life!

God still has work to do in both of us. He has made it very clear to me that I can no longer see you because I am in his way of accomplishing everything he wants for you and your wife. God also needs to heal my heart.

God told me to stand firm in his Word and I am! I am following God's commandments for my life. It's that simple!

You must not commit adultery and you must not covet your neighbor's wife! Deuteronomy 6:5–6: "And you must love the Lord your God with all your heart, all your soul and all your strength. And you must commit yourselves wholeheartedly to these commands that I am giving you today."

Milt, I have totally and completely given myself to the Lord and I am committed to loving him and serving him every day of my life. I will continue to walk a straight line which pleases our heavenly Father, and the only way I can do that is to no longer have any contact with you.

God has given me free will and it is my free will to decide that I no longer want to be tempted to sin.

I appreciate your advice on my newest spiritual gift. I sometimes let my excitement for the Lord get the best of me. The last thing I want to do is scare people! Praying in my spiritual language is very edifying! I have to respect where everyone is in their journey, but I'd be less than honest if I didn't tell you I have been praying for you to be filled with God's power. I only wish I could be there the day you start speaking in tongues.

Also, please do not concern yourself with my friends. They are my friends and each and every one of them has been a special blessing in my life!

You need to know with 100 percent confidence, certainty, and clarity that I am following God's will for my life and my life alone!

In addition, you should be happy to know that God is working mightily behind the scenes on our behalf! God has revealed a number of things to me over the last month. He is in complete control! God's message to me is twofold: 1) *Get out of my way so I can work* and 2) *Be quiet!* I believe this same advice holds true for you!

We need to continue to pray for divine protection while we are in prison, as Satan is working overtime in there! Keep your mouth shut and don't assume that anyone is your friend. God has sent me so many messages on this subject over the past three weeks, it's almost starting to scare me. I cannot tell you how important this is!

I continue to pray for you and your wife and also that our camp "sleepover" is not as long as we think it's going to be!

I'll leave you with this: A true friend walks in when the

rest of the world walks out, but a true friend also walks out when God walks in!

You will see the mighty hand of God as a result of this obedience!

May our Lord Jesus Christ continue to shower you with His blessings and love! Believe in miracles!

Then Milt e-mailed back a response:

Katie, thanks for the note and I am very pleased to know that you are still walking so close with the Lord. Like you, I have surrendered everything to him and it is very exciting to see how he is working in so many lives. I struggled with the court's decision for both of us but he has been gracious to give me peace over that also. We have come a long way but still remain a work in progress and the key is to continue to focus on the Lord.

I will be leaving for my new home next week and I appreciate your input on that as well. God has got both of us in a great place and there is nothing that I would do to screw that up.

God has been so good to answer so many prayers as of late and I have to remember that it is all in his time and not my time.

I pray for you every day and know that God has great plans for you.

If you are up to it, I would love to have a short phone conversation with you sometime just to pray with you. I will have my phone on and if you want to call please do so. If not, that is okay as I fully understand and would not want to compromise your position with the Lord.

～

My flight was scheduled to leave Milwaukee on December 30, so I decided to welcome in the New Year in Tampa. I received a second letter from Daniel and he continued to share the challenges of being incarcerated. It was a tough letter to read because it reinforced how difficult it was going to be away from my family, especially my children.

Daniel thanked me for sending the Christmas miracle story, telling me he could relate to Pete and his struggles. It was encouraging to read because I believe the tangible examples of how the Holy Spirit was working in my life were going to be the springboard and turning point in his. Daniel realized that forgiveness was a choice, and I believed he was very close to finally forgiving himself.

I was surprised when he told me the Christmas miracle story has touched many more hearts than just his. When I read, "Bet you never imagined your story would make it into a prison Christmas service, now did you?!!" I just paused and shook my head. *No, Daniel, I can't say I ever imagined that.* But God knew. I bet you never imagined your story would find its way into a book about a woman caught in adultery, now did you? Don't ever underestimate how God can use the things you are going through for his glory and your good.

Daniel's update came at the perfect time, because it was incredibly inspiring. His words of encouragement gave me the boost of confidence I needed. As I held onto Daniel's letter and reflected on everything he had written, I knew with certainty that my ministry calling and having to spend time in prison were all part of God's perfect plan for my life.

It did not, however, make saying good-bye to my family any easier. It was incredibly difficult to leave my mom and dad, who were in their late seventies. My ongoing prayer continued to be, *God, please let my parents live long enough to see all of the good that is going to come from this,* because with good time credits, the next time I would most likely see my family would be in August of 2014.

Although I knew my kids and grandkids would be fine, I hated to think about what I was going to miss during this time frame. Three years seemed like an eternity, but that was exactly where I had to place my focus. And just like the disciples, I was going to stand on the promises made by Jesus: "And everyone who has given up houses or brothers or sisters or father or mother or children or property, for my sake, will receive a hundred times as much in return and will inherit eternal life" (Matthew 19:29).

And again, Jesus said, "Those who love their life in this world will lose it. Those who care nothing for their life in this world will keep it for eternity. Anyone who wants to serve me must follow me, because my servants must be where I am. And the Father will honor anyone who serves me" (John 12:25–26). I was days away from following God into a federal prison.

~

There was one last bit of unfinished business I had to take care of while I was in Tampa. I made a promise, a promise I would keep. On New Year's Eve day, I called Milt. He was surprised to hear from me, but even more surprised when I told him I was fifteen minutes away and wanted to see him.

I turned into the subdivision where we had walked for years. When I pulled up, Milt rolled down his window, and, with a sheepish grin on his face, asked, "What in the world are you doing here?"

"I made a promise," I replied. "I promised I would say good-bye before you left for prison and I'm here to do that." We parked the cars and just sat and talked. I told Milt that the hardest thing I ever had to do was to not have any contact with him, but I knew with certainty that was God's will.

Milt went on to share that after I shut down our friendship, he got very mad with God, went into a room, and let out all of his anger and rage. After he gave God an earful, he shared that every one of his family's prayers were answered. "Katie, I can't begin to thank you enough for what you did," he said with a fair amount of excitement in his voice. "Everything fell into place after that."

And again with tears in my eyes, I reiterated how it broke my heart to no longer support him even though I knew it was the right thing to do. There will come a time in your life when God wants you to show him that you love him more than anyone or anything else, which is what God asked me to do during one of the most difficult times of my life.

Just prior to saying good-bye, I walked up to Milt and tenderly put my hands on each side of his face. Looking deep into his eyes, I confidently stated, "We will get our miracle!" I wished Milt the best and, once in the car, never looked back. I knew this was how it was supposed to end. I thanked God for giving me the closure I so desperately needed.

A short time later, I received a devotional from *God Calling*, by A. J. Russell, titled "I Clear the Path 'Wait on the Lord'" (Psalm 27:14). It was as though it had our names on it.

> I AM thy shield. Have no fear. You must know that "All is well." I will never let anyone do to you both, other than My Will for you.
>
> I can see the future. I can read men's hearts. I know better than you what you need. Trust Me absolutely. You are not at the mercy of Fate, or buffeted about by others. You are being led in a very definite way, and others, who do not serve your purpose, are being moved out of your Path by Me.
>
> Never fear, whatever may happen. You are both being led. Do not try to plan. I have planned. You are the builder, not the Architect.
>
> Go very quietly, very gently. All is for the very best for you.[1]

～

Some days it was hard to think that all of this was for the very best for me. This was especially true on Wednesday, January 4, 2012. It was time to surrender in more ways than one. I guess we will not know the depth of our character until we see how we react under pressure.

---

1 A. J. Russell, *God Calling* (Uhrichsville, OH: Barbour Publishing, Inc., 1989).

It was a relatively quiet ride from Tampa to Coleman, as I made the last of my phone calls to my loved ones. I assured my family and friends I was in good spirits, although I would be less than honest if I did not tell you I was a little bit nervous. We arrived twenty-five minutes prior to check-in time, and I sat in the parking lot talking with my friends, commenting that the building did not look like a prison.

As we were waiting, a van pulled up and two correctional officers escorted two young women out of the vehicle. The women were wearing white jumpsuits and restrained with chains and shackles. Okay, it was starting to look more like a prison. Within a few minutes, a federal officer opened the door, motioned to us, and asked if I was ready. "Do I have to come in now?" I asked.

"That would be nice," she said.

I took a deep breath. "Guys ... it's time. I have to go."

I opened the door, grabbed my Bible, gave Kim and Diana a hug, and walked up the sidewalk to receiving and discharge. This was it. No turning back. I waved good-bye, kissed my fingers, pointed to the sky, and looking upward I silently prayed, *God, this is in your hands. I know you never make a mistake, but please protect me.* I walked through the door and my next assignment had officially begun.

The two women who had been escorted inside in chains and shackles were seated behind a table, and I was asked to take a seat next to them. There was paperwork to be filled out, additional fingerprints to be taken, along with DNA samples, a picture identification card, the dreaded strip search, and a medical screening.

They brought us hamburgers and fries for lunch, and the three of us agreed the food was edible. We changed into prison clothes, which consisted of a short sleeved brown T-shirt, a khaki-colored pair of elastic-waist pants, and blue slip-on tennis shoes. Then we were taken to the medical center to be screened.

After my physical, it was time to meet my counselor. For the first time I was scared. This woman looked like "Mean Joe Greene," but only meaner. I was convinced she could kill me with one hand, so I politely answered her questions. She told me I was assigned to F4, which was her unit, and I would be bunking in 401.

I picked up a large plastic bag that contained my bedding, a towel, and night shirt, and was told to be at laundry at six on Thursday morning to pick up my uniform. When you are new, you stick out like a sore thumb given your clothes. A little before three o'clock in the afternoon, heads began to turn to see the new inmates heading to their unit. We all ended up in F4.

At Coleman, there are four buildings that house inmates: F1, F2, F3, and F4. As you enter each unit through the double doors, there are four phones in the entryway and a large lobby where mail is handed out. The building reminds me of a warehouse with twenty-foot ceilings, exposed duct work, red water pipes, and fluorescent lighting. Rooms are approximately eight by ten with five-foot-high cement block walls.

The room where I was assigned was next to the bathroom, and on an outside wall, which meant there was a window. There was one set of bunk beds and a smaller sleeping area, which was my bed, and three lockers. There was barely enough room to turn around, yet three inmates were assigned to each cell.

I was escorted to 401 and met my two roommates, April and Tabitha. Both were serving time for drug charges, and both knew the ropes. They helped me get settled in, which was a good thing given I am sure my expression resembled a deer-in-the-headlights look. There was so much to learn, which is why God told me that along with studying humility, I was about to embark on a course in "human science."

I was surprised to learn Tabitha had been in prison on three different occasions. The first time she was sentenced to three years, the second time she was sentenced to five years, and she was currently serving an eleven-year sentence, having been in federal prison for the last eight years. There are so many others like her—repeat offenders are the norm and many women have family members who are incarcerated as well.

As I made my bed, I wondered how I was going to sleep on a metal tray affectionately nicknamed "The Slab." Thank God I had plenty of practice sleeping on the floor. The facility did have e-mail, although we were not allowed Internet access. There was a cost associated with computer usage, but that did not matter because e-mail would become my lifeline with my family and friends, and also serve as my journal as I continued to write this book.

My first e-mail was sent on January 6, and I bet you are just dying to hear the first bit of news I was able to report relative to my incarceration: *Passed the first test on Wednesday ... I am not pregnant.* Yep, that's what I sent.

∼

Coleman is a work camp and we were required to get a job, but I could not begin working until I completed my orientation three weeks later. Within a few days, I finished reading my first book, *The Biblical Truth about God's Righteous Vengeance* by John Weaver. I loved what I found: "It is a refreshing consolation to realize that man is not supreme. His courts of arbitrary and perverted justice and perverse sentences are not the courts of last resort. There is a court greater than even the Supreme Court of the United States. It is the final court of appeal—the court of heaven!"[2]

I was quickly finding out about perverse sentences. Close to 75 percent of the women at Coleman were there on drug charges. Given mandatory minimum sentencing guidelines, I met many women who were serving ten-, twenty-, and thirty-year sentences. While agonizing over this fact, I wondered how they survived. How did you keep your "sunny side up" year after year? Three years seemed like an eternity, so how could they possibly still be smiling when they had been in prison over twenty years?

Unfortunately, only a handful of inmates serving lengthy sentences were able to smile—most were angry and bitter. Even

---

2 John Weaver, *The Biblical Truth about God's Righteous Vengeance* (King & King Publishers, 2000), 132.

though many women had worked their way down to camp status after serving longer portions of their sentences in higher-security facilities, the wear and tear on them physically, mentally, and emotionally was obvious.

Many were institutionalized. Prison was all they knew, which made for some significant challenges when they were asked to get out of their comfort zone. This may be why the majority of the compound was medicated. Let's just say my "human science" course was opening my eyes to a side of life I did not know even existed.

Given new inmates were easy to spot, I could not help but notice a woman who surrendered two days after I did. We said hello over the weekend, then I learned her name was Carol, we were close to the same age, and she was a lawyer. Carol told me that she prayed God would send her at least one person who would be her friend and who would understand her given her Christian faith. That friend was me.

We decided that maybe instead of writing a book, I should be writing a sitcom. Throw a corporate executive and attorney into prison with a diverse bunch of street thugs and drug dealers, and you could see how quickly things can get interesting. Another challenge we faced was the fact that close to 70 percent of the women there did not graduate from high school, and many did not speak English. Because the two of us had absolutely no street smarts and did not speak Spanish, we had our work cut out for us.

Carol and I hit it off, and we walked and talked every day. One of the things we decided to do was start a Friday night Bible study. Class would be held on the bleachers next to the softball diamond, and God had us studying chapters 14 and 15 in the book of John, learning more about the Holy Spirit and how he communicates the truth about God. There were ten other women who joined our group, and it was a nice way to spend our Friday evenings.

As humbling as this experience was, I had made a deliberate choice to make every day a good day. Women asked me why I smiled so much and how I could actually be having fun in prison.

It was easy because I served the Lord. He never makes a mistake, and I knew with certainty that this was part of my divine destiny.

Our goal, regardless of where we find ourselves, should be to live satisfying lives so we can be a living testament to God's glory, leadership, grace, and goodness. God wants and expects all of us to be happy regardless of our circumstances, having a deep sense of delight and satisfaction knowing that God is in control. God has a great plan for my life, and this was just the preparation phase for what was next.

> You suffered along with those who were thrown into jail, and when all you owned was taken from you, you accepted it with joy. You knew there were better things waiting for you that will last forever. (Hebrews 10:34)

Knowing God was in control made things easier. Additionally, I had adopted an attitude of gratitude. I took a day and wrote down ten things I was grateful for, and I challenge you to do the same in your own life.

> I am grateful for the ability to feel God's presence, for my family and friends, especially my children and grand-children, along with the fact God has given me a tender, compassionate heart. I am thankful for the ability to smile, which can lift the spirits of the women here at Coleman. I have been blessed with a positive attitude; I'm learning to be more patient. I find something to laugh about every day and I appreciate how God directs my steps so I can lift heavy hearts with kind, encouraging words. I thank God for surrounding me with angels and for a very tangible reminder that he loves me.

When I exited my building for dinner that night, there was the most beautiful white dove perched right outside the door. The dove flew down and walked with me, accompanying me all the way to the cafeteria as I prayed in the Spirit. I stopped, stooped down, and the dove came right up to me. I could not help but think of the following Bible verse: "The Holy Spirit [descended] on him like a dove" (Mark 1:10). What a great reminder that the Lord is with us no matter where we find ourselves.

Something else also made me very happy. Two days after the Holy Spirit descended on me like a dove, God delivered a special message during the wee hours of the morning. On three different occasions I heard, *Your charges will be dropped. Receive it! Speak it! Believe it!*

~

Most of my days started off much the same way. First thing in the morning I typically did my Bible study. On one particular morning, while I was standing by my locker reading my Bible and doing some writing, a young African American woman from down the hall stopped by and asked me what I was doing. "Reading the Bible and waiting for God to give me some direction as to what to do next," I replied.

"What do you mean?" she asked.

I said, "I try to keep a pretty low profile, but when God asks me to do something I do it." Then I shared that one time he had me write a thank-you note to someone for being so kind, and at other times he told me to pray for people.

She went on to say, "Well, if God talks to you about me, come down to 406 and let me know."

I did not know this girl's name, but she had *sexy* tattooed on her neck, so I nicknamed her "Sexy," which she didn't seem to mind. Sexy had a rather rough exterior, yet I believed with a little tender loving care, things would change. I talked to her in passing and she seemed to be warming up to me. My concern was that as I had been trying to get to know her, it was very apparent she was running with the wrong crowd.

For some reason God continued to lay her on my heart, which told me I needed to continue to reach out to her. After Sexy and I had talked, I went for a walk and asked God to reveal something to me about her that no one else knew. For crying out loud, I did not even know her real name.

As I was praying in the Spirit, God and I were having quite a discussion. *How do you have a conversation with God?* you may be wondering. Well, even though I was speaking in tongues and did not understand what I was praying, my capacity to think was not impacted. So I was thinking, *God, tell me something that no one knows about Sexy, so she knows the information came directly from you.*

My body language showed my excitement regarding this special request, as did the intonation and expressiveness of my prayer language. The thought of going down to Sexy's room and telling her that God told me something about her that nobody else knew was as exciting to me as making the game-winning shot at the buzzer.

During the afternoon a name popped into my head. After I heard the name, I heard another message. I kind of dismissed it and figured if it was God, then he would let me know again because I specifically asked for a God slap. "Don't let me miss it," I told him. "It is important I get this one right."

You may be wondering what a God slap is. A God slap is when God wakes you up from a nap or during the night, and you know with 100 percent certainty that it is God talking to you. Well, guess who was awakened with a God slap after a fifteen-minute power nap on Saturday afternoon? I received the same name and same message as I did on Friday.

It was time to go down to cell 406 and find Sexy. She was not in her room and I actually found her in the hallway near the bathroom. "Sexy, you are not going to believe it," I said with excitement in my voice. "I asked God to reveal something to me about you that no one else knows so that you would know it was God who told me." I went on to ask, "Does the name Tyrone mean anything to you? And is he home alone or all alone?"

With a look of shock and surprise on her face, she said, "Katie, that is my brother and he is in prison."

All I could say is, "Wow! God told me." Then I asked, "So Sexy, is there anything else you want me to pray about?"

"Yeah," she said. "Tell God to get me the hell out of here."

Well, at least I now knew her name. It was Shawnitralla, and her nickname was Shawn.

The following week I found myself talking to Shawn in her room, so I invited her to come to church with me. She was still shaking her head in disbelief. "Katie, I still can't believe what happened. No one here knows about Tyrone. No one."

"I know, Shawn," I said. "I specifically asked God to tell me something that no one else knew so that you would know it came directly from God. But I have to tell you, that word of knowledge even surprised me."

~

What I was finding was that the more time I spent with the Lord, the more often I would hear from him. So it was not a surprise that as I relaxed in my room, a familiar Scripture rose up in my Spirit: "Always be joyful. Never stop praying. Be thankful in all circumstances, for this is God's will for you who belong to Christ Jesus" (1 Thessalonians 5:16–18).

Given the fact that joy seemed to be the theme of the week, I wondered, *Are joy and happiness the same thing?* Joy is described as a feeling of great pleasure and happiness.

A few years ago I was asked to provide some biblical feedback on happiness. At the time I had just finished reading a book that provided some insight into this subject, called *Secrets of a Satisfying Life: Discover the Habits of Happy People* by David Ireland. Two important points to note from this book: first, happiness has very little to do with circumstances and has more to do with perspective; and second, the secret of personal satisfaction can be learned. The Bible verse that supports this was written by the apostle Paul:

> Not that I was ever in need, for I have learned how to be
> content with whatever I have. I know how to live on almost

nothing or with everything. I have learned the secret of living in every situation, whether it is with a full stomach or empty, with plenty or little. (Philippians 4:11–12)

Happy people have embraced consistent conduct and psychological responses to life that keep them satisfied. The most important thing to realize when you embark on a spiritual journey is that you are not competing against anyone else. Your personal journey is just that, *your* journey. As an individual Christian you are in a spiritual race against yourself, running toward the goal of being conformed to the image of Christ.

The book of Ecclesiastes provides additional guidance here. Solomon established three thresholds for personal happiness: happiness is a choice, happiness is the ability to find enjoyment out of life, and happiness results from following your heart. Each one of us can choose to be happy in our present circumstances, no matter what those circumstances are. As a result, happiness is not as elusive as many people believe. Happiness can be and is found in the measure of satisfaction one can find in the normal activities of life.

Some will argue that prison is not normal, but I would argue that the promises of the Bible are for everyone, inmates included. The gifts of God, including the ability to enjoy life, are freely given to all. The key is accepting and embracing them, recognizing that you are responsible for yourself.

Someone once told me when I was in prison, "Be happy that you are only here for three years. After a while, people forget about you." That was the problem. There was something desperately missing here. These women craved love and attention. This may be why even though I had only been there a short time, mail call continued to tug on my heart. Every weekday right after dinner, mail was distributed in the lobby of each unit, and every evening almost every inmate came to mail call hoping to hear her name called.

All these women wanted was some validation that someone cared. Anyone. It broke my heart to see so many women walk away dejected night after night. I saw the same women come every single night, even though their names were never called. It became quickly obvious that this was a ministry opportunity, and within a few weeks I rallied the troops. Through Really Good News Ministries and my family and friends, we began a letter-writing campaign sending cards and letters to inmates who would not otherwise receive mail.

I cannot begin to tell you what this did to lift spirits and change hearts. The look of surprise and excitement on the faces of these prisoners when they finally heard their names called was priceless. Many women would come to my room to show me their cards or letters because they were sent from people I knew. There was a noticeable change in all who received mail. They were much more positive and fun to be around, but the change I liked the most was seeing them smile simply because someone cared enough to send mail. All I needed was their name and inmate identification number, and God took care of the rest.

I was also busy distributing the 2012 Just One Word calendars and was coordinating requests for Bibles in both English and Spanish. Many of my friends sent in Pass It On cards, which contained inspirational messages and Scripture quotations. I handed these out individually to those who needed an encouraging word. It was amazing how quickly our prison ministry efforts were able to provide resources, improve morale, and influence such a positive change in the lives of so many women.

10

The day I was sentenced, the Lord reminded me that *humility is to be studied in Scripture*. But the question remains, how do we humble ourselves? One of the ways that we demonstrate humility and humble ourselves is through obedience to God. Humility is simply accepting the circumstances of life according to God's will, waiting on his perfect timing, and believing he has chosen certain things to happen for his good purposes in our lives.

But how can we humble ourselves regardless of where we are in life? Truly humble people only compare themselves to Christ, not to other people around them. They realize their sinfulness and limitations, understanding that God has equipped them with special gifts, talents, and abilities they should use to serve others. God asks us to be tenderhearted, always keeping a humble attitude. A humble person is willing to submit for the good of the team.

One of the things I have asked the Lord to do in my own heart is to put me wherever he needs me relative to a work assignment. Not only was God going to put me exactly where he needed me, but it was also the last place on earth I ever thought I would find myself—the kitchen. My new position as line server had officially begun, and my starting wage was twelve cents an hour.

Once again, as I have found out, be careful what you ask for because you just might get it. I couldn't say I ever thought I would be working in a cafeteria, let alone one in a federal prison, but I hoped to bring new meaning to "service with a smile." I would be serving lunch and dinner Tuesday through Saturday—Sunday and Monday were considered my weekend.

The schedule was absolutely perfect. It broke up the day, allowing time to sleep in, exercise, read, or just sit outside and enjoy the sunshine and warm weather. The daily duties of someone "called to serve" included setting up the line, dishing out the food, and cleaning the serving area. The neat thing about this position was that during the course of a given day, I would interact with virtually every inmate at Coleman.

The kitchen staff was comprised of servers, cooks, and dishwashers, along with one officer who supervised the meal preparation, food distribution, and cleanup. Twelve inmates were assigned to the p.m. shift, and my new team was a cast of characters. Most were drug dealers who continued to look for ways to make quick money. Apparently, you could make hundreds of dollars a month stealing food from the kitchen and selling it in the units. I was surprised to learn that an inmate could actually buy better food in the units than what was being served in the cafeteria.

Fruit, chicken, cheese, salads, raw vegetables, and sugar were the top-selling items. It was a big business, and, for a prison, it was an elaborate enterprise with middlemen and distributors. You had to be there to see how entertaining and creative theft could actually be. One day I saw a woman, who was rather large, get fifteen oranges into her bra, and, given her size, you could not even tell. Another time an inmate was caught with a five-pound bag of frozen cheese in her pants. One kitchen employee even put chocolate chip cookies in her underwear. There was a reason why I never ate anything that was brought back to the unit.

I was going to have to stay clear of the "transportation of stolen goods across the compound," as every once in a while there would be a shakedown, lockers would be searched, and two or three prisoners would be sent packing. After fewer than two weeks on the job, one of the officers came up to me in a very serious tone and said, "I need to talk to you."

Oh no, what did I do wrong? Or worse yet, what did someone accuse me of doing? The officers and administration handed out "shots" when you broke the rules, and three disciplinary shots would earn you a one-way trip to the nearest county jail.

My supervisor told me one of the inmates came to him about me. My heart was pounding, wondering if I was in trouble, until he shared her comment: "Katie is always so polite to us." Not five minutes later another prisoner approached me and said, "You are always so nice." As my friend Ruth Ann predicted, "the radical power of God had hit the Coleman cafeteria line and the place would never be the same."

The kitchen employees represented a wide variety of demographics. Black, white, Hispanic, educated, uneducated, and young and old. The youngest employee was twenty-three and the oldest, a silverware roller (no pun intended), was seventy-four.

When we stood to be counted at four in the afternoon, we really did resemble the Bad News Bears. We were a bunch of misfits who somehow ended up on the same team. I was determined to take these ladies to the next level by getting them to believe in themselves and also reminding them that God had a special plan for their lives. Let's just say I had my work cut out for me.

~

When Diana came for a visit on Super Bowl Sunday—she would be the first of many visitors—it felt so good to hug someone. And I think Diana was relieved that after a month in prison I looked the same. "I love your uniform," Diana said, laughing. Even though I knew she was being sarcastic, I did appreciate her comment.

We sat outdoors until about two o'clock, when we were forced to move inside because the outside seating area was closing. As we took our seats inside, it was extremely difficult to watch children say good-bye to their mothers. Quite frankly, it was heart wrenching to observe a crying child being pulled from their mother's arms, not wanting to leave. Little did I know, God was beginning to prepare my heart for something very special.

Two weeks later, my friend Eileen visited. You get pretty pumped up when you get a visitor, especially a first-time guest, and you look forward to walking into the room, having your eyes connect, seeing a smile on their face, and getting a big hug. But as I entered the visiting room, I spotted Eileen sitting alone at a table near the officer's station, and she was in tears. I was not prepared for this scene, and neither was Eileen. "What's wrong?" I asked.

"Katie, this is killing me," she replied. Eileen has the spiritual gift of mercy and compassion, so it was not a surprise that this experience would break her heart. She was grieving for the children who were longing to see their mothers.

There was one particular boy who she could not take her eyes off of. He was twelve years old and desperately needed his mother's touch and attention. But as Eileen would find out, there are rules that prevent children from sitting on their mothers' laps. There are also times when some mothers do not recognize the needs of their children. This particular day there was a combination of factors preventing this boy from getting the love and attention he so desperately needed.

As Eileen shifted her gaze to observe other family dynamics, her tears continued. This was the most difficult part of visiting, seeing the impact incarceration has on children. I was truly thankful my kids were older.

One of the real struggles families face relative to visits is the cost and distance associated with travel. Many inmates are not geographically close to home, which means even if their families are willing to travel, it is cost prohibitive. As a result, there are hundreds of inmates who never get visits at all.

Eileen sent a card telling me she had a complete meltdown before driving out of the parking lot at Coleman. She could not stop thinking of the faces of the children visiting their moms. She gave God thanks for the peaceful hours he allowed her to sit still, to visit with me, and to see the things that break his heart. It was a memory she will never forget, and she believed God wanted it that way. Eileen said it best when she said, "He's good at breaking hearts for his glory."

~

As I was walking one particular morning, God reminded me that I needed to finish writing about my walking path. To most people it would appear to be an oval of crushed sea shells and small stones that is one-third of a mile long. But to hundreds of inmates, it is the Path of Hope. Every day inmates head to the track to exercise, pray, reflect on life, and find hope to endure their remaining time in prison.

As we would walk or run, we hoped that our families were being well taken care of, we hoped we might be released early, we hoped the truth of our respective cases would someday be known, we hoped our prayers would be answered, and we hoped we could find the strength to carry on. While exercising, I heard many Christian songs sung, and saw many hugs given, many tears cried, and many lives changed, all because of hope. Zechariah said:

> "Come back to the place of safety, all you prisoners who still have hope! I promise this very day that I will repay two blessings for each of your troubles." (Zechariah 9:12)

What is hope? Hope is the anchor of the soul. It is synonymous with optimism and courage. In fact, the Bible defines hope as confident expectation. Hope is the firm assurance regarding things that are unclear or unknown, and without hope life loses its meaning. Christian hope is rooted in faith in Jesus Christ, which means that it is your relationship with God that provides hope, as the three most important virtues found in our Christian walk are faith, hope, and love.

Hope changes the way we see ourselves, what we value, and what we do with our lives. It produces joy and peace in believers through the power of the Holy Spirit, and it provides protection, strength, courage, and confidence each and every day. Hope in God's Word, hope in God's promises, and hope in God's grace give us the comfort and assurance we need on this journey.

~

Our small group on Friday consisted of twelve women from all walks of life and very different backgrounds. One of the ladies in our study was Carol's roommate Anabel.

One particular day was really tough. It started out like most Sundays. I watched Charles Stanley and enjoyed the opening song, which reminded viewers that when we suffer, we must give God praise. After watching the program, I grabbed a cup of coffee and headed to the track for some exercise. But my walk was cut short when I ran into Carol, who had a terrible look on her face. "Go get the others," she said with a sense of urgency. "We need to pray. Anabel's son was murdered this morning."

Without saying another word, I ran back to the unit and found most of the members of our small group. As Anabel sat with the chaplain, eight of us gathered on the racquetball court hand in hand and prayed. Some prayers were in English, some in Spanish, and others in our respective prayer languages. We interceded on behalf of the family, and after approximately twenty minutes a quiet peace enveloped us. At that point a few of the ladies went to wait for Anabel.

I felt compelled to continue to pray, however. Walking over to the bleachers near the softball diamond, I wondered how we were going to help Anabel get through this. Before I even sat down, I was overcome by a sense of God's presence. As the tears continued, I worshiped and praised the Lord, thanking him that it is through suffering that we grow and mature. It is through suffering that we are conformed to Christ's image, but it is through praise and thanksgiving that we learn to trust God.

As I sat there and wept, Anabel, Carol, and the others walked slowly from the chapel with their arms around each other. As I watched, I saw unity, togetherness, and an outpouring of love that only God could orchestrate. There were many lives that were immediately touched as evidenced by the love and compassion shown to Anabel that day, and countless hearts would be impacted throughout the day because of this tragedy. As I watched Anabel put one foot in front of the other, I realized she was being led back to her unit on the Path of Hope.

Waiting for our two o'clock service to begin, I knew that day's worship would be far different from what I had experienced up to that point. Most Sundays the chapel was filled with gospel music, the sanctuary was overflowing with heavenly voices and dance, and there were smiles and festive praise. That day the mood was incredibly somber as I sat behind Anabel and Carol.

Dabbing my eyes, I asked God why. *Why does it have to be this way? I know you work all things together for good, but isn't there enough hurt here? How can a mother possibly endure losing her twenty-three-year-old son while she is in prison?* I did not receive an answer that day. It was my job to trust God and persevere in prayer.

There are things going on behind the scenes that we know nothing about. We wonder why God allows something, and we question or doubt God's goodness without seeing the full picture. We must trust God under all circumstances. Jesus asks us to trust God not only when we do not understand but *because* we do not understand. God does not have to answer to anyone for what he does or doesn't do. We may never know the specific reason for suffering, but we must trust God, whose ways are perfect.

I prayed that God would give Anabel and her family strength to carry on. I prayed for justice to be served. I prayed for her family to be able to forgive. I prayed for healing and peace. I prayed for Anabel to not give up, and I prayed for Carol to find the right words and strength to comfort Anabel that night and in the days ahead. *Lord, please surround us with your love and give us the strength to bear this burden. This is a heavy load to carry.*

Obviously, some days it was very difficult to be there, but as

God told my friend Paula, *The final chapter needs to be written.*
Interestingly enough, that message was confirmed on Mother's Day
weekend when I was talking to another inmate who lived next door.
As we were waiting for the ten o'clock count, she shared a prompting from the Holy Spirit about my journey: *You are on a mission.
You will be here until you finish the book completely. Then you will
be ready to face what is next. Be at peace.*

From a biblical standpoint, the word *mission* is the divine activity
of sending intermediaries to speak or do God's will so that his purposes are fulfilled. It means to be sent like the apostles in the time of
Jesus. What is an apostle? Apostles are divinely commissioned mes-
sengers of the good news. I guess that explains why God led me to
the following Scripture where King David was speaking to Solomon:

> "Worship and serve [God] with your whole heart and a
> willing mind. For the LORD sees every heart and knows
> every plan and thought. If you seek him, you will find him.
> But if you forsake him, he will reject you forever. So take
> this seriously. The LORD has chosen you. ... Be strong, and
> do the work." (1 Chronicles 28:9–10)

~

When God tells me to take something seriously, I do. Things
began to get interesting as he was giving me some very specific
instructions: *Pray for your release.*

Pray for my release, I thought. *That doesn't make sense.* But if
I knew anything at this point, I knew God's thoughts are not my
thoughts and his ways are far beyond anything I can imagine.
God is in the miracle business, and if he wanted me to pray for my
release, then that was exactly what I was going to do.

The thought of getting out of there was exciting, and come to
think of it, the inmates had heard rumors that Coleman was going
to be turned into a men's facility and that prison camps were no
longer going to be funded given the high cost of incarcerating

nonviolent offenders. That latest information had given me hope that an early release was in the works. I was eager to share this latest communication with my Bible study group, as I was sensing in my spirit they too would be involved in praying for my release.

It did not take God long to impress upon my heart what was next. Paula was to invite those who were receiving my e-mails to her house for an evening of prayer on Tuesday, May 15. Prayer was to begin at seven that evening, and everyone was to pray for me and my release. Those who attended would be anointed with oil, the lights should be dimmed, and candles lit. The CD they played to usher in the Holy Spirit would provide background music, and everyone except Mary would be on their knees. The group was to keep praying until peace came over them. I began fasting Monday evening, and I would also be praying on my knees in my room at the exact same time.

A little before seven o'clock on Tuesday, May 15, I hit my knees and experienced an incredible night of prayer. So what was going on in Tampa at the exact same time? The group began with an opening prayer, asking the Holy Spirit to come into Paula's home and fill them to overflowing. These ladies worshiped and prayed on their knees, all except Mary. Some women wept while others were on their faces before God. Some prayed in their prayer languages, and Paula believed all were touched by the hand of God.

Peace eventually fell over the room. They continued in prayer, and it wasn't until the music ended that they began to speak. My friends shared what God had spoken to their hearts and what each of them was feeling. Paula commented, "Many witnessed about your joy in the midst of your situation and how many lives are being touched by your faith in your Father God. It was a beautiful evening of peace as we prayed for you, my dear sister. Thank you for your obedience to God. We will now wait to see the manifest workings of God brought about by this prayer agreement."

~

The end of May was fast approaching, which meant birthday number fifty-five was right around the corner. Not too many of the inmates knew that May 24 was my birthday, although my coworkers found out and surprised me with a special dinner in my honor.

Everyone sang "Happy Birthday," and CeCe, who called herself my prison daughter, came around the counter and gave me a big hug. To know CeCe was to love her. She was actually involved in the first fight I witnessed at Coleman when she let another inmate have it with a broom handle upside the head. CeCe loved to speak her mind, and she did so quite often, which was one of the reasons I love her. Of course, the real reason I loved her was because she was my bodyguard. Most everyone was afraid of her, especially when she forgot to take her medication.

One day we were serving side by side and she decided to hand out dessert. This particular day the choice was an orange or a piece of cake. As we were waiting for lunch to begin, she looked at me and asked, "Scheller, did you ever notice that all the fat women take cake?"

I laughed and responded, "I noticed that." Well, the first overweight inmate who came to pick up her dessert heard, "No cake for you today—you're fat enough!" and CeCe proceeded to put the orange on her tray. I thought I was going to die. I mean really, who did that other than our beloved CeCe? She had been involved in some interesting altercations while imprisoned and, as a result, had firsthand knowledge on how to survive time in a county jail.

CeCe, who was African American, had a very dark complexion. She insisted on calling me her prison mother because I had taken her under my wing. We made many inmates and officers laugh when we put our arms around each other and asked, "Do you see the family resemblance?" Let's just say that question always caught people off guard, and most of the time people just stood there shaking their heads laughing.

Paula and Diana came for a visit Memorial Day weekend, and the first thing Diana asked was whether or not 5:19 meant anything to me. She had been awakened by an alarm at that exact time, but the only problem was that there was not an alarm in her room. We chalked it up to the Lord because she felt strongly these numbers were for me.

When I told her that 5:19 was the time I was born, she couldn't believe it. In my spirit I was sensing I needed to read every chapter 5 verse 19 in the Bible, convinced there was a message of some sort for me personally. Well, guess what I found in the book of Galatians? "When you follow the desires of your sinful nature, the results are very clear: sexual immorality, impurity, lustful pleasures …" (Galatians 5:19).

This list begins with sexual immorality. Unfortunately, moral impurity removes holiness and makes fellowship with God impossible. In order to follow the Holy Spirit's guidance, we must deal with these sinful desires.

Guess where the study notes took me? Galatians 5:19 references Galatians 5:24, and as you already know, May 24 is my birthday. Galatians 5:24 says, "Those who belong to Christ Jesus have nailed the passions and desires of their sinful nature to his cross and crucified them there." The date and time of my birth coincide with my story. Unbelievable!

~

A few days later, I stood on the top of the bleachers, spread out my arms in prayer, and cried out at the top of my lungs, "Lord, come get me."

That very night God spoke these words to me: *Come away, my beloved.* As I began to process what God had said to me, all of a sudden it hit me when I realized what had just happened. God had just proposed!

I told God, "Yes, I'm all in."

I bet you didn't know "come away, my beloved" is in the Bible, did you? All you have to do is go to the Song of Songs, which is a book in the Old Testament that contains romantic poetry. There, the writer says, "Rise up, my darling! Come away with me, my fair one!" (Song of Solomon 2:10). God desires our hearts to burn for his Son alone, which may be why he also told me to *light a fire for Christ.*

In the Song of Solomon, it's the Bridegroom-King who is initiating intimacy. He's the one who says that we are to come away with him. This verse starts with the bride recognizing her lover's voice. In 2:13 he says it again: "Rise up, my darling! Come away with me, my fair one!" He repeats himself because of his desire to be with the one he loves. He goes on to tell his bride who she is in him and affirms her beauty, thus celebrating their love.

The Bridegroom in his kindness invites her to come away with him so he can lavish her with love, show her who he is, and speak his desires into her heart, which is exactly what God had been doing since the day I arrived at Coleman.

Right before I fell back to sleep, I asked God to reveal when I would be leaving. He simply told me to look up the word *come.* So, like a good student, I went to the subject index and there was only one verse listed, Revelation 22:17: "The Spirit and the bride say, 'Come.' Let anyone who hears this say, 'Come.' Let anyone who is thirsty come. Let anyone who desires drink freely from the water of life." And that verse had a reference to Revelation 22:20: "He who is the faithful witness to all these things says, 'Yes, I am coming soon!'"

And with that, I began to wonder. *Could I possibly figure out what day I would be released?* Given June 1 was the day God proposed to me, I began reading all of the 6:1 Bible verses I could find. First Samuel 6:1 was one of the first ones I read: "The Ark of the Lord remained in Philistine territory seven months in all." *Hmm,* I thought. *What other numbers in the Bible are significant?*

Forty is mentioned hundreds of times, and it is a number that has great significance. It rained forty days and nights when God flooded the earth (Genesis 7:12), Moses was on the mountain with God forty days and forty nights, not once but twice (Exodus 24:18; 34:28–29; Deuteronomy 10:10), the Israelites wandered in the wilderness for forty years (Exodus 16:35; Numbers 14:33–34), Jesus fasted in the wilderness for forty days (Matthew 3:17; 4:1–2), and Jesus was seen on the earth for forty days after his crucifixion (Acts 1:3).

A "forty something" time period is always a period of testing or trial, and it ends with a period of restoration, revival, or renewal. So what day is forty days from June 1? That would be July 11, and, interestingly enough, that was seven months and seven days from the day I walked into Coleman. Completion and perfection, perhaps? Only God knows, and it would be the perfect day.

I could not, however, get July 11 out of my mind, so I asked the Lord if this was the day I would be released. He sent me to every 7:11 Bible verse I could find. Well, what is the probability of finding confirmation about July 11 in a 7:11 Bible verse? "Ask the LORD your God for a sign of confirmation. ... Make it as difficult as you want—as high as heaven or as deep as the place of the dead" (Isaiah 7:11).

"Okay, Lord, I need one more confirmation," I said. "I need to feel your presence."

He then asked, *What day were you sentenced?* That would be November 23. Numbers 11:23 says, "Then the LORD said to Moses, 'Has my arm lost its power? Now you will see whether or not my word comes true!'" And Jesus said in Mark 11:23, "I tell you the truth, you can say this to the mountain, 'May you be lifted up and thrown into the sea,' and it will happen. But you must really believe it will happen and have no doubt in your heart."

As I shared this story with another inmate, she told me the Holy Spirit gave her some advice about me: *Stay close to her,* the Lord told her. *She is blessed and faithful.* She went on to say, "Katie, he sees your heart. Everything you ask for will come to you."

Father, I am asking to be released on July eleventh, I prayed. Within a few days, I received an e-mail from Paula telling me the

Lord revealed something to her: *Call that which is not as though it were.* God told her that he had much to teach each of us through my experiences concerning him. He wanted the group to call out on my behalf and seek his face, giving Paula Romans 4:16–25. There, Paul wrote:

> So the promise is received by faith. It is given as a free gift. And we are all certain to receive it, whether or not we live according to the law of Moses, if we have faith like Abraham's. For Abraham is the father of all who believe. That is what the Scriptures mean when God told him, "I have made you the father of many nations." This happened because Abraham believed in the God who brings the dead back to life and who creates new things out of nothing.
>
> Even when there was no reason for hope, Abraham kept hoping—believing that he would become the father of many nations. For God had said to him, "That's how many descendants you will have!" And Abraham's faith did not weaken, even though, at about 100 years of age, he figured his body was as good as dead—and so was Sarah's womb.
>
> Abraham never wavered in believing God's promise. In fact, his faith grew stronger, and in this he brought glory to God. He was fully convinced that God is able to do whatever he promises. And because of Abraham's faith, God counted him as righteous. And when God counted him as righteous, it wasn't just for Abraham's benefit. It was recorded for our benefit, too, assuring us that God will also count us as righteous if we believe in him, the one who raised Jesus our Lord from the dead. He was handed over to die because of our sins, and he was raised to life to make us right with God.

Romans 4:17 in the King James Version says, "Calleth those things which be not as though they were." We are to call what is not as though it already was. In other words, God wanted us to begin to speak of my July release as though it had already happened.

While showering one afternoon, God told me, *The answer you are looking for is in two seventeen.* So I read all the 2:17 verses in the Bible, and they were reminiscent of my past life with lots of warnings relative to sexual immorality, pride, and idolatry, and, unfortunately, I still couldn't figure out what God was trying to tell me.

On July 10 I received a vision, and it was as though I was standing in the driveway of my townhome in Tampa looking at the house number 4916. So I grabbed my Bible and camped out in Isaiah 49, which is entitled "The Lord's Servant Commissioned." Verse 16 says, "See, I have written your name on the palms of my hands." I was not sure what God was up to, but I knew it was good.

11

Wednesday, July 11, arrived and the thought of being released that day was exciting. I had stepped out in faith and given away everything I owned, being obedient to every one of God's promptings and specific instructions in my life. As the day progressed, so did the excitement. Many women came up to me to offer encouraging words, confident today was the day I would be set free, while others looked at me as though I was nuts, convinced I had lost my mind.

While serving lunch, the unexpected happened. Two officers with a look of panic on their faces ran to the doors and we were in lockdown. With close to three hundred women in the cafeteria, it was chaotic. People ran to the windows, trying to figure out what was going on. Did someone escape? Was there a medical emergency? All of the sudden, an incredible storm appeared out of nowhere, and it felt as though all hell was breaking loose. Whatever was happening in the spiritual realm indicated that there was a fierce battle going on.

One woman came up to me and said, "Katie, something is happening. I think you are going home." Another gave me a thumbs up. I went into the dish room and told Carol, "Don't be surprised if we see the cross in the middle of the infield and God comes to get me in a chariot." And then I thought, *Oh my God, what if this place gets leveled and God really does take me home?*

After close to an hour, the ferocious winds began to subside, the dark storm clouds receded, the rain stopped, and the all clear was given. I came back to the unit, took a shower, and waited expectantly for my name to be called. The time rolled around to three o'clock in the afternoon and there was no call, so it was time to head back to work.

At 4:25 p.m. I went to use the restroom and the Holy Spirit rose up inside of me and I began to pray. I told a coworker, "God is up to something, and he is very serious." Standing at the window near the back of the cafeteria, another fierce storm began to move in. I closed my eyes and began to pray in tongues. My hands were open, my arms extended, and my head was lifted toward heaven.

After approximately ten minutes, I sensed someone was next to me. As I opened my eyes and looked to my right, Dale, a woman who worked in the dish room, was standing a few tables away. Interestingly, God woke her up during the night and told her to pray for me.

After glancing at Dale, I closed my eyes and continued to pray. I asked Dale to write what happened next:

> As you well know, the Lord has been putting you in my heart to pray for you. But that day in the kitchen when you were by the window watching the storm come in (physical and spiritual) and praying, I was walking around behind you praying myself. Well the Lord kept pressing upon me to lay my hands on your shoulders.
>
> After about four or five times of this, I finally gave in and did what he was encouraging me to do. As soon as I touched you on the shoulders I knew it was God because it was like a surge or electrical shock going from my arms and hands into you. It was like no one was around but me and you. Time stood still for a few seconds … minutes.

Dale said when she touched me, she spoke in her prayer language, which rarely occurs. At that particular moment, I did not sense Dale was behind me, and, as a result, when she touched me, my knees buckled as I felt an incredible anointing, feeling the same power surge she did, and began to weep. Through tears, I prayed for another five minutes before being called to serve.

Called to serve? What Scripture did God give me the day before? Isaiah 49:16: "See, I have written your name on the palms of my hands." Dale opened her hands and placed the palms of her hands on my shoulders. That was the moment I was commissioned as a faithful witness to God's purposes.

As I was praying at the window, one of the most intense prayers I have ever prayed, the word *obedience* was spoken while I was in my prayer language. Biblical obedience is submitting to God's authority and trusting him in all things. I had passed the test! I had given God my entire heart throughout the last forty days, obeying every command he had given to me, which may be why he told me at seven that morning, *Now you will see whether or not my word comes true.*

God was speaking to Paula at the exact same time about my release. He told her not once but twice: *Let those that doubt, doubt no more.*

∿

The next day while having breakfast, I mentioned to my friends that God had me all stirred up about 2:17 again. Before I could tell them what I was going to do, go see who lived in 217, one woman said, "You need to go to F2." About an hour later, I came outside and shared this story with a girl who lived in that particular unit. She went inside to see who lived there, and I asked her to please tell these women that I would like to talk to them.

After lunch, I entered cell 217, not knowing what to expect. I started off the conversation by introducing myself to Crystal and Jackie, simply stating, "I have no idea why I'm here, but the Lord does. Please just start talking to me and tell me a little about yourself and your life, and I'll see if I can figure out what God is trying to tell me."

As we talked, it was apparent that Jackie and I had a lot in common. Neither of us felt loved. Jackie had been given up for adoption, and, sadly, she still struggled with feelings of rejection. While I fed my loneliness with material possessions, work accomplishments, and inappropriate sexual relationships, Jackie filled her void with food. It was an ongoing battle.

While Jackie was sharing her life story with us, she spoke about being separated from her husband and going back to care for him when he was sick. "I took my marriage vows seriously," she said. "And even though we were separated, I went back and took care of him until he died. That was twelve years ago."

As she spoke, I began to get excited. I knew *exactly* what 2:17 Bible verse God meant. The answer I was looking for was just found in cell 217. Proverbs 2:17: "She has abandoned her husband and ignores the covenant she made before God."

~

An immoral or promiscuous woman is seductive, like a prostitute, and two of the most difficult sins to resist are pride and sexual immorality. Pride says, "I deserve it," while sexual desire says, "I need it." When you combine these two, their appeal is deadly.

Pride appeals to an empty head and sexual enticement appeals to an empty heart. That is why we must rely on God's strength to overcome these sins, because only God can fill our heads with wisdom and our hearts with love.[1] God's relationship with each of us is characterized by our faithfulness, and he takes the marriage covenant seriously. That may be why from June 1 to July 11 God wanted to see if I would honor my commitment with him and obey each and every one of his commands.

Let's go back to June 1, the day God proposed. *Come away, my beloved.* How faithful and trustworthy would I be during this forty-day courtship and testing period? I was obedient to every prompting. When I had an opportunity to share my testimony, that's what I did. When others needed prayers, I prayed for them. When

---

1 Adapted from the Application Study Notes found in the NLT Life Application Study Bible by Tyndale House Publishers.

God insisted I write about certain things that made those receiving my e-mail updates think I had lost my mind, I wrote them anyway, not fearing what others thought about me. When another inmate needed a roommate, I moved in. When God insisted I give everything away, I followed his directions to a tee. As a matter of fact, one of the inmates commented, "You remind me of Abraham. I think if God would have told you to shave your head, you would have."

I had done everything God asked me to do—everything. I obediently followed every one of his instructions, doing exactly what he asked of me because I loved him, I trusted him, and I was faithful to what he had called me to be.

It seems like an appropriate time to share the story of the woman who was caught in adultery.

Jesus returned to the Mount of Olives, but early the next morning he was back again at the Temple. A crowd soon gathered, and he sat down and taught them. As he was speaking, the teachers of religious law and the Pharisees brought a woman who had been caught in the act of adultery. They put her in front of the crowd.

"Teacher," they said to Jesus, "this woman was caught in the act of adultery. The law of Moses says to stone her. What do you say?"

They were trying to trap him into saying something they could use against him, but Jesus stooped down and wrote in the dust with his finger. They kept demanding an answer, so he stood up again and said, "All right, but let the one who has never sinned throw the first stone!" Then he stooped down again and wrote in the dust.

When the accusers heard this, they slipped away one by one, beginning with the oldest, until only Jesus was left in the middle of the crowd with the woman. Then Jesus stood up again and said to the woman, "Where are your accusers? Didn't even one of them condemn you?"

"No, Lord," she said.

And Jesus said, "Neither do I. Go and sin no more." (John 8:1–11)

God is willing to give us a second chance, but a new life in Christ means we must have a change of heart. We cannot keep chasing after the things of this world and feed our fleshy desires. God's Word is very clear about this: we must be obedient. John wrote something very similar, saying:

> Do not love this world nor the things it offers you, for when you love the world, you do not have the love of the Father in you. For the world offers only a craving for physical pleasure, a craving for everything we see, and pride in our achievements and possessions. These are not from the Father, but are from this world. And this world is fading away, along with everything that people crave. But anyone who does what pleases God will live forever. (1 John 2:15–17)

There is one verse in the book of Ecclesiastes that has helped me see things in a new light too: "Yet God has made everything beautiful for its own time. He has planted eternity in the human heart, but even so, people cannot see the whole scope of God's work from beginning to end" (Ecclesiastes 3:11).

By planting eternity in the human heart, God had ensured that we will never be completely satisfied here on earth. God has placed this restlessness within us. That "more" we are continually looking for can only be found in an intimate relationship with God. What did he tell me? *The security you crave can only be found in the Lord.*

~

A written order of court was received in August requesting my appearance in the United States District Court for the Eastern District of Wisconsin to testify at the Buske trial. I was scheduled to leave on Tuesday, August 14, 2012, and I arrived at the message center at five thirty in the morning to see a rather imposing male officer who looked like he had walked out of Gold's Gym, carrying three sets of handcuffs and shackles. A female officer was with him—her jacket told me she was a member of the Crisis Support Team.

Great. They told the three of us who were leaving to wait outside. One of the two girls who was being transported with me was throwing up. At six fifteen we were brought inside and led down the hallway to receiving and discharge. It was time to be strip searched and change into our traveling clothes, which consisted of a brown T-shirt, khaki-colored elastic-waist pants, and blue slip-on tennis shoes. I was the lucky one who got to go first. I used the restroom as the other two inmates went through the same process.

For the first time I felt like a prisoner. I could laugh off many of the other things that had happened to me since I had been there, but this was no laughing matter. The chains were wrapped around my waist and pulled tight, almost too tight. My left hand went into the handcuff first while the right cuff was put through the chain around my waist and then secured on my right hand. I was only able to move my hands a few inches in any direction. It was now time for the ankle cuffs, one foot at a time. They were similar to the handcuffs but had a slightly longer chain between them. Lift one leg at a time and presto, you were now handcuffed, chained, and shackled.

At seven fifteen we were led to the van. Given the restraints, I had difficulty walking and needed help getting inside the vehicle. I chose to take the back seat because the two girls riding with me were carrying barf bags. We were taken over to another facility to be processed, which meant I got to do the shuffle one more time. I was able to get back into the van on my own, and thought, *It's going to be a long day.*

We drove back to the camp and sat in the parking lot, waiting for two buses to show up that were full of male prisoners who were being transferred. We finally departed Coleman a little after ten in the morning, heading toward the Tampa International Airport. I was surprised when we took one of the first exits off of I-75 and ended up in a McDonald's parking lot. Guess the officers need to eat too. At this point, I decided to look into my lunch bag.

How in the world did they think I could make a peanut butter and jelly sandwich in handcuffs? I'm not kidding. I opened the bag of chips and cookies and pretty much gave up on having a sandwich. Unfortunately, we did not get anything to drink.

As the vehicles headed south, I was happy to see my old stomping grounds. We drove onto airport property a little after eleven, and we were allowed to use the restroom. I was so dehydrated I could not urinate, so I found a drinking fountain and drank as much as I could.

It should not be a surprise that I was feeling the stress of the day. I had a headache because I was tired and rap music had been blaring in the van all morning long. At twelve thirty a lieutenant came over to our vehicle, called my last name, and said, "Receiving and discharge just called. The written order of the court has been canceled. You're coming back with us."

You have got to be kidding me. What in the world is God up to? The plane arrived a little after three, and it took two hours for the transfer process. Inmates had to be moved from the plane to the bus and the bus to the plane. Armed guards sealed off the perimeter.

I saw the Devil over and over again. Scary, scary-looking people. I was actually somewhat thankful to be locked inside the van. I felt safe until both officers had to be outside with the prisoners and they turned off the engine. Are you kidding me? There was one window cracked about four inches, I was chained and shackled, it was in the mid-nineties and sunny outside, and I hadn't had anything to drink for hours.

Not only was I hot, but I was also beginning to get a little claustrophobic. I know how quickly it could get to 160 degrees inside a vehicle, so I knocked on the window and asked the officer if he could turn on the air. The answer was no. After another ten to fifteen minutes, when I had sweat pouring off of me, the two offi-cers returned to the vehicle but the engine would not turn over—the battery was dead. When they finally opened the side doors of the van so I could get some air, I welcomed the ninety-five-degree breeze, relieved I did not suffer the same fate as the battery.

We were back on the road at shortly after five thirty, and I just settled in answering questions posed to me by the new inmates. The shackles finally came off twelve hours after they had been put on. One more strip search and I'd be free. I grabbed the few per-sonal items I left behind, put on my shorts and flip-flops, grabbed my bedding, and walked back into prison as a princess.

All the remaining puzzle pieces came together. As I was walk-ing the track later that week, I received the release I had been waiting for. God spoke three words to me: *chains of addiction*. I simply smiled as I remembered the book that the Holy Spirit put in my hands just two days earlier, *Codependent No More*.

How do you know when you have finally broken the chains of addiction? Joyce Meyer may have said it best in her book *Managing Your Emotions*:

Freedom from codependency is based upon the develop-ment of a sense of value apart from what a person does. If you are free from codependency you are not dependent on people, places or positions. You don't have to be in a relationship with any certain person or group of people, or to be in a certain place or occupy a certain position to feel safe, confident and secure.

If you are free from codependency, you don't feel you have to be in control of everything and everybody. You can allow others to make their own choices and not feel threat-ened or responsible for them. You don't feel you have to solve every problem or satisfy every person.[2]

2 Joyce Meyer, *Managing Your Emotions: Instead of Your Emotions Managing You* (Tulsa, OK: Harrison House, Inc., 1997), 168.

Everything I had experienced on Tuesday was in my past. The chains not only represented my sexual codependency but all of the sins that would have prevented me from inheriting the kingdom of heaven. As you know, I nailed my sinful desires of pride, sexual immorality, impurity, and lustful pleasures to the cross, and they have been crucified with Christ. It is no longer I who live but Christ who lives in me.

At the exact time God was speaking to me, guess what song came on the radio? "Amazing Grace (My Chains Are Gone)" by Chris Tomlin. My chains truly were gone and I'd been set free. My Savior had ransomed me!

~

In early October I witnessed one of the most intense thunder and lightning storms of my life. We had four lightning strikes at the camp alone. And well, let's just say God does his best work after the storm. Here is what happened, and once again it involved Dale, the woman who worked in the dish room.

Dale was ironing her clothes when the Holy Spirit told her to go find me. She went outside to see if I was on the track, and, because she did not see me there, she went back to pressing her uniform. God once again told her to go find me, so she finished up and said, "God, if this is of you, then when I walk back outside I want Katie to be there." Guess what? I was there.

She heard me talking before she saw me, and she called my name as I was heading around the corner. It was obvious she wanted to see me, so I turned around and met her on the sidewalk between our units. She told me that while she was walking toward me, God told her to bless me, anointing me in the name of the Father, Son, and Holy Spirit. She felt like she was to hold my hands and pray.

Dale prayed a quick prayer, we talked for a few more minutes, and when Dale got back to her room she received additional marching orders. God told her to go back and pray with me again, but this time she was to put a cross on my forehead (in the name of the Father), a cross on my right palm (in the name of the Son), and a cross on my left palm (in the name of the Holy Spirit). Dale found me in my room and did as she was instructed. She went on to tell me, "This is what God told me to say: *Satan, you cannot have her, she belongs to me.* Katie, you are his, and I plead the shed blood of Jesus over you."

As excited as I was, I did not know what to say. I hugged Dale, thanked her, and began to praise the Lord. As we hugged, she spoke in tongues and was so overcome with the power of the Holy Spirit that she could barely stand. It was all I could do to hold her up as we embraced. The joy we both felt was incredible.

Once I let her go, it was as if my feet were not touching the ground. I jumped up and down, spun around, and said, "Did you hear that? God said Satan can't have me—I am his!" Dale was crying and we were both filled with incredible joy. I hugged her again, knowing we had just witnessed a miracle. Dale went on to say, "You will be doing awesome work with children, and there is going to be one special child that God is sending your way."

~

A few weeks later I had a dream involving Dale. In the dream Dale brought me a piece of paper that contained an organizational chart, and of the twenty-five names on the chart, the first person listed was me. She went on to tell me that I was smart, she wanted me to take care of these people, and I was to buy each one of them a computer. Then I woke up and decided to take a shower, and the Spirit began speaking to my heart.

God revealed that what I saw in the dream was the organizational structure for The Vivian Foundation, and he told me that I had proven myself trustworthy. I got dressed and headed over to F3 to tell Dale about my dream, and Dale spoke first, saying, "God sent you over here, didn't he?"

"Yes," I said, and she just smiled.

"We need to talk," she said. Then Dale went on to tell me that she told God that she would wait for me to come to her, to deliver his last message, because she was leaving the following day. The Spirit was also speaking to Dale during the night, and keep in mind I had never shared with her how long I had been on this journey.

Dale went on to tell me that God revealed that I am his pearl, and he had been refining me and polishing me for the last eight years. It had taken God all of this time to conform me to his image. Would it surprise you to know that October 18 was the eight-year anniversary of the day this journey had begun?

I wept as I told Dale there were at least a dozen times while walking the track that I had kicked the gravel and said, "Someday I am going to find a pearl here." Little did I know the impact and significance of my words.

The second thing God told her was that there was something deep inside my heart that I had to give him, something that no one else knew about. I had buried the pain deep inside of me and it had been locked for a long time. She said it wasn't for her to know what it was, but I needed to give it to God so I could finally have the peace I needed. God promised he would take care of it for me. I stood silent for a few minutes, completely lost in my thoughts—they drifted to a few places deep inside my heart. When I got to the heartache and pain that was buried, I felt a gentle nudge in a certain direction because God actually revealed something that happened to me when I was a very young child.

The third message was exciting. Do you remember that Dale told me God was going to send me one special child? Well, he revealed, *It will be a girl; she's going to be a 'spitfire,' and have a lot of Katie in her. It's going to take everything you have to help her recover from her pain, and you are going to be successful in helping this child on her journey.*

Dale said it was time for one last anointing, and this time it was to be done with prayer oil: in the name of the Father on my forehead, the name of the Son on my right palm, and in the name of the Holy Spirit on my left palm. God's "pearl" had been polished and was ready to shine.

Matthew 13:45–46 is where you will find the parable of the pearl: "Again, the Kingdom of Heaven is like a merchant on the lookout for choice pearls. When he discovered a pearl of great value, he sold everything he owned and bought it!"

Another mystery of the kingdom is that its value exceeds all other treasures, and, as a result, everything should be forfeited to acquire it. In this parable, the kingdom of heaven is not the precious pearl but the merchant. The kingdom pays the ultimate price to possess the pearl—the price God was willing to pay to redeem us—the death of his only Son.

~

Two weeks later God told me, *There is still work to do.* That was very obvious as I walked and prayed with a woman who had been "down" for over twelve years. We had a great day of fellowship, and it became apparent that the work the Lord was referring to was my prison ministry.

But it was what took place the previous night that had me in awe of how God works. Do you remember Shawn from the Shawn and Tyrone word of knowledge story? Well, guess who walked in the door that night after being gone for six months? Yep, Shawn. We had some time to talk, and I learned she and Tyrone had gone out to testify in their case. Tyrone had originally received a ten-year sentence, and, after serving fewer than four years, he was released to a halfway house. Shawn was currently awaiting her downward departure.

As I was sharing some of what had happened while she was gone, I was feeling God's presence. Throughout our discussion, it became apparent that Shawn came back to tell me that there would be a plea deal in the Buske case and I would receive a downward departure without having to testify. I was almost certain I was hearing the Holy Spirit correctly on this one—time would tell.

The strangest part of what happened is that Shawn was called to the message center at four o'clock in the afternoon and did not return. I'm not sure if she was released or transferred. The only thing I know was that she was there for fewer than twenty-four hours and delivered to me a message from above.

~

An inmate came to see me one day and broke down in tears because her sixteen-year-old son was really struggling with her imprisonment. He had run away from home, started experimenting with drugs and alcohol, and his Facebook page said he was "lonely and sad." Those words left her feeling defeated. She went on to say, "When I came here, he lost part of his life—me."

Another woman added, "Being here is like a death, but there is no closure." It has been extremely difficult for both of these mothers and countless others as I have heard many stories of heartache and pain. It's also extremely difficult on the children who are without their mothers or fathers, and many times they have no one to care for them.

Throughout this journey I have learned to trust God. I can't say I ever thought I would have a prison ministry or want to start a foundation for children of incarcerated parents, but God has placed this desire in my heart. More than 2.7 million children in the United States have an incarcerated parent, and half of these kids are under the age of ten. To put it another way, one out of every twenty-eight children has a mother or father in prison, and 10 million children have experienced parental incarceration at some point in their lives.[3]

That is why God has asked me to help. God tells us in his Word, "Direct your children onto the right path, and when they are older, they will not leave it" (Proverbs 22:6). And Jesus said, "Let the children come to me. Don't stop them! For the Kingdom of Heaven belongs to those who are like these children" (Matthew 19:14).

Every once in a while I wondered how I was going to pull this

---

3 Rutgers University, Children and Families of the Incarcerated Fact Sheet, *http:// dept.camden.rutgers.edu/nrccfi/files/nrccfi-fact-sheet-2014.pdf* (July 15, 2015).

off. I did not have any experience with nonprofit organizations or foundations, and I had never been involved in any significant fundraising efforts. Furthermore, given my litigation expenses and the fact that I still had a significant amount of restitution to pay, I had absolutely no money to get this thing off the ground.

But that's where God came in. With Thanksgiving and Christmas just around the corner, I chose to be thankful for everything God was doing in my life, trusting his perfect plan.

~

For a child is born to us, a son is given to us. The government will rest on his shoulders. And he will be called: Wonderful Counselor, Mighty God, Everlasting Father, Prince of Peace. His government and its peace will never end. He will rule with fairness and justice from the throne of his ancestor David for all eternity. The passionate commitment of the LORD of Heaven's Armies will make this happen! (Isaiah 9:6–7)

It was Christmas Day, and as I read that Scripture, I could not help but remember the words God spoke to me quite some time ago when he told me he would restore justice. Christmas is the day we celebrate the birth of Jesus, and some of you may have wondered why Jesus was born and came to earth in the first place.

One reason—he came for us. Jesus came to earth to save lost souls, to call us into repentance, and to testify to the truth of God's Word. He also came to destroy evil and free people from the bondage of sin and their fear of death so they can live life to the fullest. The gift he has given us is the ultimate Christmas miracle—the gift of forgiveness and everlasting life.

So what did I find under the Christmas tree that morning? No tangible gifts, but I discovered something far better, gifts found in God's Word: "God saved you by his grace when you believed. And you can't take credit for this; it is a gift from God" (Ephesians 2:8).

And Paul writes, "For the wages of sin is death, but the free gift of God is eternal life through Christ Jesus our Lord" (Romans 6:23). Then he told the Corinthians:

There are different kinds of spiritual gifts, but the same Spirit is the source of them all. There are different kinds of service, but we serve the same Lord. God works in different ways, but it is the same God who does the work in all of us.

A spiritual gift is given to each of us so we can help each other. To one person the Spirit gives the ability to give wise advice; to another the same Spirit gives a message of special knowledge. The same Spirit gives great faith to another, and to someone else the one Spirit gives the gift of healing. He gives one person the power to perform miracles, and another the ability to prophesy. He gives someone else the ability to discern whether a message is from the Spirit of God or from another spirit. Still another person is given the ability to speak in unknown languages, while another is given the ability to interpret what is being said. It is the one and only Spirit who distributes all these gifts. He alone decides which gift each person should have. (1 Corinthians 12:4–11)

And Peter wrote:

God has given each of you a gift from his great variety of spiritual gifts. Use them well to serve one another. Do you have the gift of speaking? Then speak as though God himself were speaking through you. Do you have the gift of helping others? Do it with all the strength and energy that God supplies. Then everything you do will bring glory to God through Jesus Christ. All glory and power to him forever and ever! Amen. (1 Peter 4:10–11)

I bet you are wondering what an inmate does on Christmas Day. Well, I slept in and then I was off to work. The menu consisted of Cornish hens, ham, yams, cornbread dressing, collard greens, macaroni and cheese, cabbage, sweet potato pie, and bread pudding. After enjoying a delicious dinner, I washed dishes for over two hours, and just hung out with my friends. We had our Christmas program earlier in the week, so there was no church service to attend.

The highlight of the day was seeing an eagle, which is regarded as a symbolic messenger of God representing divinity. The eagle symbolizes swiftness and destruction. They have great speed and often have an element of surprise, carrying off their prey before their prey can even react. Why did I have a feeling that there was going to be a surprise for me right around the corner?

12

A second written order of the court was received in early January, and it was time to be transported to the federal courthouse in the Eastern District of Wisconsin. As I sat in the cafeteria waiting to be called to receiving and discharge, my friend Carol came in and we reminisced about what we were able to accomplish during our time together.

The two of us managed to lead a full year of Bible study, bringing many women a little closer to God. We learned a lot about ourselves and were confident there would be countless ministry opportunities in our future. There were tears in our eyes as we prayed for divine protection, knowing our friendship was arranged long before we were even born. Carol walked away saddened over the fact that I was leaving, only to return a few minutes later with a message from above.

"Katie," she began, "I know how you feel about this case and the injustice you feel you have suffered, but God sent me back here to tell you something very important. These are the Lord's words, not mine: *This journey has never been about who was right or wrong; this journey has always been about your heart.*" I broke down and began to cry, knowing God wanted only the best for me.

A little before ten in the morning, an officer motioned for me to come inside. It was time to dig down deep inside myself to find the strength and courage I needed to go through this transfer process again. As I opened the door to receiving and discharge and saw the handcuffs, chains, and shackles sitting on the table, I paused, inhaled slowly, and let out a long, deep breath.

The routine was familiar. If you had to use the restroom, now was the time to do that. When finished, a female officer escorted me into the dressing room, I stripped down to my birthday suit, and my body was searched in places where apparently criminals have been known to hide things. After the cavity search was complete, it was time to put on my traveling clothes, step back out into the common area, and have the handcuffs, ankle cuffs, and chains secured.

As I was being handcuffed, the camp administrator walked in, and I asked, "What are the top three needs for children of incarcerated parents?"

Her response: "These children need a liaison, someone who can help them when their families are not capable or able. Second, the kids need to see their parents, but the cost of transportation is prohibitive."

She hesitated and asked me to identify the third need based on my experience. "Well, given close to 70 percent of the women at Coleman have not earned their high school diploma, I believe inmates need to be educated and learn hands-on parenting skills with their children."

As the chains were being wrapped around my waist and the handcuff pin put in place, the camp administrator left and I reflected on our conversation. *How many kids will The Vivian Foundation be able to impact, and how do we go about influencing positive change in these families?*

The challenge reminded me of David versus Goliath. David was a lowly shepherd boy who wasn't afraid of the nine-foot giant who dared others to fight him. When David was ready to take on Goliath, the giant looked at him and thought he was kidding. Most of us know the rest of the story, how David conquered Goliath with a sling and five smooth stones.

What was the key to David's success? It was all about his perspective. In this story most of the onlookers only saw the giant. David, however, saw a mortal man defying Almighty God. Goliath was a target too big to miss. David knew he would not be alone when he faced Goliath—God would fight with him. He looked at the situation from God's point of view, because viewing impossible situations from God's vantage point helps keep problems in perspective.

The Vivian Foundation is a kingdom project and God will lead the way. Like David before us, we will also focus on a very big target, a giant so to speak, trying to help millions of children whose parents are in prison.

As I readied my feet to be put into the ankle cuffs, the white transport van was waiting outside, and it was once again time to venture into the unknown. The last time I left the facility, it was ninety-five degrees outside—this day, however, the skies were overcast, a light mist was falling, it was windy, and with temperatures barely above fifty degrees, it was cold by Florida's standards. Unfortunately, it does not matter how hot or cold it is, inmates are transported in a short-sleeve brown T-shirt, khaki-colored elastic-waist pants, and blue slip-on tennis shoes.

For me, the most difficult thing to endure besides the confinement was the dehydration. Although the Bureau of Prisons (BOP) provides a bag lunch, there was again nothing to drink. No water equals less bathroom breaks, and when you have more than one hundred inmates being transferred, that makes it easier on the twelve US marshals assigned to the flight.

You may be wondering why the BOP moves so many prisoners around the country. That's a good question. Most often, it is for court cases. In my particular instance, I was serving my time in Florida and needed to go to Milwaukee, via Chicago, where my testimony was needed. Given the Buske trial was scheduled to begin the third week of January, it was time to be moved.

The air fleet operations and Federal Transit Center are both located in Oklahoma City, because most inmates who enter or are transferred throughout the federal prison system come through this facility.

The ride from Coleman to Tampa was fairly uneventful. As a matter of fact, there was something comforting about seeing my old neighborhood and the places I loved to shop. I was surprised at how many changes had been made along the familiar route.

As we drove past the International Mall onto airport property, the transfer process from August came rushing back to my memory. It's not too often I get upset about things, but there was something heartless and inhumane about that experience. There I was, a non-violent offender who was serving my time in a prison camp, being treated the same as murderers, pedophiles, and terrorists.

As I stepped out of the van onto the tarmac, the cold January temperatures and brisk winds made my entire body shiver. Because I was surrounded by a dozen US marshals wearing bulletproof vests and carrying high-powered sharpshooting rifles, I stood where I was told. The marshals did not appear to be in any hurry—they were wearing winter coats, hats, and gloves.

I was so cold that I could not stop shaking. They must have known what I was thinking, because within a few minutes the marshal with the clipboard called out my name, took out his black Sharpie marker, and put an *X* on my left hand. I somehow hoped the light mist would wash away the marker because the dreaded *X* meant that I was heading to the Grady County Jail in Chickasha, Oklahoma. *Haven't I been through enough already?* I thought. *Grady County Jail will make my accommodations at Coleman look like a luxury hotel.*

As the transfer procedure began, we continued to stand on the tarmac while the prisoners who were flown into Tampa were removed from Con Air. It was a very orderly yet time-consuming process to move hundreds of inmates from the plane to transport vehicles and transport vehicles to the plane.

Finally, ready to board the plane, I was searched once again, which involved a pat down, looking in my mouth and under my tongue, and removing my shoes and checking my feet. Not the easiest thing to do when you are chained and shackled, as you can only lift your foot so high while trying to balance on the other. The marshal actually removed my shoes and put them back on. Once that was done, it was time to climb the stairs and enter the aircraft.

The men and women were segregated, with the women entering first and sitting in the front of the plane. We were given strict instructions not to have any conversation or eye contact with the male prisoners as they were boarding. If we did not cooperate, our bathroom privilege would be revoked.

It was my one-year anniversary in prison, and I was chained, shackled, and buckled into a seat on a Con Air flight that was heading to Oklahoma City. As I looked out the window, just as I had done hundreds of times before on flights departing Tampa, I wished I could somehow go back in time and change things. I wiped away a tear, wondering how in the world I was going to survive this nightmare.

Only one thing was certain: God decided we were going to do this part of the journey alone. No phone, no e-mail, and no one except the two of us, and I had no idea what to expect.

~

As we began our descent, I dreaded to think about what was next. I had never been to Oklahoma, and there was a part of me that hoped it would be my first and last trip to the Sooner State.

As the plane landed and taxied down the runway, I was surprised when we pulled right up to the transit facility. The Federal Transit Center is actually located on airport property. Most inmates on this flight would be taken inside, while I was one of a handful of not-so-lucky ones who was heading down the stairs to be transported to another location.

There it was—the Grady County Jail bus, ready and waiting. Although it looked like a normal school bus with the exception of its color, I knew this field trip was not going to be much fun at all. Similar to the time the van drove us to the Tampa airport, the inmates would be locked inside the seating area, where metal barriers and keyed locks would separate us from the officers.

Just like a dog on a short chain, it was time for the prisoners heading to Chickasha to be locked inside their kennel. Once again, the women were seated in the front of the bus, while the men were in the back. When I got onto the bus, I sat in the first row. There were two officers who accompanied us on the trip, one being the driver and the other an armed guard.

Chickasha was approximately thirty-five miles southwest of Oklahoma City, yet the ride seemed to take forever. As we approached the facility, we turned the corner and stopped in front of a large overhead door, which was the vehicle entrance. The bus pulled into a large indoor parking area and we were told to remain seated until the garage door closed and the officers were in position to allow us to move inside.

I exited the bus, headed toward the side door, and stepped inside a long hallway. One by one our restraints were removed and we were put into a holding cell. Of the ten female prisoners who now occupied that relatively small space, six of us were "feds" awaiting processing.

The body odor of the remaining local inmates who had apparently spent more than a week in that cell tested my already queasy stomach. I was nauseated from motion sickness and had a splitting headache because I was tired and dehydrated. If that wasn't enough, one of the young girls whose body was withdrawing from whatever drug she was addicted to decided it was time to throw up, vomiting in the same toilet I had to use a few minutes later to relieve myself. Needless to say, when they brought dinner I did not eat.

We remained in the holding cell for close to three hours, until one by one we were pulled out and booked. Time for another mug shot. I was weighed, asked a few questions, and given an orange Grady County pair of scrubs, two pairs of orange mesh underwear, and one pair of orange Crocs, then told to change. When I returned, the restraints were put back on and I was seated on a bench until the other women completed the same process.

Once everyone was ready, the officers told us to follow them to an elevator. We were heading to the third floor. When the elevator doors opened, it was obvious that we were near the prison laundry. There was a thick steel door that opened after the officer buzzed the command station. We entered a small holding area as the heavy door closed behind us. Another door, similar to what we just passed through, opened and we were led inside another holding area.

Prior to walking through a third door, my restraints were removed and I was handed a bag that contained a one-inch-thick mat, a blood-stained sheet, a wool blanket with holes in it, half of a towel, and some prison-issued toiletries. I had just entered a real-life episode of *Lockdown*.

Home sweet home was now cell block 3A-3, which was one of eight two-person cells that occupied this particular pod. I would be sharing this six-by-eight-foot space with a girl named Trina who was a county-jail inmate and had arrived a few months earlier. She had the lower bunk, which meant I was assigned to the upper. This bunk consisted of a very thin metal tray that hung approximately five feet off the ground. I was not able to physically climb up there without stepping on the stainless steel toilet and sink, and I quickly realized there was no way I could sleep on such a narrow surface.

I asked Trina if she minded if I slept on the concrete floor between her bed and the door. As I looked at the door, which contained a very small window and even smaller opening for a food tray, thoughts of claustrophobia entered my mind. "How long are we locked down?" I asked.

"Twelve hours a day," came her response.

"Do you mind if I leave the food-tray door open?" For some reason, I convinced myself that if that door was open I could breathe easier. Within minutes we were told to get inside our cells, the heavy door slammed shut, automatically locking, and I was about to find out what it was like to attempt to sleep on the concrete floor of a county jail cell.

I placed the paper-thin four-foot-long mat in the corner, hoping there were no insects or rodents that would be joining me. I covered the mat with the blood-stained sheet and tried to make a pillow out of the tattered towel. The ragged blanket would have to keep me warm as I was not given a T-shirt or a pair of socks. If there was ever a time I needed my friends to be praying for me, that was the time. Unfortunately, however, they had no idea where I was.

Bang, bang, bang, bang. I counted the repetition of the continual clanging that sounded as though someone were hitting a metal pipe with an aluminum baseball bat. One, two, three, four ... all the way up to twenty and thirty times before it stopped. "What's that noise?" I asked.

"That's the male inmate below who wants out," Trina responded. "He's been in solitary confinement for the last fifteen months."

"Obviously, we are not going to get much sleep," I conceded.

"You sleep when you can," she told me.

"How do you know he's been in solitary confinement for fifteen months?" I wondered out loud.

"He talks to some of the women through the air vents," she responded.

How could someone actually survive fifteen months of solitary confinement when they were subject to sensory deprivation and lack of social contact? How could a person's mental health not be impacted by such circumstances? What in the world could someone have done to warrant such harsh treatment?

I rolled over onto my side. The pounding subsided and I actually fell asleep for a short time, only to be awakened by a different noise. "What's that?" I asked again. "It sounds like chains being dragged across the floor."

"Stand up and look out the window," Trina suggested. "Those are the men who are being moved."

"In the middle of the night?" I asked, sounding a little surprised.

"Virtually every day. You'll get used to it," Trina again assured me.

I wasn't sure I could ever get used to it. It was so inhumane. As

I lay in the dark on the cold concrete floor and peered at the back wall, noticing the bars that covered an extremely small window, I realized I was not in a county jail; I was one step above hell. It was going to take everything I had to survive this part of the journey.

~

I may have slept two or three hours that night. It was four in the morning, and if I wanted breakfast I would have to get up. Because I did not eat anything the day before, I figured I'd better see what was being served. Ten trays were slid through the opening into the common area and stacked on top of a metal picnic table that was bolted to the floor. I was not given a cup, so I borrowed one and was given some sort of fruit drink.

There were four metal tables with four round bench seats attached to each table. I chose to sit at the one nearest my cell. I looked at the tray, and it could only be described as some sort of prison slop with two pieces of white bread and a single serving of butter. Trina was gathering the bread and butter from anyone who did not want theirs, and I was quickly learning that whatever appeared to be edible should be saved in case we got hungry.

Those who wanted to eat did so in a hurry because we had only a limited amount of time before having to return to our cells to be locked down until eight o'clock. Apparently, lunch was not served until early afternoon, so Trina encouraged me to eat something. I did the best I could.

~

Upon arriving the night before, I had tried to make a collect call to let my family know where I was, but unfortunately when you were on a fixed-rate plan, regardless if it's a landline or cell phone, you could not accept collect calls. After a number of futile attempts calling every number I had memorized, I gave up, hoping that caller ID would identify my location and someone would let the others know where I was.

This also meant I had no ability to order anything from the commissary, because that had to be done by someone on the outside who had Internet access. Not only was I in a county jail, but I was now an indigent inmate. My prison-issued toiletries were going to have to do, and I had no choice but to eat the food that was put in front of me, even if it was unidentifiable.

At eight o'clock on Saturday morning, the electronic lock on my cell door opened and we could now venture into the common area. There was a television, but given all of the inmates were still sleeping, turning it on was not an option. So now what? I wandered over to look at a pile of books next to the microwave and was happy to find two Bibles. I grabbed one, sat outside my cell, and started reading. For whatever reason, God began taking me to Scriptures about redemption.

One of the first I read was Romans 3:24: "Yet God, in his grace, freely makes us right in his sight. He did this through Christ Jesus when he freed us from the penalty for our sins." He then took me to Ephesians 1:7, and the theme continued: "He is so rich in kindness and grace that he purchased our freedom with the blood of his Son and forgave our sins." The Lord was reinforcing that he had rescued me from the bondage of sin. Then I turned to Isaiah:

This is what the LORD says: "Be just and fair to all. Do what is right and good, for I am coming soon to rescue you and to display my righteousness among you." (Isaiah 56:1)

Due to the fact that God was speaking to me through his Word, I knew it was time to write. So I returned to my cell, grabbed two pieces of paper and a pencil, and sat down at a picnic table. For a brief moment I felt like the apostle Paul writing some of the letters to the church he dearly loved.

Paul authored many of the books in the New Testament, and actually wrote four books while he was in prison—Ephesians, Philippians, Colossians, and Philemon. These four letters are among the most hopeful and encouraging in the Bible. They help us understand how we can find joy in our trials, peace in our suffering, and contentment in our circumstances.

Paul remained happy throughout his incarceration because he could see his circumstances from God's point of view. He focused on what he was supposed to do, not what he felt he should have done. Paul had his priorities straight, and he was grateful for everything God had given him. Once again, just like when David conquered Goliath, the answer to peace, contentment, and an attitude of gratitude lay in my perspective, priorities, and source of my power. With that said, I knew God would give me the strength to get through this.

I read for a while, jotted down a few notes, and less than an hour later returned to my cell. Because it was fairly quiet, I was lucky enough to fall back to sleep.

~

Lunch arrived at twelve thirty, and one by one the weary inmates walked from their cells into the common area. Rubbing their eyes and stretching, they got ready to eat. Many of the women chose not to eat breakfast, so this was the first time I had seen them since arriving at "Shady Grady."

I sat at a table with Trina and two women from cell 3A-4, Donna and Sasha. As we began to eat, everyone was pretty subdued. Many times inmates did not discuss the reason they were in prison, yet these three ladies began to share their stories. Just like at Coleman, illegal drug possession and its manufacturing, along with substance abuse, theft, and child neglect, were real-life problems facing these women. My heart broke as they told me their children's names and ages and how their incarceration was impacting their families.

At two o'clock I found myself sitting in my cell once again. Sasha was seated next to me at the small table near the door, and Trina and Donna were seated next to each other on the bottom bunk. I knew in my heart that this was a divine appointment, so I began to share my testimony and love for the Lord. I told them about what

God was asking me to do with The Vivian Foundation and learned a little bit more about their children.

We talked about the fact I was writing a book, and I eagerly shared how God was working in my life. They were curious to know more about how God spoke to me and what it meant to follow God's will for your life. The Holy Spirit was guiding my words and heart when I began to share what had been happening to me at Coleman.

I told them that since I had been incarcerated, I had spent hours each day in prayer. I explained that when you pray in your spiritual language, you develop an incredible connection with the Holy Spirit. God spoke to me through his Spirit and had revealed to me many things. I went on to tell them I had done everything God had asked of me, all which had been instrumental to my spiritual growth and healing.

At that point, I began to share something that I had not told anyone else before. I had a feeling that something happened to me as a youngster, like I was sexually abused as a child. I racked my brain trying to figure out if anything like this could have happened, but I had very happy memories of my childhood. I even wondered if there was a chance something occurred in elementary school because I attended a Catholic grade school, but again, there was nothing I could recall.

I shared that during the second week of October, I had the worst nightmare of my life. I was very young, about three or four years old, and I was wearing a white dress. In this dream I saw myself standing all alone and crying as I kept repeating, *Stop it, it hurts, stop it!* It was unnerving to see myself at such an innocent age, hearing my cries of despair. When I woke up I told the Lord, *I rebuke that dream in the name of Jesus. The Devil must flee!* But I also quickly added, *God, I don't know where that came from and I don't ever want to experience anything like that again, but if it's from you, bring it on.*

Less than a week later while I was walking the track and praying, I heard a name and stopped dead in my tracks. It was a name

I was familiar with, a nickname I could not have come up with in a million years. God had just revealed who had hurt me—it was the nickname of my abuser, a man who lived in our neighborhood.

Right after God revealed this to me, a woman whom I worked with in the kitchen shared that God disclosed a few things to her. God told Dale there was something deep inside my heart that I had to give him, and it was something no one else knew about. She went on to say the pain had been buried deep inside my heart and it had been locked up for a long time. It wasn't for her to know what it was, but I needed to give it to God so I could finally have some much-needed peace.

Sasha, Donna, and Trina were captivated by my story, as I recalled other encounters with Dale. God used Dale many times to speak to me, and she kept telling me that God was going to send me a special child. The day before Dale left Coleman, God revealed a little bit more. She told me this child would be a girl, she was going to be a spitfire and have a lot of Katie in her, and it was going to take everything I had to help her recover from her pain, but I would be successful in helping this child on her journey.

I paused and could not help but look at Trina as she was beginning to shake. Bringing her hands to her mouth, tears started to well up in her eyes. Sasha looked at me in disbelief, and Donna put her arm around Trina and appeared to be having a hard time believing what she was about to say. Struggling to get the words out, a wide-eyed Donna looked at me and said, "Katie, Trina is that special child."

I sat there in awe, unable to speak, realizing what was happening. Suddenly, everything started to make sense. God revealed a number of times that there would be a Christmas miracle, which is the story that focuses on the gift of forgiveness.

Donna and Sasha told me they had been trying for months to help Trina cope with the pain of her childhood abuse. For the next three hours, Trina poured out her heart to me as I heard graphic details of the sexual abuse she suffered at the hands of her father.

The abuse started when she was nine years old and continued until she was fourteen. She was certain her mother knew about her father's inappropriate behavior yet did nothing to stop it.

We talked at great length about her parents, her siblings, her children, and her struggles. I leveraged every Scripture I could to show her the importance of forgiveness. I focused on God's Word and his promises in hopes that her heart would finally begin to heal.

As she continued to cry, I continued to encourage her: "Trina, the best gift you can give yourself and your parents is the gift of forgiveness. It is a gift that is found deep within your heart and it is a gift filled with love. There is also something you must remember: forgiveness is a choice. It doesn't mean what your mom and dad did was right—it wasn't. You were deeply hurt for years and what they did was very, very wrong. But you need to leave it in God's hands so you can be at peace. He will take care of it."

I paused for a minute before adding, "God tells us to pray for those who have hurt us." So we prayed. And prayed. And prayed. And through the tears Trina decided to make a godly decision—she chose to forgive her mother and father. The burden and emotional distress she had been carrying for thirty years had finally been lifted. We had just witnessed a miracle.

∿

Later that evening, physically and emotionally drained, I sat in the dark on the floor of my jail cell thinking about what had transpired. How had God done this? Do you know all of the things that had to happen for the two of us to end up in the same jail cell at the exact same time? If you don't believe in God, maybe you should.

With my back propped up against the wall and my hands resting on bended knees, I thanked God for another Christmas miracle. I was so overcome by the presence of the Holy Spirit that I had a hard time believing what was happening. Through tears I spoke the following words out loud: "God has just climbed the fire escape with my bouquet of roses."

216

At that point, I knew with certainty that my coming to Grady County Jail was orchestrated from above. This was my final redemption, and it was also time to grieve the innocence I lost as a young child. I too had a choice to make, and, like Trina, I made a godly decision to forgive my abuser.

As I cried and the Holy Spirit spoke, God gently reminded me that no one knew about the abuse I suffered and this man was a person our family should have been able to trust. Even though he had passed away many years ago, the thought that this individual may have hurt other children in our neighborhood, possibly members of my very own family, was painfully and overwhelmingly disturbing. Yet we must find comfort in God's Word: "But if you cause one of these little ones who trusts in me to fall into sin, it would be better for you to be thrown into the sea with a large millstone hung around your neck" (Mark 9:42).

Many times victims of sexual abuse may not remember their childhood experiences, and, as a result, do not know what is wrong with them. For most of my life, I wondered why I behaved the way I did. Why did I always feel such great shame, embarrassment, and confusion toward my sexuality? Why was sex always so difficult for me to talk about? Was this why I would always find it necessary to joke about sexual intimacy or make inappropriate comments? Was the abuse I suffered at an early age the reason I never felt loved or why I had so much difficulty articulating my love? When I should have been able to find love and intimacy in my marriage, it had escaped me.

As I sat in the corner, pondering these questions, it was as though a sense of relief washed over me. It wasn't necessarily anything I had done; rather, it was what had been done to me. At a very early age, when most children learn to set boundaries, my boundaries were not respected. As a result of this, when it came time to set appropriate limits as a teenager and adult, I either could not or would not because I was paralyzed with fear. There was a reason I did not want to be alone.

That is why we need to trust God. He knows what's best for us. As long and difficult as this journey had been, I was beginning to realize that every bit of it was necessary to release me from the bondage of sin and my painful past. Who would have ever thought God would do his best work in a county jail cell in Chickasha, Oklahoma? After years and years of searching, I had finally found true love.

13

On Sunday morning the routine continued. I seemed to be the only one who was trying to stay on somewhat of a normal schedule, although there is nothing normal about being in jail. I was happy to hear that Mondays and Thursdays were transport days to Chicago, and, with any luck, I would be out of there first thing in the morning.

I fell asleep a little after eleven o'clock at night—sleeping for only an hour or two had become the norm. I was awakened by the intercom a short time later when I heard an officer say, "Scheller?"

"Yes," I responded.

"You're leaving today. Get ready."

I was now one of the inmates whose chains and shackles would wake the others. Trina told me the cell door would be unlocked after my traveling clothes were placed on the table, and to expect a bag lunch with a bologna sandwich for breakfast. Needless to say, I did not go back to sleep.

I looked out the window of the cell and my clothes eventually arrived. It didn't take long for the officer to unlock the door, and I was happy to retrieve my travel clothing and change out of the clothes I had been wearing since Friday. I ate half a sandwich, figuring I'd better eat something, yet knowing how this process played out I drank very little as I was not sure when I would be able to use a toilet again.

At about four in the morning, two officers arrived and it was once again time to be chained and shackled. I was led downstairs and seated on a bench for what seemed to be close to an hour before being escorted to the bus. I boarded the bus and sat in the first row, and it was still dark outside when we pulled out of the garage. We drove to another building that housed additional inmates, and a few other prisoners climbed aboard. It was now time to head back to Oklahoma City.

Once we arrived at the airport, we entered through two electronic fences before driving onto the tarmac near the Federal Transit Center. The plane was already out of the hanger and sitting on the tarmac. We sat in the bus for quite some time as the driver studied his clipboard. The other inmates were allowed to exit the vehicle as the transfer process began. But I was asked to remain seated.

It was apparent they were discussing something involving me. The officer turned around and asked if I had been tested for tuberculosis. I told him I had not been tested while I was at Grady County, but I had been tested within the last year at Coleman. He was on his phone talking to someone because apparently each prisoner was required to be screened for tuberculosis before being transported. I had not been in Grady County long enough to have had the proper testing done.

The conversation continued, he made a notation on his paperwork, and the deputy told me I could get off the bus and get in line to be searched. Part of me didn't want to venture outside because it was so cold, but I decided I was ready for whatever was waiting for me in Chicago, figuring my accommodations could not get any worse than they had been.

With the pat-down complete, I climbed the stairs to board the airplane and took an aisle seat near the front. I was exhausted because I had so little sleep. A US marshal boarded soon after, and when I heard him say, "Scheller?" I thought, *Uh-oh.* I let him know I was the person he had just called, and he said, "Get off the plane. They don't want you."

You have got to be kidding me ... not again. "Now what?" I asked.

"You're going back to Grady County. Get on the bus." What in the world was happening? I could not believe what I had just been told.

Did Buske take a plea deal, or was there another delay in his case?

If there was any good news, the US marshal thought I would eventually be transferred back to Coleman, but he had no idea when. That meant I had to climb back on the bus with two male officers. Two male officers from "Shady Grady," and two male officers who were all alone with a female inmate who was chained and shackled. I hoped and prayed that neither of them was thinking what I was.

Much to my surprise, the two gentlemen were extremely nice and wanted to know what I did to end up in federal prison. I laughed, commenting, "You wouldn't believe me if I told you." We could not leave Oklahoma City until Con Air took off, so we sat in a parking lot for a short time until they knew with certainty the plane was airborne. I shared my story with them, and the three of us actually had an enjoyable conversation on the ride back.

Once we arrived in Chickasha, the two officers escorted me inside, and as we entered the long hallway I told both deputies I needed to use the restroom. Neither acknowledged my request. As my chains and shackles were removed, one of the officers apologized for having to put me in this particular holding cell.

I reminded him that I needed to use the restroom, and he pointed toward the floor and locked the door. Okay, now I was feeling claustrophobic. That cell was extremely small, there was no window, and it felt as though the concrete walls were closing in on me. It smelled, the area was disgustingly filthy, and I really did have to urinate. But there was only one problem: there was no toilet. I looked into the floor drain, which contained a bloody sanitary napkin and feces, and my gag reflex was tested as I quickly looked away. I had no choice. I had to go. So I pulled down my pants and squatted over the drain as if I were on some horrific camping trip.

How long am I going to have to stay in this torture chamber? Friday night we were in the larger holding cell for three hours and for a fleeting moment I wondered what would happen if they forgot they put me in there. There was only one thing I could do. I stood in the corner facing the camera and began to pray in tongues. It was just me and the Holy Spirit, and I prayed until that door finally opened over an hour later.

I was taken into the booking area and given another pair of orange scrubs, an orange pair of Crocs, and two more pairs of mesh underwear. The chains and shackles were put back on, and I was led upstairs to return to cell block 3A-3.

The inmates were very surprised to see me, and I was equally surprised when I found a relatively clean sheet and newer blanket in my bedding bag. I was so tired, I felt like I was going to be sick. I had a splitting headache because of my exhaustion, and I had never felt so physically and emotionally sapped in my life. I set up my bed on the floor and slept until dinner.

I knew I needed to let my family know where I was, and given the fact that I could not find anyone who could accept a collect call, I wrote a letter to my sister. The mail would not go out until the next day, but if I was lucky she would receive my correspondence before the end of the week and place an order with Tiger Commissary.

I didn't care how much it cost—the first thing on my list was the travel-size pillow. After dinner I paged through the Bible and noticed that the following verses were circled:

> Then the LORD said to me, "Write my answer plainly on tablets, so that a runner can carry the correct message to others. This vision is for a future time. It describes the end, and it will be fulfilled. It seems slow in coming, wait patiently, for it will surely take place. It will not be delayed." (Habakkuk 2:2–3)

God had encouraged me with these Scriptures before.

In this particular chapter of Habakkuk, evil and injustice seem to have an upper hand in this world. Habakkuk complained to God about the situation, and God's answer to him was the same as it would be to us: "You need to wait patiently." We must trust God even when we don't understand why certain events occur.

On Thursday I finally connected with the outside world when

the Holy Spirit led me to call my friend Marsha. She was one of the few people I could always count on. When Marsha accepted the collect call, I almost started crying, relieved to hear a familiar voice.

Marsha had been in contact with my family and was able to tell me Buske had accepted a plea deal and there would be no need for me to testify. The written order of the court was canceled on January 4, the day I left Coleman. Not only was this an answer to prayer, but it was exactly what God had told me would happen. Remember when Shawn came back to Coleman and delivered that message? This was great news and it meant I would still be eligible for a downward departure because of my cooperation.

~

On Saturday, as I lay on the floor pondering everything that had happened, the Spirit began speaking to me once again. There was a reason God led me to the book of Joshua and the story of Jericho earlier in the week. For months we had heard rumors that prison camps were no longer going to be funded, and we were all praying that the walls of Coleman would tumble down and we would be released to home confinement. Obviously, that did not happen. But it was something that Trina said that kept rising up in my spirit when she told me, "I was finally able to remove the wall that surrounded my heart."

That is why I had to go there—the wall I had put up around my heart also came tumbling down, and I was finally able to give God everything he was asking of me. In return, God showed me his love, kindness, and faithfulness by giving me peace regarding my past.

Saturday evening I was watching the Green Bay Packer's game and visiting with a new inmate who was twenty-three years old, pregnant, and back in prison on a probation violation. I shared my testimony and we talked about what it meant to be born again. My intention was to build some trust as she pondered her life decisions and current situation, which she admitted were not working out too well for her.

Sunday morning the Lord woke me up and told me it was time to invite her to the best party in town. As we shared an orange, I led her in prayer and she accepted Jesus into her life as her Lord and Savior. At that moment I knew I was right where I was supposed to be.

~

Jesus replied, "I tell you the truth, unless you are born again, you cannot see the Kingdom of God." (John 3:3)

The term "born again" refers to spiritual birth, the Holy Spirit's act of bringing believers into God's family. Jesus used this concept of a new birth when he explained salvation to Nicodemus in John 3. It is a wonderful metaphor of new life from God, a gift from above.

You cannot be a Christian without a fresh beginning based on the salvation that Christ brings. All who welcome Jesus Christ as Lord of their lives are spiritually reborn, receiving new life from God. Through faith in Christ, this new birth changes us from the inside out.

John writes, "They are reborn—not with a physical birth resulting from human passion or plan, but a birth that comes from God" (John 1:13). When each of us was born, we became physically alive and a member of our parents' family. Being born of God makes us spiritually alive and now we belong to God's family, the body of Christ. To experience spiritual rebirth, a person must be completely renewed through God's power. This fresh start in life is available to all who believe in Christ. To believe means to put your faith, confidence, and trust in Jesus.

Jesus replied, "I assure you, no one can enter the Kingdom of God without being born of water and the Spirit. Humans can reproduce only human life, but the Holy Spirit gives birth to spiritual life. So don't be surprised when I say, 'You must be born again.'" (John 3:5–7)

If you have never trusted Jesus Christ as your Savior, now is the time to accept this free gift. *How do you accept this gift?* you may ask. I'm glad you asked. Paul put it very plainly for us:

> In fact, it says, "The message is very close at hand; it is on your lips and in your heart." And that message is the very message about faith that we preach: If you openly declare that Jesus is Lord and believe in your heart that God raised him from the dead, you will be saved. For it is by believing in your heart that you are made right with God, and it is by openly declaring your faith that you are saved. As the Scriptures tell us, "Anyone who trusts in him will never be disgraced." (Romans 10:8–11)

It's that easy. Jesus said, "For this is how God loved the world: He gave his one and only Son, so that everyone who believes in him will not perish but have eternal life" (John 3:16).

∼

Monday was a day of reflection. I reflected on the fact that I had never worn the same clothes for over a week, nor had I ever had to sleep on a concrete floor for eleven days. Then it hit me. I realized there are people who live like that every day, and some of them are not even in prison.

But if you think about it for a moment, aren't we all experiencing some type of personal prison? Whether or not we want to admit it, we are all struggling with something. The fact is that there is so much heartache and pain in this world. Sexual sin is destroying families. Drugs and alcohol are tearing our world apart. Broken homes, anger, bitterness, and resentment seem to be the norm. Corruption, greed, and prejudice dominate headline news. Accounts of physical, verbal, and sexual abuse, along with gang-related violence, babies born out of wedlock, public assistance, homelessness, and gun fights are all stories I have heard. Like Habakkuk, we can either complain about evil and injustice or wait patiently for God to open the door so we can do something about it.

I got facedown on the floor of my cell and prayed in the Spirit, thanking God for this experience. I needed to see this side of life. How could I help make a difference in this world if I didn't know the issues facing inmates and their families? I had seen the heartache and pain firsthand, and I was going to do something about it.

Monday night arrived. Right before we were locked down for the evening, the guard told me that I would be leaving in a few hours.

> The LORD says, "I will rescue those who love me. I will protect those who trust in my name. When they call on me, I will answer; I will be with them in trouble. I will rescue and honor them. I will reward them with a long life and give them my salvation." (Psalm 91:14–16)

Trina thanked me for everything I had done to help her forgive her parents, and it was now time to say good-bye to this special child God had sent me. Needless to say, as we embraced I had tears in my eyes.

As I changed out of my Grady County scrubs and put on my traveling clothes, I dreaded to think it was time to endure another eight hours in chains and shackles, yet I was grateful this part of the journey was coming to an end. As I boarded the plane in Oklahoma City, the female inmate seated next to the window turned toward me, and, with a strange look on her face, asked, "What in the world are you doing here? You don't even look like you would jaywalk."

I laughed and told her, "I wouldn't! As a matter of fact, I've been known to write out a check for fifty cents and send it to the state of Illinois when I missed a toll."

The US marshal laughed when he heard that comment and he too was curious. "What did you do?" he asked. "I agree. You don't look like you belong here."

"It's a long story," I responded. "And someday you can read all about it."

Touching down on the runway in Tampa brought a smile to my

face. In fewer than two hours, I would be back at Coleman. When I was finally processed and allowed to walk back into the compound, my friends were waiting for me. They knew long before I did that I would be returning to the Sunshine State, and, as strange as this sounds, it was great to be back. One woman commented, "I don't know what God did to you, but you look different! You have a sparkle in your eyes that has been missing."

~

Upon my return, I met with the chaplain to discuss the 2013 Just One Word calendars. A few days later, I met with the supervisory chaplain who oversaw the entire compound. We were going to get the Just One Word Bible reading plan into all five of the facilities at Coleman, which was great news.

Despite the momentum of God opening new doors for me to walk through, I had an overwhelming feeling of frustration over the previous few weeks. It started when I went to see the chaplain and told her I was disappointed it was taking so long to get the calendars to the camp. She insisted my aggravation was caused by the Devil and I needed to rebuke it. I wasn't about to get into a debate about how I was feeling, but I was pretty sure it was not the Devil. My irritability was fueled by my passion for the women there—I just wanted them to receive the resources they so desperately needed.

I knew that God was in complete control and the calendars would get there the day they were supposed to, yet my frustration continued—what was up with that? There are times when discontentment is placed in your spirit by God, not by the Enemy. The good news is that once you move onto the new path where God is guiding you, this feeling ends as you experience the breakthrough God has destined for you.

As Dr. Charles Stanley has taught me through his books, when you have a restless feeling deep inside your soul, it can be one of the most exciting times of your life. God is at work and getting ready to promote you into a deeper, more fulfilling role.[1] And guess what? That is exactly what happened.

Sunday, February 24, 2013—you talk about fulfilling—I got to church about ten minutes early and took a seat in the breezeway outside of the chapel. As I looked around, I couldn't help but smile as well over one hundred women were holding their 2013 Just One Word calendars. It was very gratifying to know I had played a part in blessing each and every one of them.

Our chaplain got up and spoke about the calendars and gave a shout out to Really Good News Ministries and Ruth Ann Nylen. She shared that I had a hand in their development and called me up to the front to acknowledge my ministry work. The next thing I knew, I was getting a standing ovation and was given the microphone. I simply kissed my fingers and pointed to heaven—God was going to get the glory.

I thanked God for the time he had given me to prepare the calendars, and I shared that I was excited that we had both an adults' and kids' version. I went on to explain how the Bible reading plan was structured and promised the women that if they would provide me with the names and addresses of their children and grandchildren, the ministry would see that their families received a calendar.

With a big smile on my face, I went on to share that God revealed I would be involved in a children's ministry that would be funded as a result of the book I was writing: "God told me to put a foundation in place called The Vivian Foundation. It will fund existing ministries and help develop new ministries for children of incarcerated parents."

As I took my seat, Chaplain Bass spoke about my tenacity and passion to get these calendars into all five of the facilities at Coleman, including the penitentiaries. She went on to ask everyone, "Did you ever think you could do something to bless seven thousand inmates? This girl is not playing—she's serious about what she is doing."

---

1 Charles Stanley, *The Source of My Strength* (Nashville, TN: Thomas Nelson, 2005), 197.

She then introduced our guest speaker, Chaplain Rock, and little did I know I would be used as an example throughout his entire sermon. He started out with a story from Matthew 8:1–4, which is about Jesus healing a man with leprosy.

> Large crowds followed Jesus as he came down the mountainside. Suddenly, a man with leprosy approached him and knelt before him. "Lord," the man said, "if you are willing, you can heal me and make me clean."
>
> Jesus reached out and touched him. "I am willing," he said. "Be healed!" And instantly the leprosy disappeared. Then Jesus said to him, "Don't tell anyone about this. Instead, go to the priest and let him examine you. Take along the offering required in the law of Moses for those who have been healed of leprosy. This will be a public testimony that you have been cleansed." (Matthew 8:1–4)

As Chaplain Rock spoke, he referenced Isaiah 61:1, which says, "The Spirit of the Sovereign Lord is upon me, for the Lord has anointed me to bring good news to the poor. He has sent me to comfort the brokenhearted and to proclaim that captives will be released and prisoners will be freed." Then Chaplain Rock continued, "There is a prisoner who has already been set free. Can you believe what God is doing with an inmate who has nothing? That is divine favor! Thousands of calendars? God is blessing others and will bless Scheller for her obedience." He encouraged us to be everything we could be and asked if we were persistent enough to get what we wanted. "This is more than hearing from God about Scripture on a calendar," he said. "You have to get up and be willing to do whatever he is asking you to do."

"God has given Scheller a vision." He looked at me and said, "This is the beginning," then quickly added, "May he bless you in all that you do." I was so overcome by God's presence that all I could do was put my head in my hands and begin to weep. "Scheller didn't brag about what she had done; she waited until the chaplain called her up, so God could get the glory. This sister found a way to get the calendars done, and, in the process, she's become a Woman of Elegance. It's what's on the inside, ladies—it comes from the heart. Let others see the power and the glory of God in your deliverance. You must be an extension of God's love."

~

A month later, something interesting happened that can only be explained as a God thing. I finished reading one book and decided to head over to the library to get another. *A Love Worth Giving* by Max Lucado found its way into my hands, and I got through chapter five by eight thirty that night. Given my eyes were getting heavy, I decided to take a quick nap before the ten o'clock count. There was only one problem: I tossed and turned like a fish out of water, feeling like I was going to come out of my skin. Frustrated, I asked the Lord, *What are you trying to tell me?*

Go read your book and you will have your answer, came his reply. So I got up, grabbed the book, and continued reading. One page later, I found my answer. Max talks about missing his flight due to a snowstorm in the Midwest on page 53, and when I turned to page 54 I almost fell off my bed. The stewardess told Max, "I'm afraid there are no more seats in coach. We are going to have to bump you up to first class. Do you mind if we do that?" His response: "Do you mind if I kiss you?" Max goes on to write, "So I boarded the plane and nestled down in the wide seat with extra leg room and smiled like a prisoner on early parole! Not only was I going home, I was going home in style!"[2]

At that point I was smiling because I knew without a doubt that I was going to be that prisoner on early parole. The chapter ended with this: "So loosen up and enjoy the journey. You are going home in style."

---

2 Max Lucado, *A Love Worth Giving: Living in the Overflow of God's Love* (Nashville, TN: W Publishing Group, 2006).

~

On May 9, 2013, the criminal case with SC Johnson came to an end with Thomas Buske's sentencing. Buske received six months in prison, six months of home confinement, and two years of supervised release. The motion for my downward departure could now be filed. Within a few weeks my lawyer received the paperwork and the US attorney recommended a five-month reduction. The hearing date was scheduled for July 17. We were praying and believing that I would receive an immediate release.

The phone conference was held in my counselor's office. The connection was perfect, and once the introductions were completed, the US attorney spoke first, recommending a five-month downward departure. My attorney reminded the court of what I had to endure: being taken out of there twice in chains and shackles and having to spend twelve days in the Grady County Jail. I was then allowed to read my prepared statement, and I chose to share our ministry results.

Judge Clevert asked the US attorney whether or not he had taken into consideration the fact that I was transported twice and he said that he had. My attorney and I were not so sure, and apparently the judge agreed, because without hesitation Judge Clevert reduced my sentence by eight months. The phone call came to an abrupt end and I sat there not knowing what to think.

In many ways I was surprised that I did not receive an immediate release because an eight-month reduction meant I should already be in a halfway house. I was hoping I would walk out of there that day, but God's Word tells us, "We can make our plans, but the LORD determines our steps" (Proverbs 16:9), and "You can make many plans, but the LORD's purpose will prevail" (Proverbs 19:21).

It was an emotionally draining day. When you go through this type of legal process, everything gets stirred up every time there is a major event, and you go right back to the beginning. I thought about my poor decisions. I relived the day I pled guilty and came back to Tampa a wreck. I thought about the day of sentencing and remembered when the judge rendered the verdict. I replayed what I had to endure being taken out of there in chains and shackles, and I was praying this part of the journey would finally come to an end. In fact, I had enough—I wondered why others who did the same thing I did were not punished. I just wanted it to be over.

But then I reflected on the fact that God called me; smiling, I knew this was part of my divine destiny. Hebrews 10:32–36 resonated deeply with me:

> Think back on those early days when you first learned about Christ. Remember how you remained faithful even though it meant terrible suffering. Sometimes you were exposed to public ridicule and were beaten, and sometimes you helped others who were suffering the same things. You suffered along with those who were thrown into jail, and when all you owned was taken from you, you accepted it with joy. You knew there were better things waiting for you that will last forever.
>
> So do not throw away this confident trust in the Lord. Remember the great reward it brings you! Patient endurance is what you need now, so that you will continue to do God's will. Then you will receive all that he has promised.

It took a few weeks before my new out date showed in the computer: I would be released from Bureau of Prisons' custody on January 13, 2014. I had been asking God to tell me whether or not I should go to the halfway house or stay at Coleman due to the fact that I wanted to stay in his perfect will for my life. *How in the world is God going to answer this prayer?* The same way he always did.

When my case manager informed me of my new release date, she actually hand delivered the note to my room. I was sitting on my bed when she walked past the door and stopped. "Aren't you supposed to be in 404?" she asked.

"No," I responded, "I've been in 401 for quite some time."

"The computer says you are in 404. You better go see your counselor and make sure."

When I went to see my counselor, she pulled my up my inmate number. "It says 401. See?" She showed me the computer screen. Once again, I knew there was a message from God and I would find what I was looking for in 404.

Jeremiah 40:4 says, "But I am going to take off your chains and let you go. If you want to come with me to Babylon, you are welcome. I will see that you are well cared for. But if you don't want to come, you may stay here. The whole land is before you—go wherever you like." Well, I had no desire to go to a halfway house and had made a decision to stay there given the fact that God said I could go wherever I liked. I may be one of the few people who chose to stay in prison once I was given the opportunity to leave.

~

On my day off, I crawled back into bed in the afternoon to take a nap. I was dreaming that I had to pick up my son at the Milwaukee airport, and his flight arrived at 2:13 p.m. When I woke up, I knew it was time to get out my Bible and start looking. There was only one 2:13 verse that spoke to my heart, and that was found in the book of Philippians: "For God is working in you, giving you the desire and the power to do what pleases him." It was an answer to prayer as I had been asking God why I was still there and what it was that he wanted me to do or learn.

I picked up a book by Rick Warren called *God's Power to Change Your Life*. This book focuses on the fruit of the Spirit, and Sunday evening I read the first 125 pages. Because Monday night was beautiful, I grabbed the book and headed outside to read some more. After reading for a bit longer, I just smiled, because here is what I found:

God did not save us because of our goodness but because

of his own kindness and mercy. Thanks to the saving work of Jesus Christ our Savior, God can declare us good. Our goodness is a gift from God. We cannot work for it. We cannot earn it. We do not deserve it.

The Bible calls this work of Christ *justification*. That is a big word that simply means God says you are okay because of what Jesus did for you. When you put your trust in Christ, God gives you a new nature. (It's like starting over; that is why it is called being "born again.") Then God not only gives you the *desire* to do good, but also gives you the *power* to do good. Philippians 2:13 says, "It is God who works in you both *to will* and *to do* His good pleasure" (NKJV, emphasis added). He gives you the *desire* and the *power* to do what is right. That is one of the ways you know you are a Christian.[3]

One of my friends was sitting at a picnic table, and I walked over to her and asked, "What were the numbers I told you this afternoon?"

"Two thirteen," she said. Then I showed her what I just read.

I headed back upstairs to jot down some notes, and while I was sitting on my bed, God said, *Turn to page 213.* You'll never believe what I found: "Philippians 2:13 says, 'For God is at work within you, helping you want to obey him, and then helping you do what he wants.' … God not only gives you the *desire* to do right, but also gives you the *power* to do what is right."[4]

I picked up the book and headed back outside. The group of ladies sitting around the picnic table asked, "Now what?"

I responded, "You guys are not going to believe what just happened." I then shared my latest encounter with them, and, as only God can do, I was overcome by his presence while I was giving my testimony.

---

3 Rick Warren, *God's Power to Change Your Life (Living with Purpose)* (Grand Rapids, MI: Zondervan, 2006), 203.
4 Ibid., 213.

How did God do this? How did he get me to go back into the library a second time on Sunday to find a book that was not there when I was looking for one at three thirty, yet there it was at six? Furthermore, why did I choose this book? How did I dream about a 2:13 p.m. landing time? Why did only one Scripture speak to my heart, and it was the one in the book of Philippians? How did God ensure I would read the book? How did he put all of those ladies together at that picnic table to hear his Word? Furthermore, why did I feel compelled to go tell them? How did God get Rick Warren's book to have Philippians 2:13 on page 213? And how did I hear him tell me to turn to that page?

This is why we must have God first in our life. He does it because he is God and he does it because he loves us.

14

Sunday, January 12, 2014, arrived, and it would be my last church service at Coleman. Three of us were being released during the week, and, given our ministry involvement, we were asked to come up and speak individually. I prepared a prayer of thanksgiving, using Scripture as my way to thank God for everything he had done during my time there. Here is the prayer I read that day:

> Thank you, Lord, for teaching me that when trouble comes my way, it is an opportunity for great joy. In your divine power you have given me everything I need to live a godly life. My suffering was good for me, for it taught me to pay attention to your decrees. I have studied your Book of Instruction continually and have meditated on it day and night. I honored your command to be strong and courageous and to not be afraid or discouraged, for you really were with me every step of the way. I have cared for the flock you entrusted me, not for what I will get out of it, but because I am eager to serve you.
>
> You have taught me how to forgive and reminded me that love keeps no record of being wronged. Thank you for giving me the power and desire to do what pleases you. I can move forward with confidence knowing that you will never fail me or abandon me. My old life is gone, a new life has begun. I have humbled myself under your mighty power, knowing that at the right time you will lift me up in honor. I know I will reap a harvest of blessing because I did

not give up. Although the Devil intended to harm me, you intended it all for good. You brought me to this position so I could save the lives of many people.

In fewer than twenty-four hours, I would be released after serving 740 days in prison.

～

Receiving and discharge said I should be ready as early as eight in the morning, so I was shocked when I knocked on the door at eight fifteen and the officer on duty told me he did not have any releases that day. "Is this some sort of cruel joke?" I asked, quickly pulling out the documentation that clearly stated the Bureau of Prisons was to release me on January 13, 2014. He asked me to sit in the waiting room outside of his office while he processed the paperwork.

When I stepped back into the room about thirty minutes later, my counselor and another guard were inside. As I looked out the door, their heads turned to see the same thing I was looking at. We could not believe what had just pulled up outside of the front door. I said out loud, "They didn't." Oh yes, they did.

There it was—the same type of vehicle Edward Lewis was in when he rescued Vivian while "La Traviata" played in the background—a white stretch limousine. As the back window rolled down, I saw my daughter Jenny for the first time in more than two years. With a fair amount of excitement in her voice, my counselor said, "That's what I'm talking about. My girls in F4 go out in style." Not only had God told me I would be a prisoner released on early parole, seven months and one day to be exact, but the end of the chapter said, "You are going home in style!"

This assignment had come to an end, and I eagerly opened the door and headed toward the parking lot. I was smiling ear to ear and holding my Bible in the air thanking God when Jenny opened the back door of the limo, hopped out, and ran toward me. A lost daughter received into the arms of her loving mother, just like when

we are welcomed into the loving arms of God. There is nothing better than being encircled by the light and love of Christ and resting
in the peace of his presence.

As she hugged me tighter than she had ever done before, and
as tears were flowing down her face, I said, "It's over, Jenny, it is
finally over," and we just held onto each other, not wanting to let
go. Smiling, I could not help but see the sign hanging out the window that had my name on it: "Welcome Home, My Faithful Loving
Daughter," along with the words "Receive it! Speak it! Believe it!"
My friends were wearing matching purple T-shirts that said the
same thing. When I crawled into the limo and took my seat, our
excitement could not be contained.

My smile was as big as ever. I could not wait to get off of prison
property, so much so that I forgot to take the ceremonial drive
around the parking lot, which is when all of the inmates wave
good-bye. I was focused on my daughter and my friends and the
joy and happiness we were experiencing with my release. Each one
of these special ladies embarked on this adventure with me, and
without their love and support this part of the journey would not
have been nearly as easy.

As we drove down I-75 toward Tampa, we took one of the first
exits only to end up at the same McDonald's I had experienced
twice in chains and shackles. This time it was different. I crawled
out of the limo taking in the sunshine and warm weather without a
care in the world. I was finally free.

When my friends asked me how I wanted to spend my first day
of freedom, I knew exactly what I needed to do. It was time to head
to St. James United Methodist Church in Tampa so I could thank
God for what he had done in me, for me, and through me. It was
also time to thank the women who supported me on this journey,
and so I chose to read Philippians 1:7–8:

> So it is right that I should feel as I do about all of you, for
> you have a special place in my heart. You share with me
> the special favor of God, both in my imprisonment and

in defending and confirming the truth of the Good News. God knows how much I love you and long for you with the tender compassion of Christ Jesus.

After sharing some additional testimony, we jumped back into the limo and headed to the beach at St. Pete for lunch. We had a wonderful time, and trust me when I say I will never again take anything for granted.

Because there was a party planned in my honor for Monday evening, we returned to Tampa midafternoon to relax and unwind. I found myself in one of my favorite places, a tub of hot steamy water. Do you know how good that felt after all of that time? After feeling refreshed and revitalized, there was one more thing I needed to do. It was time to visit Helen.

~

When I think of what I had to endure, it was a piece of cake compared to what Helen suffered during the same time period. Her progressive Parkinson's disease continued to hold her hostage in her very own body.

When I walked in, wondering how she would react to seeing me, I spotted her sitting in her wheelchair in the day room. Sneaking up behind her, I welcomed her with my traditional greeting, "What's happening, girlfriend?" Leaning over the back of her chair, I gave her a kiss on the cheek and a big hug.

Helen turned toward me, and the joy on her face as our eyes connected was heartwarming. She immediately perked up and smiled, gesturing toward me. I knew Helen had something to say, and because she had difficulty speaking I put my ear near her mouth and she worked hard to get the words out, "Where have you been?"

Laughing, I responded, "Up north," although little did she know that was an hour north of Tampa in a federal prison. Yet where I had been did not seem to matter. We were delighted to be reunited and picked up right where we left off. I asked if she would forgive me for not coming to visit her for the last two years, and she said she would. We spent about an hour together before I had to leave for the party, which was hosted by my friend Phyllis at her home in Tampa Palms.

It was now time to head over to see the remaining women who had supported me on this journey. It's tough to put into words how much I appreciated their friendship. When these ladies told me three years ago, "We do life together," they really meant it. This group of willing disciples, along with my family and friends, lived the words found in Hebrews 13:3: "Remember those in prison, as if you were there yourself."

During my 740 days in prison, I received regular visits from my spiritual support team. Virtually every day I heard my name at mail call. Some friends sent money for my commissary account; others were there to pick up the phone when I desperately needed to hear a familiar voice. Many stayed connected via e-mail. When I needed a word of encouragement, a hug, a shoulder to cry on, or intercessory prayer, they were there for me, putting my needs above their own. And what does the King say in Matthew 25:40? "I tell you the truth, when you did it to the least of these my brothers and sisters, you were doing it to me!" We must be willing to be an extension of God's love.

These fifteen ladies did not know the totality of their efforts, but I was excited to share our accomplishments. With their help we distributed close to three hundred Bibles in English and Spanish. Thousands of Just One Word Bible reading plans found their way into all five facilities at Coleman, and hundreds of calendars were sent to children of incarcerated parents. Over two hundred *Radical Power of God* books and study guides were being used to teach inmates about how to align themselves with God's will. More than seven hundred fifty Pass It On cards containing Scripture and encouraging words were handed out to lift the spirits of the women at Coleman, and over thirty-five Christian books were donated to the camp library. We even sent Bibles to some of the kids whose parents were incarcerated. Our letter-writing campaign touched hundreds of lives, but more importantly it changed hearts.

None of this would have happened had I not been in prison, and none of this would have happened without their willingness to be the hands and feet of Jesus. If we could accomplish what we did with such a small group of women, think of the difference we could make if everyone reading this book were willing to share God's love with just one of the 2.7 million children who has a mother or father in prison.

We called it an evening a little after ten o'clock and headed over to Palma Vista where Jenny and I would be spending the night. When I walked into the guest room at Julia's, I could not help but smile. She had set up the room like a luxury hotel, complete with soft lights illuminated, fragranced gift products awaiting my arrival, and Godiva chocolate strategically placed on the pillow. Even better, a queen-sized pillow top mattress welcomed me along with Egyptian cotton sheets and a fluffy down comforter.

I fell into bed completely worn out. I just lay there for an extended period of time, wondering if I was dreaming. *Am I really out of prison?* I eventually fell asleep, although it was going to take some time before I got used to sleeping somewhere other than a jail cell.

My morning coffee and newspaper were waiting for me when I finally crawled downstairs long after the others. We visited for a while, grabbed a sandwich, and it was time to head to the Tampa International Airport. In fewer than four hours we would be touching down in the frozen tundra of Wisconsin and heading to my parents' house for a pizza party with my family.

As we made our final descent over an icy Lake Michigan into Milwaukee, the snowy shoreline reminded me how blessed I was to be able to serve my time in Florida. In some ways it felt strange to be home, especially in the middle of winter. After we exited the aircraft and made our way through the C concourse, I spotted two familiar faces waiting for me on the other side of security. My girlfriends Mari and Julie were there to greet me with big smiles and even bigger hugs, saying, "We wouldn't have missed this for anything."

They seemed somewhat surprised that I looked as good as I did. I had a nice tan, although my hair was shorter than usual and I was carrying an extra ten pounds. They were relieved to see that I was fine and even more impressed when they realized I did not lose my sense of humor. I invited them to join us at my mom and dad's, but they respected that the night was a family night.

It was close to six o'clock in the evening, and the porch light was on when we pulled up in front of my parents' house. The front door was open, awaiting my arrival. I put my carry-on bag on the dining room table and the celebration began. Once again, there were lots of hugs and smiles. My family appeared to be surprised and even a little taken aback that I looked the same, commenting on my suntan and how relaxed I looked. "That's what happens when you spend two years at an all-inclusive resort," I said, laughing.

After the initial shock wore off that I didn't look or appear to act any differently, we too all picked up where we left off, with my sister commenting, "It doesn't even feel like you were gone." Whether or not I wanted to admit it, I was physically and emotionally exhausted and I had a busy week ahead of me having to meet with my attorneys, check in with my probation officer, and settle back into a normal routine.

Having received one year of supervised release, I had one day to relax before heading to the federal courthouse in Milwaukee to meet with my probation officer. It quickly became apparent that I was running on adrenaline the last two years, because, within ten days, my body completely broke down. I had successfully fought the stress of my imprisonment, but it was now time for my body to recover.

I pushed myself to get what I needed to begin writing, investing in a new computer and printer, and it was time to do what I was called to do in October of 2011: *Write the book*. As I sat at my desk wondering where to start, I turned the job over to the Holy Spirit and let him guide each keystroke. Within a short period of time, I had 25,000 words. In fewer than three months, I had hit 150 pages, and before I knew it the book was just about finished.

I quickly realized I was just the vessel and this book was God's, not mine. Many days I would look back on what I had written and wonder, *Where did that come from?* God was so exact in what he wanted me to write that at times he would take me back to a single sentence to make what most of us would consider a minor change, but it was always a change for the better.

~

And speaking of changes, on February 28 I must have heard at least a dozen times *Call Me Vivian*, and the title of the book became what it is today. In March of 2014 I saw my three grandsons for the first time since 2011. Nicholas, Benjamin, and Colin spent their spring break with me, and together we designed the logo for The Vivian Foundation (see page 255 and TheVivianFoundation.com).

One of their favorite activities was visiting a local candy factory. After the tour we got into the car and I challenged them, saying, "Okay, Romans 4:17 says we are to speak things that are not as if they were; so speak it over me, baby." With childlike faith, the boys began to call out on my behalf. Nicholas confidently began with this: "One of these days something crazy will happen where you'll win a bunch of money or you'll get a bunch of time and there will be no problems with your foundation. You'll be able to set it up really easily."

The camera then moved to Colin, and with a fair amount of excitement in his voice, he said, "I think your book will turn into a hit movie and the book will be a bestseller. It will be a good success!" And then it was Ben's turn: "I think you will get lots of donations for your foundation from other companies 'cause they like the idea."

With a great deal of excitement, I finished the interview with this: "I receive it! I speak it! And I believe it!" Jesus reminds us, "Humanly speaking, it is impossible. But with God everything is possible" (Matthew 19:26).

~

On Easter Sunday God revealed himself to me in a mighty way. The previous night I decided to watch the *Ten Commandments*, and near the end I kept dozing off because it was well past my bedtime. As a result, I did not turn off my cell phone, which I routinely do each night.

Well, bright and early on Easter Sunday morning, I heard a text message alert that woke me up. I got up and grabbed my phone to find a picture from a friend who was attending the Sunrise Service at St. James United Methodist Church in Tampa. I quickly responded, "Beautiful, thank you!" and crawled back into bed.

Within a minute another text alert went off. I guess God didn't want me to go back to sleep. It was another girlfriend sending me virtually the identical picture from the same service. I crawled back into bed, and when text alert number three came in, I figured I might as well get up.

When I looked at the text, I realized my first friend had inadvertently sent the photo to my old phone number too. The latest text was from my previous number, and whoever had my old phone number asked, "Who is this causing me to smile early on Easter Sunday?" I sensed in my spirit that this was definitely a God thing and that he wanted me to reply, because whoever was on the other end of that phone needed to be encouraged.

What is it that you want me to say? I silently prayed. The only thing that rose up in my spirit was a Scripture I was very familiar with, so I sent the following response: "Just God! Given he never makes a mistake, this message was also intended for the person who has my old number. I love how he works. And remember God works everything for good. Keep smiling because he loves you and has a great plan for your life. Happy Easter!"

I received another response, and, as only God can do, this was an Easter surprise I would never forget. I found a picture of an African American man waving at me, dressed in clothes that looked familiar. His response: "All I am able to do no more than just wonder. In prison there is not very much that makes me smile. Then u remind me that 'all things work together for good to them that love God' (Rom 8:28), also 'For as many r led by the Spirit of God, they r the sons of God' (8:14) and daughters. Thank you very much & u now in my prayer today. Please say a prayer for me. Clarence Gillie. That I be one of those blessed to be released from prison this July 1."

Having been in prison, I knew an inmate should not have a cell phone. I just stood there looking at my phone, shaking my head in disbelief. *Are you kidding me, Lord?* I don't imagine it would surprise you if I told you I read an article on cell phone usage in prisons just recently, and the statistics were staggering. Although there was a part of me that wanted to respond to his text message, I had no choice but to block my old number from my phone.

I decided to take a walk and talk to God. Over the course of the following two hours, I could not help but think about what just happened, and I prayed for Clarence. I also asked God what this encounter was all about, and he revealed a couple things to me.

My prison ministry will go beyond children. Although The Vivian Foundation will provide faith-based programs for children of incarcerated parents, there will also be an outreach program for inmates. God had just given me a photo he did not want me to forget, and I could not get this man's picture out of my head. This text message obviously gave him hope—I could see it in his eyes. Clarence Gillie is facing forty-eight years in jail.

For quite some time I have been praying and believing my book will open doors for speaking engagements, and I will not be a bit surprised if I find myself back in prison encouraging others with a message of hope: "But the needy will not be ignored forever; the hopes of the poor will not always be crushed" (Psalm 9:18).

The world may ignore the plight of the needy, crushing any

earthly hope they may have. But God, who is the champion of the weak, promises that this will not be the case forever. Hope requires waiting for the Lord's rescue or justice. God knows our needs, he knows our tendency for despair, and he promises to never leave us. Even when others forget us, he will remember.

And what about the two verses that God placed on our hearts, Romans 8:14 and 8:28? Romans 8:14 says, "For all who are led by the Spirit of God are children of God." All who welcome Jesus Christ as Lord of their lives are spiritually reborn, receiving new life from him. Through faith in Christ, this new birth changes us from the inside out, rearranging our attitudes, desires, and motives.

When a person becomes a Christian, he or she gains all of the privileges and responsibilities of a child in God's family. Because we are God's children, we share in great treasures. God has already given us his best gifts, his Son, his Holy Spirit, forgiveness, and eternal life. He also encourages us to ask him for whatever we need.

Romans 8:28 says, "And we know that God causes everything to work together for the good of those who love God and are called according to his purpose for them." Think of all the things that had to happen for this inmate to receive his Easter miracle. From a sunrise service in Tampa, Florida, a picture from Easter Sunday was inadvertently sent to a wrong number. My old phone number, a Wisconsin cell phone number, somehow found its way into a county jail in Mississippi. My new phone number was on the original text and my phone had to be turned on, or I would have slept through the message. Clarence had to question who was making him smile, God had to tell me what to say, and, as a result, a prisoner no longer had to wonder if God is real. He is risen and alive!

～

Patience, prudence, providence. In late May, God was speaking and Vivian was listening. These three words were repeated four times, so I knew this message was one of importance.

Patience is the ability to endure difficult circumstances without reacting in a negative way. I'm beginning to think I really do have the "patience of a saint" as I'm approaching year number ten. Patience is extremely important when you embark on a spiritual journey because mending broken hearts takes time. The secret to maintaining a good attitude while you are being conformed to God's image is trust and obedience. I am living proof that God works on behalf of those who wait for him.

Prudence is having good sense in dealing with practical matters. It means that you think carefully about the consequences of your decisions, because being prudent is synonymous with being wise, careful, and cautious. I have been giving a lot of thought to what will be expected of me moving forward. God has specifically told me three things: *just be yourself, always be humble, and have a gentle and quiet spirit.* That's great advice for all of us.

As I was researching the definition of providence, I just smiled. Providence means that God is in control. We must remember that life's events have been arranged in such a way as to bring about God's perfect plan. "'For I know the plans I have for you,' says the LORD. 'They are plans for good and not disaster, to give you a future and a hope'" (Jeremiah 29:11).

It's all about trusting our heavenly Father: "Trust in the LORD with all your heart; do not depend on your own understanding. Seek his will in all you do, and he will show you which path to take" (Proverbs 3:5–6). Why? "Who knows if perhaps you were made queen for just such a time as this?" (Esther 4:14). One thing is certain: this book and The Vivian Foundation are kingdom projects for which God will provide everything I need on his timetable, not mine.

In early June, I wrote out my final restitution payment and decided to go for a walk before heading to the post office. While I was walking, God laid Matthew 5:25–26 on my heart:

When you are on the way to court with your adversary, settle your differences quickly. Otherwise, your accuser may hand you over to the judge, who will hand you over to an officer, and you will be thrown into prison. And if that happens, you surely won't be free again until you have paid the last penny.

As I was thinking about those two verses, I looked down at the sidewalk, and what did I find but a shiny new penny. God would not allow me to move forward until my financial obligation was met. Only he could orchestrate what was about to happen.

∾

In May of 2012, when God told me to pray for my release, I was confident based on the Scriptures he revealed that July 11 was the day I would be set free. "Ask the LORD your God for a sign of confirmation. ... Make it as difficult as you want—as high as heaven or as deep as the place of the dead" (Isaiah 7:11). And, "Has my arm lost its power? Now you will see whether or not my word comes true!" (Numbers 11:23).

When I was not physically released from prison on July 11, 2012, my son Mike simply stated, "Mom, maybe you just got the wrong year."

I had been praying for years that SC Johnson would forgive me and settle this case. On Friday July 11, 2014, my attorney called to tell me that he received an e-mail time and date stamped that very day relative to my final restitution payment, which stated, "The victim, SCJ, considers itself paid in full." That took place 3,554 days after this journey began—I had been released, and on July 11 of all days.

My probation officer, however, told me I could not set up The Vivian Foundation until my supervisory period ended. My first day of complete freedom would be January 13, 2015. And I knew in my heart that date would coincide with God's perfect timing.

∾

Remember the March visit with my grandkids? Do you recall what Nicholas called out on my behalf? "One of these days something crazy will happen where you'll win a bunch of money or you'll get a bunch of time and there will be no problems with your foundation. You'll be able to set it up really easily." Well, something crazy did happen.

In November of 2014 I received something in the mail from the United States District Court for the Eastern District of Wisconsin. Without my knowledge, I had become a plaintiff in a class action lawsuit against SC Johnson's retirement plan, and, as a result, I would be receiving monetary benefits. As I looked at the amount, I could not believe my eyes. When I had no idea where the money was going to come from to establish The Vivian Foundation, God opened the windows of heaven and poured out a financial blessing so great it could only be described as a miracle. The hearing for the approval of this settlement had been set. Can you guess the date? January 13, 2015.

Little did I know at that time that God was going to provide me with much more as a result of this blessing! I chose to take the settlement in the form of a lifetime annuity, which means I will be receiving a check every month for the rest of my life. Not knowing exactly when I would receive the first payment or exactly how much it would be after deductions, I was thrilled when I went to the bank the end of July and found out a deposit had been made. The monthly annuity amount after taxes is $816.18.

Throughout this journey, God has used numbers to speak to me. As I drove back to where I was staying to prepare for the first Vivian Foundation board meeting, which was held the same day I learned the money had hit my account, I had a sense in my spirit that God had something special for me!

So I asked, *What are you trying to tell me, Lord?* His answer was, *Go to the book of Deuteronomy.* Deuteronomy 8:16–18 will be my heavenly reminder every month for the rest of my life:

> He fed you with manna in the wilderness, a food unknown to your ancestors. He did this to humble you and test you for your own good. He did all this so you would never

say to yourself, 'I have achieved this wealth with my own strength and energy.' Remember the Lord your God. He is the one who gives you power to be successful, in order to fulfill the covenant he confirmed to your ancestors with an oath.

As I wept in his presence and thanked him for everything he had done for me, God reminded me of those three little words he spoke to me in May of 2014: *Patience, prudence, providence!*

In this life we cannot be flawless, but we can aim to be as much like Christ as possible. We must separate ourselves from the world's sinful values. We must be devoted to God's wishes rather than our own, and carry his love, mercy, grace, and forgiveness into the world.

We cannot achieve Christlike character and holy living all at once, but we must grow toward maturity that will manifest itself in words and deeds throughout our life. Just as we expect different behavior from a baby, a child, a teenager, and an adult, God expects different behavior from us, depending on our stage of spiritual development.

~

And so, dear brothers and sisters, I plead with you to give your bodies to God because of all he has done for you. Let them be a living and holy sacrifice—the kind he will find acceptable. This is truly the way to worship him. Don't copy the behavior and customs of this world, but let God transform you into a new person by changing the way you think. Then you will learn to know God's will for you, which is good and pleasing and perfect.

Because of the privilege and authority God has given me, I give each of you this warning: Don't think you are better than you really are. Be honest in your evaluation of yourselves, measuring yourselves by the faith God has given us. Just as our bodies have many parts and each part has a special function, so it is with Christ's body. We are many parts of one body, and we all belong to each other.

In his grace, God has given us different gifts for doing certain things well. So if God has given you the ability to prophesy, speak out with as much faith as God has given you. If your gift is serving others, serve them well. If you are a teacher, teach well. If your gift is to encourage others, be encouraging. If it is giving, give generously. If God has given you leadership ability, take the responsibility seriously. And if you have a gift for showing kindness to others, do it gladly.

Don't just pretend to love others. Really love them. Hate what is wrong. Hold tightly to what is good. Love each other with genuine affection, and take delight in honoring each other. Never be lazy, but work hard and serve the Lord enthusiastically. Rejoice in our confident hope. Be patient in trouble, and keep on praying. When God's people are in need, be ready to help them. Always be eager to practice hospitality.

Bless those who persecute you. Don't curse them; pray that God will bless them. Be happy with those who are happy, and weep with those who weep. Live in harmony with each other. Don't be too proud to enjoy the company of ordinary people. And don't think you know it all!

Never pay back evil with more evil. Do things in such a way that everyone can see you are honorable. Do all that you can to live in peace with everyone.

Dear friends, never take revenge. Leave that to the righteous anger of God. For the Scriptures say, "I will take revenge; I will pay them back," says the Lord.

Instead, "If your enemies are hungry, feed them. If they are thirsty, give them something to drink. In doing this, you will heap burning coals of shame on their heads."

Don't let evil conquer you, but conquer evil by doing good. (Romans 12:1–21)

~

It all came together just like God said it would. In February of 2009 God made Vivian a promise, a promise he intended to keep: "I will never fail you. I will never abandon you" (Hebrews 13:5). Like Abraham, when there was no reason to hope, I believed this journey was part of my divine destiny. As a result, my faith grew stronger, which brought God glory.

I never wavered in believing God's promises and completed each assignment regardless of its difficulty. As a result of my faith and God's unfailing love, my heart has been transformed. I have been strengthened in faith. What is faith?

Faith is the confidence that what we hope for will actually happen; it gives us assurance about things we cannot see. (Hebrews 11:1)

It is impossible to please God without faith. Anyone who wants to come to him must believe that God exists and that he rewards those who sincerely seek him. (Hebrews 11:6)

Three things will last forever—faith, hope, and love—and the greatest of these is love. (1 Corinthians 13:13)

Are you ready to run into the loving arms of your Savior? It's the only way to live happily ever after. My lover said to me, "Rise up, my darling! Come away with me, my fair one!" (Song of Solomon 2:10). And the book of Revelation assures us:

"For the time has come for the wedding feast of the Lamb, and his bride has prepared herself. She has been given the finest of pure white linen to wear." For the fine linen represents the good deeds of God's holy people.

And the angel said to me, "Write this: Blessed are those who are invited to the wedding feast of the Lamb." And he added, "These are true words that come from God." (Revelation 19:7–9)

Not only did Vivian get her fairy-tale ending by receiving everything her Bridegroom-King promised, but she also proved all things are possible with God if we simply have the faith to believe. Go ahead, call me Vivian. This is not the end—it's only the beginning. Wait until you see what God has planned next.

Acknowledgments

To the many authors, teachers, and Christian leaders whose words of wisdom changed my life: thank you. I would especially like to acknowledge those people who will find pieces of their work embedded in this book: Glenn Beck, Robert Heidler, David Ireland, Charlotte Davis Kasl, PhD, R.T. Kendall, Dr. Mark Laaser, Joyce Meyer, Beth Moore, Max Lucado, Ruth Ann Nylen, Priscilla Shirer, Dr. Charles Stanley, William B. Turner, Rick Warren, John Weaver, and Bruce Wilkinson as well as Angie Smith and the Women of Faith team. I am eternally grateful for your books, Bible studies, and faith-filled events, all which were relevant, timely, and instrumental in transforming my heart.

To my attorneys: Mike, you were a God-send and always there for me. Michael, your encouragement to go read the book of Ecclesiastes helped me understand the truth of God's Word. Thank you both for your kindness and generosity.

To the management team at WC Bradley: I sincerely appreciate the support I received from the Turner family. You displayed the servant leadership preached by your founding father.

To the remarkable mighty warrior princesses at Camp Coleman: Thank you to each and every woman I met on this journey. Susan, you taught me how to give God the glory and renew my mind with the Holy Spirit. Together we anointed doors, hit our knees in prayer, shook off the dust, and worshipped face down. To Carol and our Friday night Bible study group, please remember that as I carry this story to the world, each of you goes with me. Thank you to those who delivered prophetic words, especially Dale, Ivory,

KK, Kerry Ann, and Shawn. Your obedience fueled my passion for writing and helped me stay the course. To all of my friends, especially Christy, Erika, Collette, and Lisa who kept me laughing and provided hours of entertainment and enjoyment, we found out that no matter where life takes us we can have fun.

To my loyal friends: When others walked out, you walked in and stayed there. Jane, Marsha, Marilyn, Anne, Belinda, Mari, Julie, Nancy, and JoAnn, thank you. Your love, care, and concern are examples of what true friendship is all about.

To the amazing people of Tampa: My sincerest appreciation to Julia, Joe, Kim, Eileen, Diana, and Bob whose unconditional love has sustained me since the day we met.

To all of the people at St. James United Methodist Church, River of Life, and Really Good News Ministries: thank you.

To my girls at Hearthstone, especially Helen, Frankie, Grace, and Margaret who are now in heaven, and to Nick: you helped me become the person God intended me to be.

To my spiritual support team: Bonnie, Deanne, Debra, Eileen, Gloria, Jonie, Josie, Laura, Linda, Lorrie, Mary, Patrice, Paula, Phyllis, Ruth Ann, and Wendy, your friendship means more to me than you will ever know.

To my airplane angel Mary Ann and her son Daniel: thank you for allowing me to share your story.

To my family who weathered this storm and remarkable journey with me: may you treasure this book.

To my mom and dad, Ginny and Kazzy; my brothers and sisters Jerry, Joe, Nancy, Susie, and Kris and their families as well as my former husband, Tom, and our children Mike, Jenny, and Brian and their families including my grandsons Nicholas, Benjamin, and Colin, there is only one thing to say: "Low day cho da leet te a da pa!"

And to Jesus Christ, the love of my life who assured me he would never fail me or abandon me: this is our story and to God be the glory!

Receive it! Speak it! Believe it!

About The Vivian Foundation

The Vivian Foundation is a 501(c)(3) nonprofit charitable organization established in 2015 to help the children of incarcerated parents. Our mission is to raise money and provide Christian resources to children with incarcerated parents, to prison ministries, and to other nonprofit organizations dedicated to helping these families.

The American criminal justice system holds almost 2.3 million people in 1,833 state prisons, 110 federal prisons, 1,772 juvenile correctional facilities, and 3,134 local jails. There are 2.7 million children in the United States who have a mother or father behind bars, and approximately ten million children have experienced parental incarceration at some point in their lives. Will you prayerfully consider sharing God's love and supporting our mission to help inmates and their children?

The Vivian Foundation is dedicated to improving the well-being and quality of life for these individuals and doing whatever it takes to positively impact these families. Please visit our website at www.thevivianfoundation.com. Tax deductible donations can also be mailed to: The Vivian Foundation PO Box 44601, Racine, Wisconsin 53404–7012.